Handbook of
Political Science
Methods

Handbook of Political Science Methods

G. David Garson

Department of Political Science
Tufts University

Holbrook Press, Inc.   Boston

to Cindy

Contents

Preface

An introductory text is a curious work, validly subject to the criticisms of tempting the student into pat formulas and "instant analysis" on the one hand, and of numbing him with the enormity of the field on the other. This book is specifically an introduction, and presumes further study. Not dependent on any particular text, it is designed as a supplementary handbook for beginning and intermediate political and social science methods and statistics courses. Various general topics, such as structural-functionalism, are raised for purposes of methodological instruction, for illustration and discussion, for what can be obtained from them. To deal with each of these on their own terms, in their own complexity, is beyond the scope here.

In my first years as a graduate student, I made what was for me an enlightening discovery—I found simply that my understanding of political questions profoundly improved when I approached a problem from several different viewpoints before attempting my own synthesis. Called upon to address the question, "Why do periods of corruption arise from time to time in the polity?" my initial reaction was that of the empiricist, seeking out the literature, particularly behavioral literature, on that topic. Not only was there remarkably little such literature, but what I did find seemed disjoint, fragmented, not helpful in grasping the question. For some reason, perhaps because this was a course in political theory, I chose the strategy of thinking first how a Marxist would view this question, then a writer in the psychoanalytic tradition, and so on. Using these great traditions in an applied manner certainly involves abuse of their complexity, but, without denying that, I found this criticism somewhat beside the point.

In this experience, I also developed new insight into the relation between political theory and behavioralism. Political theory is an essential aid in creatively forming hypotheses—the first step in any sound political science research project. Though this seems commonplace, nevertheless, it is a belief not commonly acted upon in the discipline. The present volume is a modest attempt to remedy this, reemphasizing the rightful role of political theory as an integral part of political science methodology. The two have long been divorced, but I believe that the thoughtful student will find this approach fruitful.

Although part of the content of this book is not to be found elsewhere, in general it seeks to explain and apply the work of others. The list of authors to whom I and all political scientists are indebted would itself fill a book; many of them are indicated in the readings that head each chapter. I am, of course, indebted to many of my former teachers, including Frederick Mosteller and H. Douglas Price, both of Harvard. Appreciation must also be expressed to the authors and publishers who kindly gave permission to use the tables that appear in the Appendix, including the Literary Executor of the late Sir Ronald A. Fisher, F.R.S., to Dr. Frank Yates, F.R.S., and to Oliver & Boyd Ltd., Edinburgh, for permission to reprint Tables IV, V, and VI from their book *Statistical Tables for Biological, Agricultural and Medical Research*.

G. D. G.
Roxbury, Mass.
October 1969

Introduction

There are now available several excellent volumes for the student wishing an introduction to the theoretical aspects of political analysis. These include Ithiel de Sola Pool, ed., *Contemporary Political Science: Toward Empirical Theory* (published in 1967 by McGraw-Hill, in cooperation with the American Political Science Association; contributors include Almond, Dahl, Deutsch, Eckstein, Eulau, Pye, Shils, and Simon); Robert A. Dahl, *Modern Political Analysis* (Prentice-Hall paperback, 1963); and Robert T. Golembiewski, William Welsh, and William J. Crotty, *A Methodological Primer for Political Scientists* (Rand McNally, 1969). An elementary introduction to quantitative aspects of political science is contained in Oliver Benson's *Political Science Laboratory* (Charles Merrill paperback, 1969).

More critical views of political and social science are contained in Barrington Moore, Jr., *Political Power and Social Theory* (Harvard University paperback, 1958); Robert S. Lynd's classic work, *Knowledge for What?: The Place of Social Science in American Culture* (Grove Press paperback, 1964; originally published 1939); and C. Wright Mills, *The Sociological Imagination* (Grove Press paperback, 1959).

For an instructive example of the theoretical and methodological debate in political and social science, G. William Domhoff and Hoyt B. Ballard, eds., *C. Wright Mills and 'The Power Elite'* (Beacon Press paperback, 1969) usefully presents some classic essays on both sides of the important elitism-pluralism debate in the field.

1

The study of politics is not a science, and there is no one "correct" political science methodology. In fact, political scientists are as often behind as they are ahead of informed journalists in their ability to anticipate important political changes. Yet the study of political science methods is rapidly becoming virtually mandatory for graduate and undergraduate students in the field. Why is this so?

Some have attributed the changes in the field to a desire to construct a complicated intellectual framework as a form of protection from charges that political science merely deals with the obvious. No doubt there is some truth to the argument that frustration in our attempts to answer the classic political questions of democracy and welfare, for example, has led the field to retreat into narrow techniques in order to learn lesser things about our political system, if only because these things *can* be determined. Perhaps there is even a measure of status-seeking involved in the spread of complicated political methodologies as well.

These, however, seem only subsidiary reasons for the change. The paramount reason for the emphasis on method is simply that as larger issues are dealt with more and more systematically, the ways of gathering information, processing it, and interpreting it have become increasingly complex. The fact that many have used old or new methods for trivial or even misleading purposes should not obscure the greater purposes involved.

THE CHALLENGE TO POLITICAL SCIENCE

Strange as it may seem, there is a romantic dream at stake here. That dream envisions the use of information about the past and present to predict and shape the future. It conceives of the ability to specify the likely consequences of alternative policies, alternatives the consequences of which are now only dimly perceived. B. F. Skinner, a founder of behavioralism, emphasized that social planning requires a predictive social science. The meaning of democracy will always have a flawed aspect until the practical implications of existing and proposed political actions and policies can be stated with greater clarity and assurance.

As political scientists, we need not accept the full challenge of this dream, which equates science with the ability to employ predictive theories, but we must recognize that it is a challenge of substantial importance. Explanations of the past and present, and predictions of the future will occur regardless because decision-making requires it. A president claims his foreign policies will bring peace. Unions proclaim that current business practices will bring economic depression. A local editor asserts that the permissive policies of the national government are leading to urban rioting. How are we to respond to these assertions?

Fortunately, the challenge to social scientists is not to immediately construct a total explanatory system, but only to improve upon the results of current reasoning. As political scientists, we share a part of that task; many have already begun through methods described in this book.[1]

POLITICAL SCIENCE AND OTHER SOCIAL SCIENCES

The study of politics has no clear boundaries and is not clearly differentiated from other social sciences. Many of the methods used in political science are also used (and even originated) in history, economics, sociology, psychology, philosophy, mathematics, and engineering. Increasingly the student needs a smattering of several of these fields, especially sociology. While recognizing the arbitrariness of any fine distinctions between fields, it may nonetheless be shown that political science is differentiated in two areas, although more in the first than the second.

Power

The primary domain of political science is the study of rule, authority, and power—terms that have been defined in many ways. The questions raised by these concepts permeate our political system: distribution of power, control over policies, effect on the "public interest," the competition and cooperation of public and private powers, power used for narrow or long-term self-interest, power used directly or indirectly, formally or informally, with or without

[1] Further reading: Thomas S. Kuhn, "The Historical Structure of Scientific Discovery," *Science* 136 (June 1, 1962), p. 761.

intended results. Questions are raised of how decisions are made and "who benefits?, who decides?, and what difference does it make?"

Policy

The first domain easily merges with the second, that of policy. The study of decisions is not easily divorced from the study of decision outcomes. Just as the study of power is made complex by the fact that actors may participate in decisions individually or by way of groups or even social classes, so policy results may be narrow and technical or highly diffuse. Political scientists have traditionally been more inclined to focus on areas where policy outputs are diffuse, such as foreign policy, rather than on areas like transportation policy where technical factors become prominent. The student must decide for himself to what extent he is competent to enter the many technical fields that impinge on political science from all directions.[2]

POLITICAL SCIENCE AND THE REAL WORLD

The *basic method* of political science and of all science is simplification. In essence, political reality is so complex that the human mind cannot perceive it directly, but may understand it only by means of simplifications. Whether a concept or hypothesis is a simplification or an oversimplification depends on its usefulness for the purposes at hand. The division of the American population into Democrats, Republicans, and Independents may well be a useful simplification for analyzing the recent national elections, but is unlikely to be useful in analyzing the civil rights movement, for example. What is a simplification in one context is often an oversimplification in another.

Simplification begins with the naming of variables and the development of typologies. Just to talk about what interests us we must attach labels, and these place items or people into categories the boundaries of which are almost always arbitrary. For example, the same citizenry may be divided into conservatives and liberals, moral-

---

[2] Further reading: The relations among the social sciences are explored in a classic collection of essays edited by Daniel Lerner and Harold Lasswell, *The Policy Sciences* (Stanford: Stanford University, 1965; originally published 1951).

ists and amoralists, voters and nonvoters. These and any labels carry analytic implications that need to be made explicit.

The dividing of a citizenry into conservatives and liberals often implies that the researcher considers a partisan policy dimension most salient, while the moralist-amoralist distinction emphasizes cultural and psychological causes. What is labelled a drunken brawl from one perspective may be labelled class struggle from another. No label or typology is invalid in itself, but some are more helpful than others. Usefulness has to do with the extent of clear operational definitions, comprehensiveness of scope, ideological connotations, and many other factors discussed in the sections that follow.

Simplification continues with the development of hypotheses. We may assert that X causes Y, but we must then specify whether necessary or sufficient causation (or both) is involved, whether causation occurs only in a limited context, under what conditions exceptions occur, and many related issues. A hypothesis that is appropriate in one research situation may not be useful in another. In one time period, for example, it might be true that capitalism leads to imperialism, while the same relationship might not hold in another.

The fine line between necessary simplification and oversimplification is difficult to draw. The researcher must consider not only labels and typologies, and the causal nature of the hypothesis, but also the level of generalization on which he wishes to operate. He must seek to identify the dynamic element in his overall explanation: are political changes to be linked to changes in production, to demographic changes, to "great events" or "great men," or perhaps even to changes in "human nature"?[3]

CHAPTER OUTLINE

In the brief chapters that follow, outlines of many but by no means all political science methods are presented. At the beginning of each chapter is a set of annotated readings, emphasizing the nature of this book as a supplement and handbook designed to accompany (but not parallel) introductory texts. Its purpose is to give the student a concise, comprehensive overview of political and social science tech-

[3] Further reading: Arthur L. Stinchombe, *Constructing Social Theories* (New York: Harcourt, Brace & World, 1968), especially Chapter 3, "Complex Causal Structures" and Chapter 4, "The Conceptualization of Power Phenomena."

niques without detailing formula derivations, the numerous variations on the basic methods, or the major case studies employing each method. That is done in the suggested readings.

This book attempts to present basic information about a wide range of conceptual approaches and techniques in an applied, how-to-do-it manner needed by the beginning student. As such, the student should realize that each of the approaches and techniques is associated with a lore of rather complex literature; reading this brief volume alone will not confer mastery of political science methods. It should, however, enable the student to begin applying what he has learned to his papers and other course work.

The ability to discover and apply useful categories and relationships requires creativity, which is not taught easily if at all. Throughout the materials that follow, however, are examples of the creative use of political science methods. We start by studying three "methodologies," that is, those aggregations of conceptual approaches and associated techniques that claim a universal world-view. The methodologies presented are dialectical materialism, psychoanalysis, and structural-functionalism, all frequently encountered in political science. Their necessarily brief presentation involves oversimplification from a theoretical point of view, although not for the purposes of illustrating methodological problems for the introductory student.

After a discussion of basic views and criticisms of each of the methodologies, the major methodological issues raised by each are analyzed. Many of the issues of analysis facing Marx, for example, still face political scientists today. Each of these three chapters concludes with an example of analysis by means of that methodology, using the same subject (rioting) throughout.

In Chapters 4 and 5 certain "approaches" are studied. By approaches are meant those sets of concepts and techniques that, while widely used, are expressly limited in scope, but are not simply techniques for processing data. The major example here is systems analysis, used both to evaluate government policy alternatives and to construct theories of comparative development. Thus, it is sometimes conceived as limited in scope and sometimes not. As before, stress is placed on general research issues raised by this approach and on procedures of research application. In Chapter 5 a potpourri of approaches are discussed, including sociometry, interaction analysis, case studies, and participant observation, along with certain quantitative techniques such as coding procedures and content analysis.

The remaining chapters deal with quantitative analysis, stressing general information at an applied, introductory level. Chapter 6 on survey design and sampling raises basic issues about data collection and the results of one's sample in relation to what one would "normally" expect. A chapter on scaling follows, dealing with the problem of measurement of abstract variables so common in political science. Once variables are measured and data collected, it is necessary to determine if the relationships observed are significant, strongly associated, and valid; Chapters 8 and 9 deal with this area. More advanced methods of data analysis and model construction are presented in the last chapters on correlation, regression, and factor analysis. Further reading is suggested for those desiring more depth in any given area.

1

Marxism
As Methodology

C. Wright Mills, *The Marxists* (Dell paperback, 1962) provides a basic review. A convenient collection is Karl Marx, *Selected Writings in Sociology and Social Philosophy,* edited by T. B. Bottomore (McGraw-Hill paperback, 1964; originally published 1956), particularly Part 1, "Methodological Foundations." Lewis Feuer, ed., Marx and Engels, *Basic Writings on Politics and Philosophy* (Doubleday Anchor paperback, 1959), provides useful longer excerpts or entire works. In addition to the "Manifesto," particularly helpful readings included are "On Historical Materialism," "Socialism: Scientific and Utopian," and "The Class Struggles in France." A standard biography is Franz Mehring's *Karl Marx: The Story of His Life* (University of Michigan paperback, 1962).

Students may wish to follow up special topics. Economics is treated in a manner sympathetic to Marx in *Marx and Modern Economics,* edited by D. Horowitz (Monthly Review paperback, 1968) and critically in Murray Wolfson's *A Reappraisal of Marxian Economics* (Pelican paperback, 1964). Interests in psychology are pursued in the essays of one of Freud's Marxist colleagues, Wilhelm Reich, in "Dialectical Materialism and Psychoanalysis" and "Psychoanalysis in the Soviet Union" (*Studies on the Left* 6:4, July–August, 1966, pp. 5–57).

From a sociological point of view, the student might read Ralf Dahrendorf, *Class and Class Conflict in Industrial Society* (Stanford University paperback, 1959), especially Chapters 1 ("Karl Marx's Model of Class Society") and 4 ("A Sociological Critique of Marx"). In history, Herbert Aptheker's *Toward Negro Freedom* (New Century paperback, 1956) represents a view favorable to Marxism, especially the essays "Marx and Engels on the Civil War" and "The Central Theme in Southern History." In contrast, the historian Jacques Barzun has argued that Marx greatly impeded the development of social science, in *Darwin, Marx and Wagner: Critique of a Heritage* (Doubleday Anchor paperback, 1958; originally published 1941). Students interested in philosophical aspects might read Erich Fromm's *Marx's Concept of Man* (Ungar paperback, 1961), emphasizing the "Economic and Philosophical Manuscripts of 1844."

The readings listed are but a handful of the vast number dealing with Marxism. With rare exceptions, however, there is little to be found explicitly dealing with how Marxism may be applied to contemporary political analysis. Perhaps this is partly due to our having just emerged from a period of "cold war scholarship" during which the subject was virtually ignored. Since C. Wright Mills' call for a "celebration" of Marxism, however, the pendulum has swung somewhat in the other direction.

Much of the new attention has emphasized humanistic aspects of Marx, focusing on the "Economic and Philosophical Manuscripts of 1844," recently translated by T. B. Bottomore and edited for the American public by Erich Fromm, a noted socialist psychoanalyst. The alienation theme in particular has been used to place the *Communist Manifesto* in a new light, emphasizing a Marxism far more complex than economic determinism. Students of politics interested in methods, however, should be primarily interested in how a Marxist orientation might be applied to analysis of political events.

THE MARXIST PERSPECTIVE

Before turning to methodological aspects, what *is* the Marxist perspective in general? This question calls for a simplification of Marx, and hence a distortion, but recognizing this the following is a useful summary.

Marx argued that man as a being is by nature productive, rather than evil (as Luther), bellicose (as Hobbes), or rational-calculating (as Bentham). In this sense Marx was in the romantic tradition, viewing man as having lost his strengths to idols of his own making —religion, the state, the market. "Things are in the saddle and ride man," he wrote. Whereas liberal man was a consumer and the image of politics was that of the free play of groups and ideas in the political marketplace, Marxist man was a producer, his political nature forged by his relationship to production.

Marx was perhaps most romantic in his attacks on the division of labor, describing a day in the life of a socialist man as one in which he might hunt in the morning, farm in the afternoon, and write poetry in the evening. That was the vision of a future socialist world about which Marx wrote little.

In brief, Marx adopted an approach that divided history into epochs distinguished from one another by changed relationships of men to the means of production. He devoted his greatest attention to the most recent stage, that of capitalism. Under capitalism citizens were divided into owners (and their agents—the intellectuals, the managers, the politicians) and workers (not counting the lumpenproletariat subclass of criminals and riff-raff). Capitalism was seen to deny man his product and hence his natural fulfillment (his species-life) as a basically productive being. Marx argued that it was this capitalist relationship which had to be changed, not just inequality as implied by Proudhon and certain other utopian socialists. The socialists were not interested in "better pay for slaves." This issue was central to Marxists, since for them, unlike liberals, property relations were understood to relate directly to the inner essence of man.

Change in society was believed to occur through the natural development of the forces of technology, precipitated by the seeds of destruction harbored within each social stage in the form of internal contradictions. Each stage, such as feudalism, at first greatly facilitated the development of productive forces, but later impeded that development, at the same time generating the forces that would create the next stage. For example, the overthrow of feudalism was attributed to bourgeois needs to establish a liberal market in labor, goods, and capital, free of aristocratic and monarchic restraints. With

regard to the capitalist stage, Marx predicted the growing immiseration of the masses, revolution, dictatorship of the proletariat, and
abolition of exploitation by socialism. The withering of the state
under socialism referred to the predicted demise of government in its
aspect as agent of class rule, since class distinctions became abolished
with the end of exploitation.

Criticisms

One of the readings, that by C. Wright Mills, conveniently summarizes many of the criticisms of Marxism. The concept of society
constituted by an economic "base" and a political "superstructure,"
with the former somehow determining the latter, was crucial to Marxist interpretations of political development, but, as Mills emphasizes,
this relationship is very vague and the mechanisms relating the base
to the superstructure are not specified. Mills also notes that property
relationships (as owner-worker relations) were inadequate even to
understand economic stratification, where income and status relationships are also important.

Similarly, it is possible to interpret all history as class struggle, but
only if that struggle is seen as very intermittent and extremely multi-
formed. But, if interpreted this flexibly, class struggle may not be
very useful as a simplification. Mills also feels that in comparing bourgeois revolutions against feudalism with the anticipated proletarian
revolution against capitalism, Marx made a bad analogy: if it were
parallel bourgeois institutions growing within feudalism that led to
its overthrow, so parallel socialist institutions growing within capitalism, not necessarily workers' organizations, should lead to the
socialist revolution.

Mills also mentions the more common criticisms directed against
Marx's economic predictions. The economic crises of capitalism are
not clearly getting worse: unionism *has* proved a viable alternative
to revolution, because it can institutionally guarantee workers' interests. In general, growing immiseration has not occurred; class structure does not seem to be becoming more (or less) polarized.
Wageworkers, a "class-in-itself," does not necessarily become the
proletariat, a "class-for-itself," because men do not always act in
terms of their long-run interests. The state is not merely the coercive
instrument of the owning classes; political and military leaders have
power in their own right.

The student has no doubt already been exposed to these criticisms of Marxism on numerous occasions. Critics usually credit Marx with emphasizing the role of conflict at a time when there was much focus on harmony and equilibrium. Similarly, Marx's concept of class, although certainly not without precedent, stood in useful contrast to liberal emphasis on rational individuals as units of political action. These, however, are not the focal points of this discussion. Instead let us examine the theoretical issues faced by Marx that must still be faced by researchers today.

CONTEMPORARY METHODOLOGICAL ISSUES

Nearly all political studies contain explicit or implicit theories of the nature of man, the structure of political life, and the way social change occurs. Failure to make these underlying assumptions explicit may lead the researcher to fail to consider all the relevant issues, and lends itself to misunderstandings among political scientists.

Historical Epochs

Proof of various hypotheses is often sought by comparing similar phenomena across cultures in the same time period or by making comparisons over time. If the latter historical path is chosen, then as the length of time considered increases, the need to divide the historical period into epochs grows. That is, history must be divided into categories that simplify history for purposes presumably useful to analysis.

The crucial question is, "What criteria are to be chosen as bases for placing the historical dividing lines?" In one sense, all history is transitional and the process of dividing it into periods is arbitrary; again, however, simplification is inherent in analysis. Marx used the technology of production as the criterion, establishing time periods like feudalism and capitalism. Of course, other criteria might be used instead, such as great events, changes in forms of government, political boundaries, or intellectual currents.

Of these alternatives, the great events approach has been the traditional mode, used even in primitive societies. For example, among the Buku islanders of the South Pacific, history is divided between "the time of the fighting" and "the time of the white man," the great event dividing the two periods being the arrival of German imperialists. As with other approaches, there is nothing intrinsically wrong with using great events to distinguish time periods, but it is an approach that rarely serves to clarify analysis. Preferably, the criterion should grow out of the historical process being described. Using wars to set off periods in the development of foreign policy might conceivably serve analysis in one instance, whereas the same criterion applied to the development of Supreme Court decisions would be purely arbitrary. Rationale for the great events approach was given by the German sociologist Max Weber, who emphasized such events in history as instruments of widespread attitude changes; if used in this light, the approach may serve analysis in a non-arbitrary way.

The criterion of changes in political territory or government has been used by many political scientists. Machiavelli, for instance, developed a cyclical theory of the state, revolving from classic to despotic to republican forms, a movement based on the impulse to participate leading to success and wealth, and from this to corruption and decline, followed by the awaiting of resurrection through great men. Generally, however, such divisions are characterized by little description of the dynamic by which one stage leads to the next; it is this issue that is at the heart of the problem of categorization of time periods.

The use of intellectual currents as a criterion raises a problem central to Marxism: are ideas to be considered products of material culture, or do ideas cause social change? All sides on this issue admit mutual causation, but primary emphasis is often given to one or the other. Seymour M. Lipset, for example, emphasizes ideal factors in his interpretation of American social-political history in *The First New Nation*. Emphasis on material factors might lead to divisions such as "the age of commercial capitalism," "the age of industrial capitalism," "the age of monopoly capitalism," and the like; whereas emphasis on ideal factors might lead to stages like "the age of enlightenment," "the age of ideology," "the age of analysis." It is entirely possible to use ideal divisions and hold to a theory of material causation, but then the author may expect confusion in the minds of his readers. Usually criteria should be consistent with the underlying theory of development; if there is no such theory, this too should be made explicit.

The Marxist criterion of technology of production is explicitly related to a theory of change. As a criterion it has problems, but so do all the alternatives. Whether it is oversimplified for the student's own purposes is a question to be decided in each case, but the central issue of how to categorize time periods will continue to arise with insistent regularity.

Social Classes

The class concept is one that appears in a great variety of political works. One would do well, however, to keep firmly in mind Weber's distinction between class measures and status measures. Common measures of social status are income level, education, and occupational prestige. Class is a related but distinct concept, depending in the Marxist definition on relationships to the means of production.

For example, a man may work on an assembly line, be paid $15,000 a year, and still be in the working class; the same man, still on the assembly line, may earn $5000 a year from his job and have a $10,000 annual income from inherited stock, in which case he would be classified as a capitalist. By status measures this man would be classed the same in either event. Thus the real question is empirical: how important are production relationships to political behavior? In the above example, would the source of income significantly influence the man's political attitudes, for instance?

Production classes are not the only possible type, of course. One might want to speak of "status classes," arguing that those with significantly higher status differ crucially on political matters from lower social status groups. Dahrendorf has argued for a class concept based on authority cleavages, with political behavior and attitudes related more to political status vis-à-vis authority than to socio-economic status per se.

The concept of class contains many problems. The various measures of status may be discrepant; the same individual may have, for instance, a high education and a low income. Or in the example in the previous paragraph, perhaps the individual should be considered two-thirds capitalist and one-third worker! Beyond this, people may objectively belong to certain classes yet lack class consciousness or even identify with another class. In the United States, for example, many wealthy people will identify themselves as middle class when queried on surveys. Moreover, as our economy has developed, property income has ceased to be a clear class criterion, and beyond this, economic conflict does not in the least exhaust the varieties of political conflict.

These issues are reviewed in T. B. Bottomore's *Classes in Modern Society* listed in later readings. Bottomore concludes that there is no clear evidence that inequality is changing relatively, that the vast majority of people do not shift in social class, and that most mobility is of the inter-generational type which is in turn due to the changing occupational structure of the economy. He argues that while it is true in several countries that the correspondence between classes and specific ideologies has been weakened, ideological differentiation is still strong with regard to production relationships. He suggests that the real undermining of the Marxist class concept lies in the increasing importance of nonproduction relationships, which is in turn related to increasing affluence. In a crisis, classes might again dominate political events even in countries now marked by status politics.

The central issue for the political scientist is how to conceive the general structure of political action. Classical liberals seemingly implied a system dominated by anomic individuals all acting rationally and individually, but somehow tending to the common good. More recently, political science has been dominated by the various group approaches, notably David Truman's classic work, *The Governmental Process*. The class approach is prepared to explain why the National Association of Manufacturers is more important than the National Association of Contract Bridge Players, however, and those who adopt the group approach must be prepared with their own explanations. That is, there is the danger of portraying politics as being the result of the competition of a great many more-or-less equal groups, overlooking differentials in the power base of groups and in their institutionalized relationships to government.

The issue of social classes in Marxism thus raises the general methodological issue of how to describe the units of political action. As units, the individual, the group, and the class each have problems. Indeed, the whole literature on elitism and pluralism is largely devoted to this complex issue. Certainly the Marxist unit, social class, is not to be dismissed lightly until the student has formulated explicit alternatives.

Dialectic of Change

Marx believed that social change occurs through a dialectic process, in which material forces are formed, generate their own antitheses, thereby causing a clash of forces, and resolve into a new synthesis more favorable to the next stage of development. This theory contrasts with that of Hegel, from whom it derives. Hegel held that social change occurs as the result of the clash of ideal (intellectual) forces in a dialectic manner. Both of these theories are more complex than earlier theories of social change as simple progress (or decline) or as cycles. The theory that political relationships never change at all or do so at random may seem to be the implied view if issues such as this are not explicitly met.

Class Struggle

Aside from the issues of historical stages and the units of political action, there is the more general issue of whether the researcher is assuming a system in equilibrium, in which change is deviant (a view often ascribed to Talcott Parsons and other structural-functionalists), or whether he assumes conflict and views the seemingly stable regimes of such men as Louis Bonaparte as temporary balancing acts enabled by special circumstances. Although any topic can be forced into either format, the student will no doubt choose one or the other according to the subject matter.

Scientific Method

Although Marx did not make politics a science, he did face and attempt to resolve many issues having a direct bearing on scientific method in political research. Few know, for example, that one of the earliest plans for a mass questionnaire survey was projected by Marx. More important, however, was his recognition of the need to make explicit the relevant variables and relationships leading up to his predictive hypotheses. As we shall later see, some modern methodologies, although more rigorously defining their variables, have undermined their own usefulness by failing to clarify a dynamic of social change. That is, Marx did develop a predictive, empirically-testable causal model bearing on substantively important matters. As Louis Hartz has noted, others have said that everything is related to everything else. That has been said before and will be said again. It more closely corresponds to reality, but it is not useful.

When asked if a civil war will break out in India, for example, the Marxist can consult his theories, look at the known facts, and attempt an answer; many others will be so lost in complexity they will only be able to give the true but not very useful answer that it all depends on a hundred different factors. The job of political scientists interested in scientific method is not to accurately describe the overwhelmingly complex nature of political life; rather it is to develop workable simplifications more useful than Marxism and other contemporary explanatory theories.

Objectivity

Marx wrote, "The philosophers have only interpreted the world; the point, however, is to change it." Some have argued that an activist position undermines objectively; others, like C. Wright Mills, argue that we all stand inside history and can never be truly objective. Many would agree that activism does not necessarily sacrifice objectivity, although it may pose a threat. Chester Barnard's work on organization theory or Schlesinger's work on the Kennedy administration are but two of many important works by authors active in the practical affairs they describe as "objectively" as authors not so involved. In fact, one could argue that the disengaged position breeds isolation from "reality" and hence encourages ideological distortion. Regardless, the issue of engaged observation and social relevance of research must also be faced by all political scientists.

Example

T. B. Bottomore distinguishes between Marxian (pertaining to the man, Marx) and Marxist (in some manner taking off from Marxian writings) analyses. Here, concerned with the latter, our intent is not to determine what the orthodox Marxian approach would be. Rather, the student of political science must learn to think about a problem of analysis from a number of divergent points of view before attempting his own synthesis.

As a methodology, Marxism directs attention in certain directions. In choosing issues to study, it focuses on conflict and class-related areas. In choosing groups to study, it focuses on social classes. In terms of history, it emphasizes production epochs; its perspective is materialist and dialectic. The general method involves a historical model based on the tension between the dynamic of technology and the contradiction between the means of production and the social relationships of production. For example, Reconstruction in America might be interpreted as ending because a victorious Northern business class traded rejection of radical reform interests for acceptance by the South of a tariff structure and other political arrangements favorable to the North.

Many variations of class analysis are possible. For example, one may specify many more classes than simply owners and workers, yet retain an emphasis on relationship to the means of production (intellectuals, managers, women, criminals are examples of possible additional classes). Alternatively, class may be defined in terms of one or more socio-economic indicators, or Dahrendorf's suggestion about the use of authority cleavages may be pursued.

Figure 1.1 uses a Marxist method of analysis to illustrate a possible explanation of rioting.

Figure 1.1

Analysis	Example
1. Focus on an issue emphasizing conflict and change.	1. Why have riots occurred during the 1960s in American ghettos?
2. Specify the classes involved.	2. Primarily black lower class and white lower middle class (police).
3. Note historical changes in the relationship of each to the means of production.	3. Blacks: shifting from rural, peasant-like status into the marginal proletariat (as service workers), beginning shift into working class and to a much lesser extent to middle class status. Whites: shifting from working class into white collar and allied middle class positions.
4. Note changed interests resulting from altered relationships.	4. Blacks: new work relations forge greater responsibility and discipline, resulting in greater class consciousness. Whites: those remaining in working class and marginal middle class positions (as police) feel threatened.

Analysis	**Example**
5. Note direction of change suggested by changed interests.	5. Blacks: greater assertiveness of class issues, such as demands for equality and power for the poor. Whites: resist challenge to former class arrangements.
6. Note interaction with super-structure, including effect on the political event studied.	6. Black assertion of class demands leads to civil rights organizations and then to conflict with white working class and marginal middle class; norms of nonthreatened white upper classes invoked by blacks to gain legitimacy; assertiveness further encouraged. Failure of upper classes in control of government to meet demands in a tangible way (because major re-allocation of resources not in their interest) leads to frustration and struggle through illegal means, and rioting.

One could no doubt elaborate greatly on this sketchy possible Marxist explanation of rioting, perhaps emphasizing World War II in explaining the timing of changed race relationships to class structure, and hence explaining the timing of race conflict. The war, in turn, could be related to the international conflict of economic systems antithetical in nature.

One can challenge this interpretation of rioting, but it is used here to illustrate how Marxism might be adopted as a starting point to generate hypotheses about contemporary political phenomena. Later, explanations of rioting will be attempted from entirely different viewpoints. To repeat, the emphasis is not on searching for one "right" methodology, or even on working toward a unified political "science"; rather, these initial chapters are meant to jar the student out of preconceived solutions and stimulate him toward a creative, pluralistic way of thinking about political issues prior to attempting a synthesis of the most nearly "right" analysis.

2

Psychoanalytic Theory
As Political Methodology

A thought-provoking introduction is provided by Erich Fromm, *Sigmund Freud's Mission* (Grove Press paperback, 1959). Clinical aspects are emphasized in Paul Roazen, *Freud: Political and Social Thought* (Alfred A. Knopf, 1968), especially Chapters 4 and 5; and John Rickman, ed., "Group Psychology and the Analysis of the Ego," in *A General Selection from the Works of Freud* (Doubleday Anchor paperback, 1957). Another also edited by Rickman is *Civilization, War and Death: Selections from Five Works by Sigmund Freud* (Hogarth Press, 1953), especially "Civilization and Its Discontents." Students needing a basic review might start with the first two chapters in J. A. C. Brown, *Freud and the Post-Freudians* (Pelican paperback, 1961).

For the more advanced student wishing to explore the relation of Marxism to psychoanalysis, in addition to the articles by Wilhelm Reich cited in Chapter 1, Herbert Marcuse's *Eros and Civilization: A Philosophical Inquiry into Freud* (Beacon Press, 1955) presents the contrary view that Freud is relevant to political interpretation. Harold Lasswell's *Psychopathology and Politics* and *Power and Personality* (Viking Press paperbacks, 1960 and 1962) are both classic examples of the use of psychology in political analysis. Erich Fromm's *Escape From Freedom* (Avon paperback, 1969; originally published 1941), Erik Erikson's *Young Man Luther*

(Norton paperback, 1958), and Eric Hoffer's *The True Believer* (Harper & Row paperback, 1951) are also illustrative.

An introduction to the vast body of politically relevant literature in the field of social psychology may be gained by reading Hans Toch, *The Social Psychology of Social Movements* (Bobbs-Merrill paperback, 1965) or Hadley Cantril, *The Psychology of Social Movements* (Wiley Science paperback, 1963). Other readings include Fred Greenstein, *Personality and Politics* (Markham paperback, 1969); H. Stuart Hughes, "History and Psychoanalysis" in *History As Art and As Science* (Harper & Row paperback, 1964); and Richard Hofstadter, *The Paranoid Style in American Politics and Other Essays* (Random House paperback, 1965). Finally, the classic contribution of social psychology to political science is John Dollard, Leonard Doob, et. al., eds., *Frustration and Aggression* (Yale University paperback, originally published 1939).

The vocabulary taken from psychology infuses the writings of many political scientists: displacement, repression, identification, regression, sublimation, catharsis, projection, internalization, etc. Political scientists speak of *identification* with a leader, *internalization* of an organization's goals, or the *cathartic effect* of collective violence—yet these are rarely explicit applications of psychology. In spite of this, the psychoanalytic heritage has been one of the most important for political scientists, altering as it does their very image of man.

THE FREUDIAN PERSPECTIVE

If liberalism is understood in its 19th century sense, Freud may be seen as a spokesman for a post-liberal perspective. His concept of the unconscious constituted a fundamental challenge to the liberal concept of rationality, and through rationality to democracy. Once the importance of erotic and aggressive human tendencies became apparent the possibilities of disinterested rational choice seemed much reduced. Political man came to be seen not as the logical calculator of possible pleasures and pains, but rather as a much more animal being whose needs for sex, aggression, power, and other selfish ends could be reconciled with "the greatest good for the greatest number" only in the most tenuous ways, and that with the aid of a considerable amount of civilized repression.

After Freud, and especially after World War I, a great pessimism developed over man's aggressive instincts and over the high cost of social repression of these instincts. Freud himself was seen by contemporaries as a reformer, perhaps primarily because of the attack on Victorian sexual morality that his writings represented. He also asserted the need to rid civilization of unnecessary repression (what Marcuse terms "surplus repression") and was sympathetic to the needs of the working class. Nevertheless, as a liberal, Freud still believed in the necessity of a ruling elite; his was a liberalism without the usual democratic underpinnings.

PSYCHOANALYTIC APPROACHES TO POLITICS

Freud's writings contain several different perspectives on history. In discussing religion, for example, Freud noted three epochs: the animistic, in which the self is seen as omnipotent; the religious, in which father figures are seen as omnipotent; and the scientific, in which omnipotence is no longer a necessary idea—libido is invested in other adults. In his famous letter to Albert Einstein, Freud saw the history of war as a progressive rejection of instinctive goals and a scaling-down of instinctive reactions. He could even foresee the possibility that pacifism might become part of man's "instinctive nature," as he believed it might already be for himself and Einstein. In his essay on "Civilization and Its Discontents," Freud saw a continuing trend toward greater repression to overcome man's aggressive drives, as society's increasing complexity forced men into ever closer contact with one another.

Psychoanalytic writing presents four main developmental themes which may be used for political analysis: psychoanalytic stages, complexity-repression, dynamic normative orientation, and assimilation of experience.

The developmental sequence associated with the psychoanalytic stages (oral, anal, latent, genital) is perhaps the most familiar. According to Freud, the natural history of the human being from infancy to maturity involves a series of definite stages. The oral stage is passive in its early phase and aggressive, biting, incorporative in its later phase. The anal stage that follows is also aggressive, selfish, and retentive. The latent stage, in which mental development is said to remain under the dominance of the pleasure principle, and the genital stage, in which the reality principle replaces the pleasure principle, complete the sequence.

The second theme involves the argument that civilization contains a drive toward complexity, which in turn results in an intensification of social interactions. This intensification, in view of man's aggressive impulses, endangers social organization unless civilization responds by heightening the general level of repression in society. The third developmental sequence, like the first, is a natural history of the individual, who develops from self-orientation through parent-orientation to peer-orientation. Finally, Freud sometimes expressed the view that just as past experiences forge present human nature, so current experiences forge the human nature to come. The difference in this last theme is between the way the city obliterates the town which preceded it, on the one hand, and the way, Freud believed, the child lies submerged but whole in the adult mind.[1]

Criticisms

Paul Roazen has noted that Freud "was tempted to construct historical stages on scanty evidence." Indeed, psychoanalysis is today a minority tradition even within the field of psychology, in part because of the impossibility of documenting its theoretical constructs. Since Freud was *not* concerned with the development of political theory, he cannot be faulted for the shortcomings of some of his more politically-minded followers. Nevertheless, it is useful to examine psychoanalytic approaches from the point of view of the methodological themes mentioned in the discussion on Marxism.

With regard to historical epochs, the psychoanalytic approach to politics might be criticized for ahistoricism. Lacking clear institutional or other tangible referents in history, the psychoanalytic developmental stages (self-parent-other orientations; oral-anal-latent-genital stages) are merely post facto analogies from what is controversially alleged to be the natural history of the individual. But even assuming

---

[1] For terminology the student is referred to the extensive glossary appended to John Rickman, ed., *A General Selection from the Works of Freud* (Garden City, N.Y.: Doubleday Anchor, 1957).

that such stages are useful in analyzing individual development, it would be an ecological fallacy to assume relevance for political groupings. Although the organic analogy in politics (cf. Hobbes' *Leviathan*) attests to the importance of this heritage, there is no reason to believe that what is true for the individual will be true for the group.

Regarding the unit of social or political action, the psychoanalytic approach tends to emphasize primarily the individual in isolation, and secondarily the individual and his peers in collective relation to the leader, in contrast to Marx's use of social classes as the unit of action. The psychoanalytic approach, then, is most congenial to theories of "mass society," such as those advanced by Kornhauser, or theories that emphasize the translogical attachment of followers to leaders, as in Tucker's theory of communism as religion. A psychoanalytic approach would, for similar reasons, be less at home in a theory of interest groups, for example.

In terms of an overview of social change, Freud's views were contradictory. The pessimistic dominant theme, which points to increasing repression of civilization, is one of unilinear development toward an ultimate crisis. On the other hand, any of the other three development themes points to a more optimistic development. While a theory of social change is not stated with the self-assured finality of Marx's pronouncements on dialectic materialism, Freud's views on social change seem to assume a very simplified model that suffers by being made explicit.

A common criticism of writings in the political psychology tradition is that they use psychoanalytic concepts such as neurosis, paranoia, zenophobia, etc. to interpret historical figures such as Stalin, Hitler, or Woodrow Wilson on the slimmest evidence. In this way, the critics claim, psychoanalysis is used as a post facto slur on the character of the man studied, attributing his actions to something much less than rational decision. Such has been the general judgment of the book on Woodrow Wilson to which Freud himself contributed. The charge is that, as with the developmental themes, supposedly specific terms like "schizophrenia" or "paranoia" become mere metaphors when used in political analysis.

CONTEMPORARY METHODOLOGICAL ISSUES

The psychoanalytic approaches raise a fundamental issue of general methodology: what constitutes valid explanation in political science?

This essential question of validity will be dealt with more extensively in a later chapter. For now, however, generally accepted political science explanations involve three parts: a plausible hypothesis, one or more supporting case examples, and general data supporting the hypothesis *and* not supporting the major alternative hypotheses.

The psychoanalytic approaches may certainly be used to generate plausible hypotheses, as even the critics admit, and attempts have often been made to demonstrate these hypotheses for particular cases (often great men). It is on the third point that validation seems almost impossible. How can one estimate the general level of repression in society, much less surplus repression? Since erotic and aggressive drives may be sublimated, repressed, projected, displaced and otherwise disguised, how can any act be interpreted? That is, the psychoanalytic vocabulary contains so many counter-concepts (concepts that mitigate the effect of original concepts) that the general theory is often untestable. Riots, for example, may be explained in terms of an instinct to aggression, while absence of riots may be explained by displacement of aggressive drives onto socially-acceptable objects. Although such an explanation might be true enough, it cannot be used to predict the occurrence of future riots because the variables are contradictory in tendency and unmeasurable for the most part.

Nevertheless, the study of psychoanalytic explanations of political events raises several general methodological issues not discussed in the previous chapter.

Level of Analysis

Variation in political events is usually explained by the variation in other political or social phenomena. The researcher should be aware, however, that there are other possible levels of causation that may be operating instead or in addition. The psychological level, the focus of which is the human personality, is the subject of this chapter, but other levels exist as well.

The most elementary level is the *inorganic*. Even political events may be caused primarily at the level of physical forces. Here, one may recall the theory that the Roman Empire declined not because of the pressure of barbarians or the decadence of its wealthy class, but rather because the leaded wine flasks used by the elite of the Roman Republic caused lead poisoning and physiological deterioration in the ruling class.

This leads to a second level of analysis, the *biologic*. No reminder is required for the various racial theories of politics advanced in the nineteenth century. Rioting, for example, is known to be a predominantly male phenomenon, and although this is usually attributed to cultural causes, genetic explanations have also been advanced.

Above the biologic level of explanation, which includes physiological factors, is the *ecological* level. This deals with factors such as density of population, relationships between population groups, and relations of population groups to the environment. For example, "territoriality," or the tendency of animals to defend their territory against intruders, is an ecological factor sometimes used in explaining aggressive human behavior.

The ecological tends to merge with the *social* level of explanation, overlapping particularly in demographic explanations. An example of a demographic explanation is contained in David Riesman's *The Lonely Crowd*,[2] in which Riesman argues that shifting birth and death rates together with increasing economic plenty are responsible for a shift in American character from "inner-" to "other-directedness." Another demographic explanation is the argument attributing manifestations of Chinese aggressiveness to Chinese population expansion.

Another kind of explanation at the social level are those analyses focusing on group structure. For instance, the theory of "mass society" attributes the instability of such societies to the relative absence of mediating organizations between the rulers and the masses; American stability is attributed to the proliferation of secondary groups in the "middle levels" of American society.

Economic and *political* level explanations are sometimes considered explanations at the social level, though are more often regarded as distinct but coordinate levels of explanation. In fact, the "social level" is often a residual category for institutional explanations not focusing on predominantly economic or political institutions. For example, explaining the changes in American farm policy by reference to changes in the Farm Bureau Federation and other farmers' organizations would be of such a residual "social" type. On the other hand, explaining farm policy change in terms of the changing role of agriculture in modern capitalist society would be an economic level

[2] David Riesman, et. al., *The Lonely Crowd: A Study of the Changing American Character* (New Haven: Yale University, 1950).

explanation, while explanation in terms of power relationships among federal departments would be a political level explanation. The researcher should be aware that explanations at these different levels need not be incompatible at all; in fact analysis at several different levels of explanation may be highly fruitful if conducted explicitly.

The *cultural* level of explanation is considered the most general level (if one does not count the religious-magical level). Study of culture is the study of forms of social, political, and economic action *as* forms. A work of art, the U.S. Constitution, and a factory are all culture objects from which the researcher may infer the culture of our society. The study of culture often revolves around the study of values which, in cultural level explanations, are often presumed to be the molders of the forms of social or political action. Seymour M. Lipset's *The First New Nation,* for example, interprets American history in terms of the interplay between the values of equality and achievement.

In conclusion, the political science researcher must face the problem of level of analysis and not assume that a political level explanation is necessarily the only or the most appropriate level.

Developmental Sequences

The most general issue raised by psychoanalytic approaches to political interpretation is whether or not events are to be analyzed in terms of natural history. This is similar to the issue raised in the previous chapter with regard to historical epochs, but in a slightly more specific sense. That is, does the researcher wish to assume that the historical period he is studying can be divided into "natural" sequences, each of which develops out of the former? Is there, for example, a "natural history of riots" or a "natural history of organizational growth" in a sense analogous to the natural development of the human organism, or for that matter, the human personality?

The implication of such an assumption is that political explanation is akin to biologic explanation. That is, first, that "riots," "organizations," or whatever is being studied have a fundamental unity akin to the unity of the human species. Second, development is seen as largely the result of the inner dynamic and structure of the personality, organization or whatever, and is only secondarily a function of environmental variables. And third, resulting from the first two, "natural history" explanations are usually phrased in universal terms, independent of time or cultural background. In each case the researcher will need to judge whether his subject is compatible with these implications. If the term "natural" is used as a mere figure of speech, this should be made explicit.

Appearances

A third major methodological issue raised by the psychoanalytic tradition is whether things are what they seem or whether they are the reverse of what they seem. This is not a trivial issue in political science as the following examples may suggest. In a political campaign, if a politician repeatedly emphasizes his integrity, is that to be taken as evidence that his integrity is secure or as evidence that his integrity is in question? If an organization's house newspaper contains many assertions of how happy its employees are, is this to be taken as evidence of high morale or of great need to overcome discontent?

The legacy of Freud is a pervasive skepticism toward outward appearances. Emphasis on the unconscious, on projections of feelings onto others, on reversal of images in dreams, and the argument that the actions of maturity are built on the fears and desires of childhood have made succeeding generations cautious in interpreting "reality." Particularly in political interpretations of statements and attitudes contemporary researchers encounter the issue of the validity of face appearance. "Face validity" or "surface meaning," while a useful first test of validity, cannot be the only test; every hypothesis requires multiple confirmation.

Motives

Another change brought by the Freudian "revolution" is the widespread assumption that all actions are ultimately based on selfish motives growing out of the basic human drives of sex and aggression, plus instincts such as hunger. Because of the concepts of sublimation and displacement, interpretation of motives becomes much more complex than identification of the dominant drive. Indeed, the subject can quickly become so muddy that most researchers choose to avoid the issue altogether. Since motives are an important part of many political explanations, however, the method often used by those who do confront this issue is acceptance of the face validity of self-declared motives. (This, of course, raises the issue of appearances.) Beyond this, the only alternative has seemed to be in-depth interviews as a crude approximation to psychoanalytic techniques. Again, the use of all three techniques—observing objective behavior, noting self-declared motives, and using rough psychological tests—may be needed to explore the complex issue of determining the motivation of political actors.

Importance of the Past

Beyond the issues of historical epochs and developmental sequences, the psychoanalytic approach raises another problem for researchers. If many political matters are conceived of as existing in stages, are the early stages to be considered determining or is every stage a transitional one? Ultimately this issue becomes the familiar philosophical issue of free will. Its importance is that if earlier stages in a given political matter are causally more important, then in most political analyses the researcher will want to place heavy emphasis on historical evidence. If this is not true, or is not true in a particular case, then the researcher is free to limit his methods to those such as survey samples which usually bring to light relatively little historical data.

Example

As methodology, the psychoanalytic approach directs attention toward irrational behavior, toward the personal stakes in public matters, and the development of relationships between the individual and the polity over time. It invites a wariness of surface appearances, watchfulness for and even expectation of hypocrisy or divergence of ideal and practice, and it is a reminder to relate political analysis ultimately to the individual, who is by definition the only possible actor. That is, it is a warning against reification.

Because of emphasis on identification with a father-figure in analysis of groups, the psychoanalytic approach has been used to justify study of a group through study of leaders; that is, seeking to understand a group in terms of its leaders rather than, for instance, its class composition. The example for political analysis by this method depends on which of the four developmental themes is selected by the researcher as most appropriate. Figure 2.1, however, is illustrative of the way in which psychoanalytic concepts may be used to generate hypotheses about a political subject, in this case the explanation of why riots happen when they do.

Figure 2.1

Analysis	**Example**
1. Ask a question of the type "How has X developed?" where X would ordinarily involve a matter not explainable at the strictly rational level.	1. What is the developmental origin of riots?
2. Specify the groups involved, noting the individual's relation to the leader.	2. Various black groups, often led by visionary, even messianic leader, usually with religious association.
3. Note the relationship of complexity of civilization, social needs for repression, and changes in social spacing.	3. Increasingly complex urban America requires proportionately greater repression in economic roles, which are quite rigid. Since black men are routinely assigned to lower, more rigid roles (for non-psychological reasons) they suffer relatively great repression.
4. Note the relationship of groups involved to historical development.	4. As repression increases, falling disproportionately on blacks, aggressive energy is increasingly displaced into existing messianic groups traditionally sanctioning emotive behavior; riots result.
5. Consider alternative psychoanalytic variants.	5. (a) *Natural History Theme:* Riots are due to the tension and frustration associated with the shift from self-orientation (Africa) to child status and parent-orientation (slavery and Reconstruction) as shown in the slave revolts documented by Herbert Aptheker, and the shift from child status to peer-orientation (currently being fulfilled) shown in the riots of the 1960s.

Example

(b) *Assimilation of the Past:* Violence inflicted on the black man over the years gradually became part of his life experience and nature. The residue of past violence accumulated to critical levels and was eventually expressed in rioting, which will decline only with a similar long-term process of abatement.

Again, other research on rioting may refute these explanations. Nevertheless, the psychoanalytic approach is fruitful in generating hypotheses about many political matters. Hypotheses thus generated may be used by the researcher either directly or as examples of possible alternative hypotheses; the researcher must then show that his hypothesis is supported by the evidence he has gathered, while other plausible explanations are not. Creative generation and well-documented rejection of plausible alternative hypotheses is absolutely essential to valid explanation in political science and in the social sciences in general.

HYPOTHESIS EVALUATION

When is a theory true, and when is it merely so much plausible hogwash? Beginning (and older) students of politics are often overwhelmed by the problem of evaluating explanations various authors propose. Where does one begin? Obviously this depends on the particular case; however, the following is a good standard procedure for evaluating any political hypothesis:

1. Identify the *dependent variable(s)*. Keep asking questions until you determine just what it is that is being explained. Is it the historical timing of riots, location of riots, the types of people involved in rioting, objectives of the rioters, or all of these?
2. Identify *other important variables* in the analysis. Forget for a moment the relationships and just concentrate on listing the various factors that are considered important parts of the explanation. For rioting, these might include variables such as past

persecution of blacks, relative deprivation, Supreme Court decisions, and many others.

3. Identify *main relationships* among the variables as these relationships are asserted in the theory in question. Often researchers do this by representing the various variables as labeled circles and the relationships as arrows denoting causation. Mutual causation is shown by arrows going in both directions, and plus or minus signs tell whether the relationship is positive or negative. A diagram made in this way constitutes the *model* implied by the theory.

4. Give each of the variables an *operational definition.* We may wish to talk about "industrialization" as a variable, for instance, but how do we know it when we see it? How could we measure it? By the ratio of animal to total energy consumed in a society? By the extent of concentration of manufacturing capital? By the number of telephones per 100,000 population? By some combination of *indicators?* Some variables may not be operationalizable. This does not mean the theory is bad, but only that it cannot be tested with regard to relationships involving such variables; one cannot know.

5. *Data* is gathered to show trends in the indicators of the model's variables.

6. The hypothesized relationships (each illustrated by an arrow in the model) are *tested* by the data. This involves four questions:
   a. *Significance.* An apparent relationship is said to be "significant" if there is any relationship really there, even though it may be weak.
   b. *Association.* An assessment is made as to how strong the relationship is.
   c. *Validity.* The relationship is investigated to see if it is based on methodological error, logical fallacy, or spuriousness due to relations to variables not mentioned in the hypothesis.
   d. *Importance.* Ultimately, the researcher must assess whether anyone does or should care about the hypothesis, even if he is right. Does it matter?

7. *Alternative explanations* of the same dependent variable(s) are examined in a similar manner. This step is essential. The researcher should assume that any given set of data may be "explained" by more than one hypothesis. Merely because the data fit one theory does not mean the theory is right. Competing hypotheses must also be shown not to fit the data.

The purpose of these first few chapters is to help the student creatively arrive at several possible explanations of a given set of political data as one of the beginning steps of political analysis.

3

Structural-Functionalism As Methodology

Political scientists have both drawn from and criticized structural-functionalism. For general background the student might read "Functional Causal Imagery," pp. 80–101 in Arthur L. Stinchombe, *Constructing Social Theories* (Harcourt, Brace & World paperback, 1968); and A. James Gregor, "Political Science and the Uses of Functional Analysis" *(American Political Science Review* 62:2, June, 1968, pp. 425–439). The basic framework of structural-functionalism is set forth in Talcott Parsons and Edward Shils, eds., *Toward a General Theory of Action,* Chapters 4–5 (Harper & Row paperback, 1951), or "The Point of View of the Author" by Talcott Parsons in Max Black, ed., *The Social Theories of Talcott Parsons* (Prentice-Hall, 1961).

For a critical point of view read Barrington Moore, Jr., *Political Power and Social Theory* (Harper & Row paperback, 1958), especially the essay on "The New Scholasticism and the Study of Politics." Other readings might include Max Black, "Some Questions About Parsons' Theories" and Andrew Hacker, "Sociology and Ideology" in Black, ed., *supra.*; Karl Mannheim, "American Sociology" and Daniel Foss, "The World View of Talcott Parsons" in M. Stein and A. Vidich, eds., *Sociology on Trial* (Spectrum paperback, 1963). A useful and careful summary is contained in Marion Levy, *The Structure of Society* (Princeton University paperback, 1952), pp. 543–568.

Political science writings that have borrowed from the functionalist tradition include O. R. Young, *Systems of Political Science* (Prentice-Hall paperback, 1968); W. Mitchell, *The American Polity* (Free Press paperback, 1962); and G. A. Almond and G. B. Powell, *Comparative Politics: A Developmental Approach* (Little Brown paperback, 1966). None of these very different books is entirely uncritical of structural-functionalism.

The vocabulary of structural-functionalism, including such terms as function, system, adaptation, equilibrium, etc., has infused political science; on the other hand it is virtually impossible to find a political scientist who is not critical of the approach to some degree. Because political scientists have been so eclectic in what they have borrowed from structural-functionalism, this chapter examines the methodology in its "pure" form, with a view toward determining to what extent it might be used to generate interesting hypotheses. That is, we wish to ask whether structural-functionalism has a true explanatory value or whether it is an elaborate check-list typology useful only to store and retrieve general information.

VOCABULARY OF STRUCTURAL-FUNCTIONALISM

To begin, here are some of the terms that make up this system and the ways they are related. **Structures** are observable uniformities of action; it is the existence of these regularities that makes social science a possibility. **Functions** are the results of structures; they are not purposes or needs. Because the definition of function is tied to potentially observable results rather than imputed intent, that is, to actual behavior, this general method is compatible with behavioralism.

Institutions are defined as structures which, in their basic composition, are ideal (conform to social norms), actual (conform to reality), and enforced. A **tradition** is an institution whose perpetuation is institutionalized, even without regard for the functional implications of the tradition's operations. In this system of definitions, traditions are more stable than institutions, and institutions are more enduring than structures.

Functional requisites are results, usually generalized conditions, that are necessary to the maintenance of the unit with which they are associated. **Structural requisites** are patterns of actions necessary to fulfill functional requisites. **Equivalents** are structures that yield the same results (serve the same function). **Eufunctions** and **eustructures** are results or patterns leading to the maintenance or increase of adaptation, and hence to the persistence of the unit (where adaptation is any process that aids the survival, functioning, maintenance, or achievement of purpose of the unit considered). **Dysfunctions** and **dysstructures** are results or patterns leading to the lessening of adaptation and hence to failure of the unit to persist.

Functional prerequisites are results, usually generalized conditions, necessary for a unit to come into being. **Structural prerequisites** are structures leading to fulfillment of functional prerequisites. **Concrete structures** are capable of physical separation in time and/or space, whereas **analytic structures** are not.

Manifest functions are intended and recognized results, whereas results that are unintended and unrecognized are **latent** functions. Similarly, **IUR** functions are intended and unrecognized, and **UIR** functions are unintended but recognized.

Example

Robert Merton's classic analysis of the role of the city political "machine" can be employed to illustrate the use of structural-functional vocabulary in the analysis of a political subject:[1]

The old city machine was a *structure* that served the *function* of adjusting immigrants to urban America. Its *functional prerequisites* included prior urbanization and immigration, the *structural prerequisites* for which included foremost the development of steam industry (which in turn had the *functional prerequisite* of inexpensive labor). Continuation of immigration was a *structural requisite* of the urban political machine (presence of immigrants was the *functional requisite*). Decline of immigration and the growth of professionalization were among the *dysstructures* resulting in the

[1] See Robert K. Merton, *On Theoretical Sociology* (New York: Free Press, 1949), pp. 127–136.

dysfunctions (for the *unit* of the political machine subsystem) of fewer immigrants and fewer patronage jobs. Lacking these *structural-functional requisites,* the unit has failed to persist. The problem arises because only recently has the hitherto *latent function* of political machines in aiding the low-skilled adjust to urban life become manifest. The poverty program is an effort to find a *structural equivalent* to fulfill that *eufunction* formerly fulfilled by the machines.

This example, though presented in an abbreviated and oversimplified form, suggests some of the strengths and weaknesses of structural-functional analysis.

Procedure

The following is a step outline of the procedure of structural-functional requisite analysis, showing specific applications to the previous example of the city political machine:

1. Identify the unit to be studied, e.g., the urban political machine, defined by party dominance of city politics and personal dominance of the party.
2. Identify the unit's setting. **Setting** is the set of factors limiting the range of variation of the unit. For the political machine, crucial aspects of the setting include the American constitutional framework and American capitalism.
3. Specify whether one is interested in why a structure persists or in how it came into being. If the former, discuss requisites; if the latter, discuss prerequisites.
4. Determine the functional (pre)requisites, e.g., urbanization, immigration.
5. Determine the structural (pre)requisites, e.g., steam industry.
6. Specify the eufunctional and dysfunctional structures affecting the unit at the time studied, e.g., professionalism, decline of immigration.
7. Identify possible structural equivalents for the eufunctions noted.
8. Throughout the analysis, try to recognize all types of functions, not just manifest (or latent) functions.
9. Finally, avoid **functional teleology;** that is, asserting that the presence of a structure is due to its being a functional requisite of the unit in which it is found. Being a necessity does not guarantee a structure's existence.

Criticisms

Among the strengths of the structural-functional requisite method are rigorous definitions carefully interrelated, avoidance of a focus on governmental-institutional aspects alone, and systematic consideration of many possibly relevant types of variables. Weaknesses include definitions that are difficult to operationalize, absence of a criterion for determining which variables are more causally relevant than others, and hence a more restrospective than predictive usefulness. That is, structural-functional requisite analysis tends to be a typology, not a theory, and is better used to categorize variables than to predict relationships.

Structural-functional requisite analysis has been accused of a conservative bias because of its emphasis on equilibriating forces, often of a socially diffuse sort not amenable to intentional control, and for its emphasis on incremental change. It may lead researchers to overemphasize latent eufunctions to what are generally regarded as "social evils" (the city boss was good because he serviced immigrants; apathy is good because it prevents overpoliticization of social life; corruption is good because it enables flexibly circumventing rigid rules), and not emphasize latent dysfunctions or, for that matter, manifest and other functions. (The attraction to latent eufunctions is that the political scientist often would like to assert something resulting from his research that is not "common sense.")

On the other hand, structural-functional requisite analysis does have some potentially anti-conservative aspects. If structural equivalents are emphasized, then the implication is that no existing political structure is necessary. Every structure must be examined to determine if it is more eufunctional than dysfunctional, and if there is a superior structural equivalent that might replace it.

LEVELS OF STRUCTURAL-FUNCTIONAL ANALYSIS

Beyond the structural-functional requisite analysis discussed above, there are three related types of analysis that fall within this tradition. These are *universal requisite analysis, pattern variable analysis,* and *AGIL system analysis.*

Universal Requisite Analysis

As a result of structural-functional requisite analysis, some scholars have attempted to delineate the functional requisites of any society in any place or time period. This list of "universal requisites" is sometimes used, often in abridged form, as a checklist procedure for studying society. This type of analysis is common in the study of comparative development in political science. Each of the ten functional requisites of any society may be used as a chapter in analyzing a society as a whole. These ten areas are:

1. Provision for adequate sexual *recruitment* and physiological relation to the environment. This functional requisite is so basic it is often assumed rather than discussed.

2. Provision for adequate *role differentiation* and role assignment. Roles are positions that are differentiated from one another in terms of a given social structure, and may be either *ideal* (normative definition of the role) or *actual* (role as defined by behavior). A particularly important part of role differentiation is differentiation by *status,* where status is the sum of the individual's ideal roles, as opposed to *social standing,* which is the sum of the individual's ideal and actual roles. If the same *role cluster* that exists in an individual also exists in a great many other individuals, the role cluster defines a *station* in life. A *stratum* is a mass of persons holding the same station, while *stratification* is role differentiation by higher or lower social standing.

3. Provision for adequate levels of *communication*. Here vocabulary is often borrowed from communications theory, and authors speak of a system composed of *input, transformation, output,* and *feedback* sectors.

4. Provision for adequate levels of *shared cognitive orientations.* That is, any society must provide for minimum levels of information common to all or most citizens if it is to function. *Basic* cognitive orientations are those which are functional requisites.

5. Provision for adequate levels of shared, articulated *goals.* This raises the possibility of tension among multiple goals or goals

that entail dysfunctional aspects. The emphasis is usually on patterns resulting in adequate *consensus* about social goals.

6. Provision for the *regulation* of the choice of *means*.

7. Provision for adequate *regulation of affective expression* is also considered to be a functional requisite of any society, suggesting the importance of structures encouraging *conformity* in social behavior.

8. Provision for adequate *socialization* of individuals. Socialization is considered adequate if a sufficient number of socialized individuals exist to permit the structural requisites of society to operate. Socialization involves both the *education* and training of the young by the family, church, and school, and also the *assimilation* of outsiders into the dominant culture.

9. Provision for effective *control of disruptive behavior*. (Contrast 6, which deals with allocation problems). The role of regulatory forces in maintaining *stability* is emphasized here.

10. Provision for adequate levels of *institutionalization*. Every society institutionalizes some of its basic structures, that is, assures that they be ideal, actual, and enforced. This involves eliciting adequate levels of *support* for and *commitment* to social institutions.[2]

Here again the strengths and weaknesses of structural-functionalism are revealed. The researcher has the advantage of a comprehensive set of categories in which to fit his data and which he may use as a mnemonic device for remembering if he has treated all relevant aspects. On the other hand, critics argue that all aspects of a society are not included, and that there is a conservative bias involved in the focus on regulation, stability, conformity, assimilation, socialization, and the study of social stratification in its aspects as a functional requisite.

One might compensate for this bias by studying "provision for adequate levels of conflict" and "adequate institutionalization of innovation-generating structures." However, even with these adjustments the researcher should be aware of the bias involved by the implicit posing of the question, "How have things come to be the way they are?" rather than the question raised by a focus on structural equivalents, "How might things be different?"

But even though structural-functionalism may be used to categorize non-institutionally bound areas of study, for example, of a developing

---

[2] See Marion J. Levy, *The Structure of Society* (Princeton: Princeton University, 1952), Chapter 4.

nation, and even if the biases of the method are kept in mind, the method of universal requisite analysis is much more a typology than a theory. There is here no dynamic element akin to Marxist dialectical materialism rooted in the evolution of technology, nor to the psycho-analytic development sequences rooted in the assumed relevance of biological and personality development. Hence there can be no "paradigm for analysis" equivalent to that given in the previous chapters for the case of rioting.

Nevertheless, it is not true that structural-functionalism is a mere typology, as is clear when the remaining two structural-functional methods of analysis are considered.

Pattern Variable Analysis

Universal requisite analysis is appropriate for studies undertaken at the level of societal units; pattern variable analysis is appropriate for study at the level of individual interactions. **Pattern variables** are ideal points marking the extremes of several continua used to represent dimensions of individual interactions. For example, self-orientation and collectivity-orientation mark the extremes of one of the pattern variable dimensions. The idea of the pattern variables may be traced back to Ferdinand Tonnies' work *Community and Society,* and through Tonnies to Marx. The underlying conception is that traditional communities tend to be characterized by collectively oriented, functionally diffuse, hierarchic behavior patterns, whereas modern societies are more self-oriented, nonhierarchic, and universalistic. A look at each of the pattern variables will make this clearer:

1. *Universalistic v. particularistic:* Relationships are universalistic if admission to them is by germane criteria without social barriers. Relationships in modern organizations tend to be more universalistic than relationships in tribal organizations, for example.

2. *Affective neutrality v. affectivity:* This is sometimes also called the avoidant-intimate dimension. In more modern, impersonal organizations relationships do not tend to elicit strong affective interactions; instead affective neutrality is the rule.

3. *Self-orientation v. collectivity-orientation:* This is sometimes referred to as the individualistic-responsible dimension. Modern organizational relationships are often said to be self-oriented, where each individual is expected to calculate his own advantage in a given relationship.

4. *Functional specificity v. functional diffuseness:* Here, in modern relationships rights and obligations are more often precisely defined. For example, one is treated specifically as a customer by the modern shopkeeper, whereas the traditional shopkeeper treated one not only as a customer, but also as a person of a particular religion, nationality, etc.

In addition to these four pattern variables, three others are occasionally used, although they are not always acknowledged to be universally-applicable:

5. *Achievement v. ascription:* Modern societies are often seen as relying more on achievement as a criterion for relationships than on ascriptive factors like family background. Talcott Parsons used this pattern variable, but later substituted the term "performance-quality" as more descriptive. Others have rejected this pattern variable because it seemingly overlaps universalism-particularism.
6. *Rational-arational:* Marion Levy set forth this dimension, defining rational as the circumstance when objective and subjective ends are identical and the means are empirical. Irrational relationships occur when objective ends and subjective ends are not the same, although the means may be empirical. Arational behavior occurs when the means are not empirical, e.g., magic.
7. *Hierarchic-nonhierarchic:* Levy also set forth this dimension, noting that traditional relationships are more often hierarchic than are modern relationships.

Conceivably these pattern variables could be used as a dynamic part of structural-functional theory, based on a natural development sequence from traditional to modern pattern variable relationships. These assumptions sometimes underlie theories of personalism or clientelism in the administration of developing countries. Or one might attribute rioting to a period of anomie between the keeping of traditional pattern variables characteristic of the rural American South, and the holding of modern pattern variables characteristic of Northern city life.

Parsons himself, however, explicitly denies that he holds the conception of a shift from traditional to modern pattern variables. Instead of seeing the ideal points of the pattern variables grouped into two main sets, traditional and modern, Parsons asserts that the various dimensions may vary independently. He does, however, link universalism and specificity, particularism and diffuseness, achievement and neutrality, and ascription and affectivity. He refers to the first two of these pairs as orientation or attitudinal dimensions, and the second two pairs as modality or object-categorization dimensions. This more complex view tends to severely undercut the possibilities of a developmental sequence dynamic akin to the Freudian developmental themes that might be used to give structural-functionalism a predictive value.

Table 3.1   The AGIL System

ADAPTIVE	**GOAL-ATTAINING**	
General Action Level: organism	personality	
cultural system	social systems	
	economy (industry)	polity (government)
	religion- family (church)	societal community (voluntary groups)

PATTERN MAINTAINING   **INTEGRATIVE**

Structural Components of Society

roles	collectivities
values	norms

AGIL System Analysis

The AGIL system is perhaps the best-known aspect of structural-functional analysis. It is a set of **functional analytic aspects** which are *hierarchically arranged* and associated with certain *general processes.*

The analytic aspects are used to describe the predominant function of the parts of any system. There are four such aspects: the *adaptive* (adjusts the system to environmental changes), *goal-attaining, integrative,* and *pattern maintaining* (protects basic structural patterns of a system). Originally the last aspect was termed "latent pattern maintaining" and together the beginning letters of the four aspects formed the acronym "AGIL." (Confusion is further compounded by the occasional use of the term "analytic aspects" to denote the pattern variables.)

Using these functional aspects, structural-functionalists may for purposes of analysis divide any system into four parts as illustrated by Table 3.1. For example, the action system is divided into the organism, personality, social, and cultural systems each predominantly associated with the adaptive, goal-attaining, integrative, and pattern-maintaining aspects, respectively. The social system (Table 3.2) in turn is divided into the economy, polity, societal community (manifested, for example, in voluntary groups), and the religion-

Table 3.2   AGIL Subsystem Attributes of the Social System

Subsystem	General Symbolic Medium	Ultimate Base	Standard	Unit
Economy	Money	Gold	Utility	Dollar
Polity	Power	Physical Force	Effectiveness in goal-achievement	Vote
Societal Community	Influence	Ascriptive Membership	Solidarity	?
Religion-Family Complex	Commitment	?	Integrity	?

family complex, each associated predominantly with the respective AGIL aspect. Any of these subsystems might in turn be divided into the **structural components** of any society—roles, collectivities, norms (rules specifying values), and values—each of these associated with the AGIL aspect of the corresponding order.

Systems and subsystems are seen as related through a **cybernetic hierarchy,** a term drawn from information theory denoting the principle by which higher-information, lower-energy systems tend to "control" lower-information, higher-energy systems. For example, men control machines; collectivities control roles. In fact, the AGIL aspects stand in control hierarchy relationships to one another, with the pattern-maintaining aspect associated with the system or subsystem at the top of the control hierarchy. The implication would seem to be that components of the cultural system, primarily values, in some sense control the social system, of which the polity is a subsystem. For example, Parsons speaks of the important role of the value of "instrumental activism"—using society as an instrument in asserting control over environment—in determining the course of American society. Similarly, Seymour M. Lipset in his *The First New Nation* talks of changes in American development as a function of the interplay between the values of equality and achievement.

On the other hand, in spite of Lipset's praise of Parsons as "perhaps the foremost contemporary exponent of the importance of value systems as causal factors,"[3] Parsons himself does not equate cybernetic control with causation. He points to the role of "feedback" in information systems to show that causation flows both up and down the cybernetic hierarchy. Critics charge that cybernetic control is meaningless if it does not imply greater causation down the hierarchy than up.

Thus another conservative bias of structural-functionalism is revealed in the AGIL system. Parsons' thought, clearly in opposition to Marx, places material factors low in the control hierarchy. It places the economy under the control of the polity, and the polity ultimately under the control of the religion-family complex as mediated through a vaguely-defined "societal community."

An additional conservative bias is introduced into structural-functionalism in discussion of the *medium* and *base* of the four social

---

[3] Seymour M. Lipset, *The First New Nation: The United States in Historical and Comparative Perspective* (Garden City, N.Y.: Doubleday Anchor, 1963), p. 4.

subsystems. Here an analogy is built between the enonomic market and the political system, and a basis laid for a competitive market theory of politics. Besides the implications for predictive theory of the pattern variables, the cybernetic hierarchy, and the market analogy, Parsons and other structural-functionalists discuss at least four *general processes* of the social system: *differentiation, specification, inclusion,* and *upgrading.*

Processes

Differentiation is a process whereby a former unity becomes divided into heterogeneous parts. An example at the social system level is the breaking up of the traditional family, farm, and business into the modern, separate farm, family, and firm. Here one may contrast **segmentation,** whereby the family-farm-firm splits into the family-farm-firm of son #1 and the family-farm-firm of son #2. At the personality system level, the mother-child perception becomes differentiated into the mother-father-daughter-son perception, and is then further differentiated to take account of still others. At the cultural level, the church-state-school of traditional society becomes differentiated into separation of church, state and school.

Specification is the historical process in the social system whereby values (highly generalized goals) are translated into particular norms (heuristic rules for attaining values). **Inclusion** is another historical process whereby the societal community confers rights of community on new groups and imposes the obligation not to disrupt community solidarity. In this regard, one may contrast *assimilation,* whereby the included group members are dispersed throughout the system. **Upgrading** is the process whereby norms are improved to better fulfill values. Each of these four processes is predominantly associated with one of the AGIL aspects, in the usual order (differentiation with adaptation, specification with goal-attainment, etc.).

Examples

1. Changes in Black Status. The *value* of equality remains but *norms* have been *upgraded* and Negroes included in *collectivities* and their *roles* have become more *differentiated* (for instance, contrast the old, undifferentiated Negro role of black, nonvoter, menial laborer, ghetto resident). Improvement in the *status* of blacks is attributed to the social system processes of upgrading, inclusion, and differentiation, a change in which the role of value changes as mediated by value specification is crucial. (Note that if one accepts the premise that specification, upgrading, etc., are natural social processes inherent in the social system, then changes in norms need not be explained in turn).

2. Why Do Riots Happen? The divergence of *ideal norms* and *actual norms* relating to the central *value* of equality became crucial when central *pattern-maintaining institutions* like the Supreme Court handed down authoritative decisions sanctioning *upgrading* of actual norms. Although whites recognized the need for *inclusion* of blacks by conferring community rights, this involved breaking the *obligation* of not disrupting community *solidarity*. That is, the process of *inclusion* in the course of its natural development was threatening the *functional requisite* of minimum levels of shared, articulated goals, or *consensus*. Out of this conflict a crisis precipitated in which norms or goals bearing on inclusion became highly salient. Although the basic values of American society remained largely unchanged, the crisis reordered the hierarchy of conflicting norms specifying those values. In this reordering adequate levels of consensus about the most salient goals were not reached, and the functional requisite of goal consensus was not met. Therefore, there was a disintegration of the *societal community* at the *boundary* where that subsystem was *articulated* with the group to be included. That disintegration took the form of rioting. Dissolution and regrouping enables a higher level of consensus resolving friction.

Paradigm for AGIL System Analysis

1. Specify the unit to be studied. If the unit is societal, place it in the context of the universal requisites. If the unit is individual, place it in the context of the pattern variables.
2. Specify the relationship of the unit and its subsystems to the central values of the society and to norms assumed to be in the process of continuous specification and upgrading. Relate these normative changes to the social processes of inclusion and differentiation.
3. Assume the AGIL system cybernetic control hierarchy indicates

the central flow of causation. This will ordinarily involve imputing high causal priority to normative factors.
4. Make explicit the biases noted elsewhere in this chapter.

Structural-functionalism is the last of the grand methodologies considered in this book, but a similar presentation might be made for social Darwinism, market equilibrium theories of politics, phenomenology, or a number of other approaches. From the methodologies that have been explored in the last three chapters, the student may now have greater insight into the ways of formulating creative alternative hypotheses.

4

Systems Analysis
As An Approach

The term "systems analysis" covers several approaches.
Sometimes it is based on a wedding of structural-functionalism
to information theory, sometimes it is a conceptual framework
posited in opposition to structural-functionalism, and sometimes
it is used in a much more specific, value-engineering sense.

Regarding the first usage, the student might read Oran R.
Young's *Systems of Political Science* (Prentice-Hall paperback,
1968), or David Easton's earlier, now almost-classic work,
The Political System (Alfred A. Knopf, 1953). The academic
tradition that sees systems analysis in opposition to structural-
functionalism is represented by Walter Buckley, *Sociology
and Modern Systems Theory* (Prentice-Hall, 1967),
especially Chapter 2.

The engineering tradition of systems analysis is presented
in Harold Hovey's lucid book, *The Planning-Programming-
Budgeting Approach to Government Decision-Making* (Praeger
special studies, 1968). A seminal work related to the origins
of systems analysis in the Defense Department is Charles Hitch and
Roland McKean, *The Economics of Defense in the Nuclear Age*
(Atheneum paperback, 1965), especially Part 2. Insight
into the applications of systems analysis in the Department
of Health, Education, and Welfare may be gained by examining

the Public Health Service's programmed instruction course, *Health Planning* (HEW/PHS paperback, 1968).

A book somewhat in the applied tradition of systems analysis but building connections with more generalized frameworks is Robert Boguslaw's *The New Utopians: Modern Systems Design and Social Change* (Prentice-Hall, 1965). The student wishing to follow up on applications of systems analysis to government might follow the Hovey reading by looking at the December, 1966 issue of the *Public Administration Review,* which was devoted entirely to program planning systems, as well as later articles in the same journal, including the March–April, 1969 symposium on PPBS.

Systems analysis vocabulary, like that of structural-functionalism, has become heavily cliché-ridden in political science. It is an umbrella term covering many variations, some asserting world-view methodologies and others asserting practical techniques to aid in problem-solving. As such it is an approach, or set of approaches, ordinarily not as universally framed as the grand methodologies discussed in the previous three chapters, nor as specific as the quantitative techniques to be discussed later. Many, however, consider it a perspective of great potential for analysis.

Pitfalls of systems analysis are suggested by an article in the *New York Times,* "Systems Analysts Are Baffled By Problems of Social Change."[1] It reports a convention of systems analysts attempting to face the problems of social change and city life in America. Jargon from the panelists included the assertion that analysis could aid administrators' "decision-making when faced with multidimensional functional alternatives," while another participant added that analysts could "present a synthesis of very diverse networks of non-homogenous complexities."

This vocabulary is presented to suggest analogies that are often made in systems analysis. In the engineering tradition the analogies are usually to electronic systems composed of networks, flows, circuits, inputs, feedback, noise, channels and the like. In the academic tradition analogy is more often to the organism as an adaptive system, speaking of system boundaries, articulation with the environment, homeostasis, equilibrium, and regulation. On the other hand, systems analysts are quite aware of the biases and pitfalls involved

[1] *New York Times,* March 24, 1968, 28:1.

in this vocabulary. What concerns the political scientist in the study of methods is the system analyst's attempt to develop an applied social science mediating the general methodologies and the merely quantitive techniques that are also a part of political science method.

THE ACADEMIC TRADITION

Whereas the applied tradition of systems analysis is concerned with aiding the decision-maker achieve his policy goals, the academic tradition is concerned with providing the researcher with a general framework for analysis. It departs from the concern for developing the concept of a "system" shared by functionalist and information theories.

Information Systems

The concept of an information system is not antithetical to structural-functionalism (see Chapter 3); in fact, it is intimately bound to the concept of the cybernetic hierarchy that serves to relate the parts of the AGIL analytic system.

An **information system** is a set of interrelated structures that receive an *input* of *data* through *receptors* and *process* this data by comparing it to *memory* and *values* and submitting it to *decision*. Decision leads to *storage* of data in memory and, if appropriate, to implementation of decisions through *effectors*. This affects the *environment* beyond the system *boundaries,* causing *feedback* as part of the data input of the next *phase* of the *input-transform-output* process.

Moreover, this information input may contain unneeded information or *noise,* as well as information at varying levels of importance. For this reason the receptors must *scan* and *select* data received prior to processing. This selectivity introduces the possibility of *perceptual biases* and errors, especially as the *load* of data input increases. Load may also involve either *lag* in processing or reduction of *lead* in forecasting from received data.

Information systems are subject to certain patterned **distortions.** One of these is *amplification of positive feedback* in a spiral of implementations eliciting positive and negative feedbacks, of which only the positive are selected, leading to further implementations of the same sort. Of course, negative-only selectivity is also a possible distortion. Another is *channel drift,* where a system attuned to one channel of information input may gradually shift in frequency toward another channel with unintended system consequences. *Short-circuiting* is a distortion where data is not subject to all phases of the input-transform-output system; for example, implementation may occur without data being subjected to memory recall.

Despite the overlap with structural-functionalism, this tradition of systems analysis does contradict or at least revise structural-functionalism on some points. The most outstanding difference is over the concept of "equilibrium." Systems analysts in the information systems tradition prefer to substitute the term "stability," which is seen as less mechanistic. The kind of stability involved in an information system is **homeostasis**—an interrelated set of adaptive processes tending to preserve system structure in the face of changing environmental conditions. To contrast, **equilibrium** is an interrelated set of regulative processes tending to preserve the entire system in a steady state.

Certainly the structural-functionalists conceive equilibrium in broader terms than some systems analysts would suggest, but the analytic framework of systems analysis is focused more on processes of change than is structural-functionalism. The essential question asked by structural-functionalists is, "By means of what structures is a system maintained?", whereas the question in systems analysis is, "By what processes does a system adapt to change in order to preserve its basic structure?" This distinction can easily become overexaggerated, but the information systems approach does place the researcher in a somewhat different context.

The context of information systems is more limited than that of structural-functionalism, in that it is even less helpful in sorting out pertinent research data from the unimportant. Precisely because the categories of information systems are universalistic and all-encompassing, too much is taken in. By more closely reflecting reality, it is less helpful in making simplifications (theories). A positive way of saying this is to note that the approach requires greater creativity and less rote application.

Procedure

For example, suppose the researcher asks, "Why was such-and-such a decision made?" The information systems approach suggests a number of steps toward answering this question:

1. Examine relevant information inputs prior to the decision, including stored inputs, and place this in the context of a field of competing inputs.
2. Examine the structures that have been set up to receive, scan, and select information, noting the distortions introduced at this point.
3. Determine the formal and informal structures established for comparing received data with memory, determine the values of the system, and specify the manner in which processed data are evaluated.
4. Determine the procedures by which implementation outputs are assigned to evaluated data (e.g., is the procedure to work through a limited number of implementation strategies in a repertoire until a satisfactory one is found? are all strategies in a repertoire considered and then one selected by some criterion? etc.).
5. Specify distortions involved in the implementation phase, after the decision is made but before implementation defines the decision in practice.

This is a very large order, precisely because it rightly suggests that in answering the original question above, all factors must be considered. Information theory gives no help in selecting relevant factors and, in fact, even points to the importance of competing "noise." This task is not an altogether impossible one, however, and several respectable attempts to use this approach have been made.[2]

Sometimes information systems approaches do use certain criteria to narrow down the field of investigation, but these criteria are usually inconsistent with the general theory of information systems. One such criterion is **rationality**—there may be a tendency to treat information systems as rational systems processing relevant information in ways calculated to effect the desired result. In fact, there is no reason to assume that study may be confined to rational factors or to formal patterns of decision-making. A second criterion sometimes used is the **quantifiableness** of inputs and outputs. There may be a tendency to look at inputs in terms of *quantities* of messages, with selective distortion being a function of load, without examining less quantifiable sources of distortion such as *cognitive dissonance*—the tendency to

[2] See Roberta Wohlstetter, *Pearl Harbor: Warning and Decision* (Stanford: Stanford University, 1962).

adjust one's perceptions and behavior to be consistent with those of positively-valued others.

Neither criterion is consistent with information theory. In each case, all inputs, transforms, and outputs must be examined because all coexist in an interdependent field of mutual relationships. Not even the criterion of face relevance to the question is wholly valid, since information theory posits the relevance of even random noise to decision outcome.

Example

Using the five steps outlined above as a basis for information systems analysis, the question of explaining rioting may be again considered.

1. *Memory and inputs.* Memory: Past violence against the black race, crime and violence of lower class life, past promises and hopes for future, repertoire of methods used in the past to settle grievances.

   Inputs: Marginal gains of civil rights movement; messages of legitimacy of protest, illegitimacy of status quo; plus competing inputs of changes in dress, music, work styles.

2. *Receptors and scanning and selecting.* Word-of-mouth inputs given priority; rumor distortion; selective accumulation of grievances; retention of inputs of dramatic, exciting, or shocking nature.

3. *Recall and evaluation.* Inputs related to grievances are selected, compared with a rich lore of past grievances, and assigned a very negative value associated with slavery and later racial and class exploitation.

4. *Selection of implementation options.* Grievance inputs, although heavily weighted negatively, are ordinarily stored in memory, later to reinforce the negative value assigned to further grievance inputs. When the load of grievance-inputs reaches a certain critical level, a repertoire of implementation options is searched. Violent crime is one of these options. Selection of lesser options, such as nonviolent protest activity, generates an increasing load of grievance inputs. The store of grievance inputs in memory increases, more than compensating for the loss of similar information from memory through routine forgetfulness. As the store increases, the negative evaluation assigned incremental

grievance inputs increases. Higher negative values are associated with stronger implementation options.

5. *Implementation.* An amplification spiral is thus established leading to escalating implementation options and ultimately the selection of the violent crime option. In a collective context, selection of this option appears as rioting, which is an adaptive response tending to preserve the structure of the black community.

Morphogenetic Systems

Comprehensive as it is, the information systems approach is not the most general. Just as homeostasis as a concept was compared to equilibrium, so morphogenesis may be proposed as a superior conceptual scheme. **Morphogenesis** involves a set of interrelated pattern-maintaining processes that tend to preserve a system's central values in the face of changing environment through structural elaboration. In contrast, homeostatic systems tend to preserve structure. Morphogenesis is said to be a better social model because society in fact does much more than preserve its central structures; it is continually in the process of elaborating and changing them so that institutions will still serve central values even when conditions change.

In a morphogenetic system, if relevant variables exceed certain parameters the system structure changes. In contrast, given the same situation in a homeostatic system like the organism, structure disintegrates. The importance of this difference for research orientation is that in morphogenetic systems such as society, deviance, conflict, and change are as integral to the system as structural maintenance. Where a homeostatic approach such as structural-functionalism or even information systems tends to focus on institutional persistence and maintenance of central structures of a society, the morphogenetic approach tends to focus on persistence of values through institutional and structural change.

Again, there is no clear distinction of this approach from structural-functionalism, and, indeed, the overlap with the idea of cultural values as controlling factors in system evolution is retained, with the concomitant biases mentioned in the previous chapter. This bias toward the analytic primacy of values may be removed by defining morphogenesis in an even more general way, as Buckley does, as a system characterized by a set of structure-elaborating processes not clearly tending toward anything. This definition, of course, comes at a price.

Such a definition usefully serves to deny any overriding importance of norms, values, roles, and institutions, and to upgrade the importance of informal processes, conflict, tension, and change. It removes the assumption that institutions are eufunctional and legitimate. On the other hand, such a definition also removes every dynamic from a system except the vague process of structural elaboration. At least in equilibrium theory one could posit that any given deviation from the normal state would be undercut by unintended consequences of the change, consequences tending to preserve the basic structures of the existing system. It is even further from the Marxist theories of social change as they relate to institutions and groups. That is, although systems analysis in the morphogenetic tradition is a truer description of reality, the price paid for this accuracy is a level of generality that fails to aid the researcher in selecting important factors from among the myriad unimportant ones.

The usefulness of the morphogenetic approach for the researcher depends on drawing upon the implications of a structure-elaborating system. Buckley suggests that an ideal complex adaptive system of this sort would have five characteristics:

1. Sources for continuous introduction of "variety" into the system, where variety includes deviance as well as norm-conforming behavior.
2. Processes tending toward maintenance of both an optimum level of tension in society (e.g., cognitive dissonance, incongruent roles) and a relatively high level of individual satisfaction.
3. A full two-way communications system throughout the entire system.
4. A decision-making system sensitive to both external environment and its own internal state.
5. Mechanisms for preserving and propagating current information sets and symbolic meanings systems.

Followers of this approach need to accept the challenge of translating these and other criteria associated with morphogenetic systems into an operational paradigm for researchers. Until then, while this approach is helpful in understanding the shortcomings of other approaches, it may not serve the needs of the researcher attempting to devise useful theoretical simplifications of reality.

THE APPLIED TRADITION

The academic and applied traditions of systems analysis are linked in their common determination to assess the importance of all relevant variables in their collective relationship to what is being studied. That is, there is the determination to understand a system as a whole, as more than the sum of its analytic parts. On the other hand, there is also the common failing that neither tradition offers clear help in selecting the important from the unimportant variables and in relating these to theories of change. In practice the academic tradition of systems analysis tends to stress the rational and to emphasize cultural values as important factors; the applied tradition usually employs economic costs and benefits as criteria. In neither case is such emphasis a necessary implication of the general conceptual framework.

It should be clarified at the outset that applied systems analysis is intended as a prescriptive theory of decision-making. That is, its usefulness is intentionally limited to questions of improving decision-making. It is not useful, nor is it intended to be used for study of questions like the explanation of why riots occur. In this sense it is a limited approach and not a universal methodology.

Cost-benefit Analysis

Cost-benefit analysis,[3] as its name suggests, is concerned with the evaluation of decisions and programs in terms of their positive results in proportion to alternative positive results obtainable by expending the same amount of energy and resources elsewhere. As also implied, followers of this approach tend to deal with quantified variables and hold economic efficiency as the dominant evaluative criterion.

Such a bias is not inevitable, of course. The main thrust of Urgoti's article, for example, is the argument that cost-benefit analysis has been too narrowly quantitative, formal, and economic-oriented. Urgoti calls for more consideration of political, geophysical, and

[3] Reading: Nicholas Urgoti, "Survey of Cost-Benefit Analysis: Its Present Applications to Urban Renewal Decision-Making," *Planning Comment* 4:2 (Spring, 1967).

social factors, even if this results in a predominance of nonmeasureable and intangible elements in the analysis.

Evaluation of Hardware

Without discussing this technical level at length, the researcher may wish to be aware that detailed procedures have been worked out in some government agencies[4] for breaking down the costs of a given piece of hardware and for comparing the cost of this with alternatives. The questions involved are:

1. What is the function of the product?
2. What alternative products serve the same function?
3. For the product and its alternatives, what are the cost breakdowns by material, labor, and fixed (overhead) factors?
4. What is the benefit of using the product or its alternatives in terms of reliability, serviceability, safety, or other desired qualities?
5. Considering the product and its alternatives, which has the best ratio of costs to benefits?

Evaluating Service Programs

The problems involved in quantifying and comparing hardware are formidable. When the subject to be evaluated is a service or a package of services and hardware, evaluation becomes extremely difficult. Direct measurement of every cost and benefit becomes impossible, and instead cost-benefit analysis focuses on a search for useful indices of costs and benefits as indirect measures.

For example, in measuring the benefits of urban renewal, *one* of the indices might be increase in area tax revenue adjusted for increases in comparable areas not renewed. An indirect measure of the benefits of a national health program might be years increase in life expectancy, or changes in a certain disease rate, adjusting for trends predating the program. Every such index may be challenged, and ordinarily many indices would be used in a given evaluation. The indices need not be quantitative. For example, in evaluating how much an experimental school is satisfying parents' needs, in the absence of objective

[4] Department of Defense, Joint Course, *Principles and Applications of Value Engineering*, Vol. I (U.S. Superintendent of Documents, $2.00).

measures of satisfaction, subjective satisfaction increases might be measured by opinion surveys.

Procedure

The paradigms for cost-benefit analysis vary, but the following two are prominent:

Cost/gain ratio approach:
1. Evaluate the package directly or, if necessary, indirectly in terms of gains minus cost.
2. If gains and cost are not expressable in terms of common units, either (a) determine the least cost for a specified gain, or (b) determine the maximum gain for a specified cost.
3. When gain is intangible, use 2(a); when costs are intangible, use 2(b) above.
4. Examine the consistency of the gain criterion with higher-level values.
5. Be careful to include in gains any spillover effects, and exclude from costs historical sunk costs.

Paired cost/gain ratio approach:
1. Enumerate the "producers" of the services studied and pair them with the "consumers" of the services.
2. Itemize the costs and benefits of the present "without services" situation and the future "without" situation.
3. Itemize the costs and benefits of service under alternative "with services" situations.
4. Compare the net differences between step 3 and step 2 situations.

The fact that extreme creativity and effort are required to implement these steps does not alter the fact that full evaluation requires such procedures. In practical political analyses, the general procedure is often followed in a non-rigorous way. For example, in considering the suggestion that the United States propose to China that the two countries exchange newsmen, the political scientist may follow cost-benefit procedures. He will list, for each country, the costs and benefits of both accepting and not accepting the proposal. If he is sufficiently thorough he may do this for the present period and some projected future period. Among the costs to China in accepting, for example, is the perceived threat of additional foreign agents. Benefits include a greater likelihood that the U.S. will be responsive to later Chinese initiatives. Among the costs to the U.S. would be poorer relations with Taiwan; among the gains would be perceived better relations with China. The researcher could then go on to distinguish among costs and benefits in the short and long run.

In sum, cost-benefit analysis can vary from value engineering precision about hardware to a simple checklist summary of costs and gains. Although not demanded by the approach, there is often a certain bias toward quantifiable variables and the present period. It may tend to underemphasize important but intangible benefits and avoid making projective evaluations needed for future-oriented planning.

Management Systems

Much of applied systems analysis was developed for business purposes, growing out of the industrial engineering tradition of Frederick Taylor. This tradition covers such matters as organization hierarchy charts, product flowcharts, benchmark time-and-motion studies, data processing and inventory control.[5] The business management systems approach is also a checklist-oriented paradigm, focusing on the following criteria:

1. *Purpose.* Have conditions changed since the operation was instituted? Are other operations equivalent in function but superior in performance?
2. *Equipment.* Does volume justify investment in data processing systems?
3. *Organization.* Is there a functional write-up of organizational units? Are goals set for various jobs and units?
4. *Procedures.* How adequate are manuals and training of personnel in various job descriptions?
5. *Measurement.* Can management evaluate performance?
6. *Schedule.* What is the lag in processing? Is the most efficient flow sequence utilized?
7. *Facilities.* Is the assigned area adequate?
8. *Records.* What is the memory capacity and recall rate of files?

[5] A good introduction is Stanford L. Optner, *Systems Analysis for Business Management* (Englewood Cliffs: Prentice-Hall, 1968).

9. *Budgeting.* In addition to performance measures, are there functionally-itemized cost measures?

The management analyst covers these and similar points prior to designing existing and ideal operations flowcharts. While the approach takes the form of a checklist, the systems management analyst seeks to understand the relationships of all the factors taken as a whole. This is often epitomized by the operations control plan. Again, although not logically inseparable from the approach, management analysis tends to emphasize quantifiable variables, formal relationships (as opposed, for example, to effects of informal work groups), and economic-tangible product criteria.

Program Planning Systems

Program planning and budgeting systems (PPBS) has been established in many branches of the federal government as an attempt at systems analysis of government decision-making. It is an effort to rationalize decision-making, facilitate more comprehensive planning, and provide government officials with better information and clearer criteria with which to make judgments.

If a policy package is conceived as a set of inputs that have *costs* and yield outputs that have *benefits,* the *program planning budget* presents benefits in cost terms. That is, instead of a military budget listing expenditures for airplanes, tanks, pay of personnel, etc., the program planning budget groups costs by benefits—cost of the Vietnam war, cost of Latin American military support, cost of European military presence, etc. By presenting a budget in the latter manner, the decision-maker is in a better position to judge the worth of various programs. The point may seem trivial, but the former materials budget has been the standard approach until recently and has greatly thwarted evaluation of benefit costs.

Procedure

The program budget is the end result of systems analysis, the plan for expenditures for the next fiscal year, and for usually the next five years to follow. The problems involved are great, if only because of the question of allocating such things as overhead costs to various specific program benefits. Leaving this aside, what is the procedure by which the systems analyst arrives at a program budget?

1. The first step involves specifying the *goals* of the organization, the long-run states of accomplishment toward which programs are directed. Sometimes this is part of an explicit legislative mandate; more often it emerges, if at all, from arduous discussions between planners and administrators. (In practice, goals may be determined as a result of later steps.)

2. For each goal, planners consult with agency staff and others to determine a set of program *objectives*. Objectives are measured, and specific kinds of progress showing movement toward a goal in a stated time period are identified.

3. For each objective, various *indicators,* usually of a quantitative nature, are devised as measures of progress toward objectives. Sometimes these indicators are combined into a single objective *index.*

4. After the planner has clarified goals as best he can, specified objectives, and determined one or more indicators for each, he then goes through an analogous process for organization activities. The activities of the organization are separated into *general activity areas,* each of which is divided into *program categories,* which in turn are composed of *program elements.*

   For example, in Public Health Service planning, the *service* areas are considered to be normal development, repair, containment, and basic research. Activity areas for each of these are direct operations, facilities, research, and training. Then, for instance, the direct operations activity area of the normal development health service contains the program category of "public education in health," of which one of the program elements is "technical information services."

5. The service areas and their components down to the program element level may be coded. The code for the above example is 110105, where the first digit stands for the service area, the second digit stands for the general activity, the next two digits represent the program category, and the last two the program element.

6. A coded list of all output measures for each of the program elements (i.e., one master code for all elements) then is prepared. For example, code 041 corresponds to the output measure "number of community sources inspected," code 049 corre-

sponds to "number of insulin samples tested." Over time, codes tend to become standardized.

7. The program element measures are then related to the indicators of objectives. This involves not only finding which measures are equivalent to or indices of which objectives indicators, but also translating the units used in element measures into units used in the indicators of objectives. It also entails setting up special procedures for handling nonquantitative measures and indicators.

8. *Performance accounting* (program budgeting) procedures are then used to allocate organization costs to the various program elements. This completes the planning process of establishing an *information system,* ordinarily geared to data processing, that relates costs to programs to goals to benefits.

Program planning systems involve many problems, but the procedures described above (much simplified) leave the planner in a better position to evaluate the activities of his agency. It enables the formulation and review of performance (program) budgets.

The systems analyst ordinarily will do more than establish an information system, however. Other tasks involve establishing a *liaison* between the program planning office and various relevant departments and agencies. Sometimes various advisory committees and consultants must be integrated into the liaison network. In addition the data processing department itself must be organized, including bodies responsible for establishing *standardized* budget, program element measurement, and other forms, the manuals and *training facilities* to teach administrators the use of the new evaluative planning system, and even writers and designers to aid in presentation of information system results.

Also in addition to the basic information system, an office of *program analysis* may be established to do cost-benefit studies of programs alternative to the existing ones, so that a constant review of proposals occurs, phrased in terms comparable to the terms used in the basic information system. Working closely with this office would ordinarily be an office of *finance planning,* seeking to uncover new sources of funding for the organization and capable of both writing grant proposals and detailing how proposed grants would be integrated into the organization's total acitvities. Other groups must be charged with the all too unscientific tasks of coordinating public participation and political or other institutional interests in the organization. These activities involve great discretion and value choices, and are therefore ordinarily carried on by, or closely subordinated to the organization's higher leadership.

Criticisms

The main *strength* of program planning systems is provision of more and better information for decision-makers, which forces administrators at all levels to keep goals and objectives in mind, compels cost evaluation of each program element, facilitates the systematic study of possible alternatives, and does all this across traditional organizational lines. It enables political decisions to be made on a more reasoned basis.

Weaknesses of PPBS include its sometimes erroneous assumption of the absence of frequent politically-originated, unplanned interruptions, delays, and changes; the belief that planners can get administrators and legislators to articulate their goals and specify objectives; its further assumption that finances can be counted on for a year or more in advance; and, for that matter, its conclusion that it is possible to plan for the future in some specific way.

It provides the decision-maker with no value criteria, although there is a certain presumption that the cost criterion will predominate. Like other applied systems approaches, there is a certain tendency to neglect unmeasurable, intangible factors. In practice, outputs of programs are extremely difficult to define and costs are not easily allocated to program elements. Although PPBS sometimes claims to represent comprehensive planning, it tends in practice to be aggregative planning—that is, total activities are rarely evaluated as more than the sum of the parts. There is a bias against risky experimentation, or evaluation by criteria of political or social rather than economic efficiency. Finally, by the very fact of enabling decision-makers to make better judgments, it may have a centralizing effect on the organization.

The systems approach ordinarily claims to be free of any worldview and to be sometimes limited in applicability. On the other hand, like all qualitative approaches to political matters, its vocabulary and paradigm for research inevitably carry the researcher more into certain concerns than others. Certainly it is more value-laden than the quantitative techniques, although even they may contain research biases. Although the following chapters will become increasingly applied and narrower in scope, the researcher should always seek to make explicit the assumptions, strengths, and weaknesses of any methodology, approach, or technique.

5

Other Approaches
and Techniques

Severyn Bruyn's *The Human Perspective in Sociology*
(Prentice-Hall, 1966) is a comprehensive treatment of participant
observation. A more concise presentation is given in Matilda White
Riley, *Sociological Research: A Case Approach* (Harcourt,
Brace & World, 1963), pp. 62–75. For a political example, one
might examine Richard Bolling, *House Out of Order* (Dutton,
1966); on urban life, see Elliot Liebow's *Tally's Corner*
(Little, Brown paperback, 1967).

The best-known approach to case studies is represented by
the Inter-University Case Program (ICP). Over one hundred ICP
cases are available from Bobbs-Merrill in pamphlet form.
An ICP companion text is Edwin A. Bock, ed., *Essays on the Case
Method in Public Administration and Political Sciences* (Chicago:
Public Administration Service, 1965).

Eugene J. Webb, et. al., *Unobtrusive Measures: Nonreactive
Research in the Social Sciences* (Rand McNally paperback, 1966)
presents many of the creative ways political scientists and
others have found to quantitatively measure different variables.
A standard of presentation of ideal types, property space,
and coding is contained in Riley, *supra.*, pp. 328–352, and a good
complement to this is Julian Simon, *Basic Research Methods in*

Political Science, Chapter 14, "Choosing Appropriate Empirical Variables" (Random House, 1969).

A general introduction to content analysis is Chapter 19 of W. Goode and P. Hatt, *Methods in Social Research* (McGraw-Hill, 1952), and an application to a political topic is Frederick Mosteller and D. Wallace, *Inference and Disputed Authorship: The Federalist Papers* (Addison-Wesley, 1964). Robert C. North, et. al., *Content Analysis* (Northwestern paperback, 1963) provides a good handbook.

A standard presentation to sociometry is again contained in Riley, *supra.,* pp. 141–152 and 173–181. A political application is Floyd Hunter, *Top Leadership, U.S.A.* (University of North Carolina, 1959).

For a discussion of interaction analysis see Riley, *supra.,* pp. 98–111 and 119–131. A more recent and detailed presentation is contained in E. Borgatta and B. Crowther, *Workbook for the Study of Social Interaction Processes* (Rand McNally paperback, 1965).

The remaining chapters of this text will deal with the many techniques and approaches used in the study of politics and other social phenomena. Some of these, like participant observation, are general approaches to gathering data, while others are techniques for treating data—coding, for example. The various topics treated in this chapter are quite explicitly a potpourri. While often found in the repertoire of methods used by the political scientist, they bear no clearly-structured relationship to one another. Each approach or technique is limited in scope, intended for the study of particular types of behavior, and involves certain types of assumptions. Those listed here by no means exhaust the many such approaches and techniques that could be discussed.

PARTICIPANT OBSERVATION

Participant observation raises the methodological issue of objectivity discussed in the chapter on Marxism. Ostensibly this is a straight-forward technique—by immersing himself in the subject being studied, the researcher is presumed to gain the greatest understanding. Arguments in its favor are reliance on firsthand information, its ability to convey a vast wealth of data to the researcher, the avoidance of sophisticated but data-losing transformation techniques (such as factor analysis), its "face validity" as a procedure for gathering information, and its relatively simple and inexpensive research procedures.

Arguments opposing participant observation usually mention its tendency to gather data unsystematically, the relative lack of procedures for assuring "value-free" information collection, reliance on subjective rather than objective measures, and its involving an observer effect (the observer's presence may affect the behavior of the observed). In addition, the very emphasis on myriad details and intimacies may lead the researcher to present his findings in a journalistic or novelistic fashion without proper regard for underlying premises and theories. For example, one study of life in Mexico City selects quotes suggesting the theory that absolute deprivation leads to alienation from government. At the same time alternative theories (relative or changing deprivation, characteristics of leaders) are not explicitly considered, nor is the underlying absolute deprivation theory itself explicitly defended. That is, participant observation may tempt the researcher into anecdotal writing rather than theory testing.

Procedure

This method does require considerable skill and creativity, its simplicity of approach notwithstanding. William F. Whyte, in his study of *Street Corner Society* (University of Chicago, 1955), presents several methodological considerations. First, he urges users of this method to make their initial expectations clear (he himself expected to find lower class organization, not disorganization). Second, he stresses real participation, not just observation (he learned Italian, took local girls to dances, campaigned for a local politician, and lived with a local family). Third, he recommends that determining vocabulary concepts be an explicit process (Whyte sought to define the concepts of role, hierarchy, social distance).

Fourth, it is necessary to secure clearance. That is, the participant observer's entry into the community or other research context must seem legitimate to the actors studied. Sometimes official sanction will be necessary or appropriate; at other times disguise and infiltration may be required. More typical, however, was the approach of Herbert

Gans,[1] who presented himself as a researcher seeking to record the history of the organizations and groups of an area, and was accepted on this basis.

Fifth, routine procedures must be established to record and classify information received. This overlaps with simply defining terms, but it also suggests the desirability of employing a comprehensive set of defined concepts. For example, if a riot group were being observed, various role-types could be defined such as inciter, observer, missile thrower, negotiator, or rumor carrier. That is, a list of such ideal role-types could be constructed to facilitate the recording and classifying of received information. In listing the classes of observations to be made, the following should not be overlooked, as Bruyn notes: people's interaction with their physical environment, experiences of the same people under contrasting circumstances, experiences of contrasting people under the same circumstances, observations of the relation of language (such as slang) to social meanings, social openings and barriers to others encountered by the researcher, and observations of psychological barriers and openings encountered by the researcher himself.

In summary, participant observation can be a valuable approach to gathering data. It is especially appropriate to community or group studies (as opposed, for example, to policy studies), and in this area is frequently used as an exploratory technique, uncovering in detail many hidden or latent patterns in their natural context. Because of the strong possibility of personal biases and observer effects, the researcher must take great pains to define and relate terms, make systematic observations, and relate observations to existing political or social science theories. This requires considerable methodological preparation on the part of the would-be participant observer if the study is to be of theoretical value.

CASE STUDIES

Case studies carry many of the same disadvantages and advantages that participant observer studies do. At one time the case study method dominated certain sectors of political science, particularly the area of public administration, partly due to the success of the case method of teaching pioneered by the Harvard Business School. Today,

[1] Herbert J. Gans, *Urban Villagers* (New York: The Free Press, 1962).

however, the case approach is less favored as a preoccupation of the discipline, and like participant observation is considered a valuable but limited exploratory approach.

Limitations

The reason that case studies, including participant-observed case studies, are considered limited is twofold. First, it is logically invalid to generalize on the basis of a particular case or even several cases; logical inference requires information from a random sample of all possible cases. Second, case studies are amost always static; that is, they usually deal with a single point in time and for this reason may mislead the researcher. Moreover, case study meets the methodological criterion of duplicatibility only slightly better than does participant observation. If used for more than one case, this method can become extremely time-consuming.

In short, the case study, although a familiar format, is a limited one, and for that reason the restrictions on theoretic generalizations from data must be made explicit. Moreover, in collecting the data that constitute the case study, the intuitive approach is rarely sufficient. Instead, it is necessary to construct a systematic list of required information and, often, to devise and test an interview schedule as clearly thought out as that in a survey sample poll to assure comparability, completeness, and clarity of data. Construction of such a survey is discussed in a later chapter; for now, four considerations can be listed.

1. The case study researcher must explain how and why people (or other information sources) were selected for the interview.
2. How do subjective responses to an interview (or other "soft" data) relate to objective behavior?
3. How are the parameters (the "givens") set?
4. Explain the nature of the previous history of the setting and the socialization experience of the participants.

Example

This can be made more explicit by considering some problems involved in studying decision-making to determine "Who has power?" What seems simple on the surface is in fact an extremely difficult

question. If power is defined as control over the distribution of benefits, the case study researcher must seek to measure three factors: first,
he must assess the value of the decision outcome for the participants
whose power he wishes to determine; second, he must assess the value
of the opposition to these participants; third, he must assess the value
of the supports received. That is, the amount of power of a particular
decision-maker is a function of how much the outcome is worth,
increased by the strength of the opposition he must overcome, and
diminished by the value of the supports he received to accomplish
this. And even then, the researcher has only estimated the decision-
maker's power exercised in a particular matter, as opposed to potential power or power over time.

The study of decisions to investigate who has power thus involves
not only problems of definition and conceptualization, but also formidable difficulties in measurement if the case study is done systematically. Consider the problem of assessing the value of a decision-
maker's opposition, for example. This might involve not only the
strengths of opponents in the decision-making body, but also the
worth of opponents (such as hostile newspapers) outside the decision-
making body, and even indirect factors such as the values instilled in
all the actors by the society's educational system. Nondecisions as well
as decisions must be considered. In explaining the "givens" in any
case, it is necessary to explain the historical development of the case
setting. For example, urban renewal laws, and for that matter, the
capitalist system were given in Robert Dahl's study[2] of New Haven
politics of urban renewal. Ultimately, the explanation of any case
tends toward requiring an explanation of history itself. What starts
out as a study of power in a particular decision is apt to become the
study of a total power system as an entire entity.

The case study approach thus raises again the need for *multiple
approaches* to any given political topic, such as rioting or power.
Because the mind cannot directly comprehend a tremendously complex reality, researchers are pressured toward selecting a small bit
they can grasp, perhaps by the case approach. However, because any
case is intricately related to the whole and cannot be understood in
isolation, the researcher is then pressured back toward grand theory.
Political scientists need not choose between grand theory and case
studies; on the contrary, both of these approaches and points in

[2] Robert Dahl, *Who Governs: Democracy and Power in an American City*
(New Haven: Yale University, 1961).

between are necessary to the development of political theory. These are contrasts only if methodology is understood narrowly; for political science as a whole they are complements.

QUANTITATIVE MEASUREMENT METHODS

Some things, such as number of votes, can be measured directly, while others such as power must be measured indirectly. All abstractions—justice, order, efficiency, or happiness—must be measured indirectly, which is to say by **indicators**. For example, the number of riots or the crime rate might be used as indices of lack of order. Ultimately there is no way to prove that any indicator actually measures what it is supposed to, although it is possible to gather evidence one way or the other. Evidence bearing on the merit of indicators is, in the study of social science methods, the question of *validity*.

Validity is discussed more fully in a later chapter; for now, a few points may be suggested. A measure of power may be partially validated, for example, if it intuitively seems to measure power (face validity). Or it may be partly validated if it shows to be powerful persons who are proven powerful by other accepted measures. If power is assumed to be linked to some other factor, such as multiple membership in important civic groups, then the measure of power should show to be powerful persons holding several memberships in civic groups. That is, a measure may be validated only by reference to some other factor assumed to be valid, such as intuition, by another measure of the same variable, or by the measure of a related variable.

Measurement also raises a second crucial methodological question, that of *creativity*. While creativity cannot be reduced to a method, it is certainly essential for the researcher seeking to apply political science methods. Webb, Simon, and other authors cited in the readings seek to convey insight into creativity in the only way possible—by citing examples of creative use of measures. Webb in particular is concerned with *nonreactive* or unobstructive measures, i.e., those in which the measurer does not affect the measurement.

Concern with nonreactive measurement is in part an attempt to get away from sole reliance on survey data, which can be affected by subject awareness of the test (effect of being studied on workers' productivity in the famous Hawthorne studies, for example); role selection (only the "best side" may be presented); skills of the subject (language misunderstandings, for example); and interviewer bias among others. Again the point is not that one method or another is right or wrong, but rather that there is need for creative use of *multiple measurement* in political science.

Examples

The following are examples of creative indirect measures:

1. A researcher was refused social class data on military cadets in a Latin American country. Noting that the lower classes of the country tended to be of Indian descent and hence of shorter stature, the researcher concluded that the military leadership was becoming more open socially, as evidenced by the declining average height of cadet classes over time.
2. *Physical traces:* Webb cites the example of using size of tombstones as measures of family status.
3. *Continuous archives:* One researcher interested in parental preference for sex of children they might have measured this by looking at vital statistics, taking the ratio of male to female last children of mature families as an indicator of sex preference, and controlling for factors such as the Depression, when the last child might well be economically dictated.[3]
4. *Episodic archives:* Sales of John Glenn and Robert Kennedy stamps as a measure of popularity, or alcohol consumption at the U.N. delegates' lounge as a measure of international tension.
5. *Simple observation:* This recalls the Mass Observation movement in England, which at one time enlisted ordinary people all over England to submit reports on everything they observed on a certain day. Although haphazard, valuable data were gained on popular culture, dance crazes, and effects of political campaigns. In another context, oriental jade dealers have been known to use pupil dilation as an index of customer interest.
6. *Contrived observation:* Tape recorders, cameras, electric-eye counters and use of "stooges" in research have all been employed, usually covertly but often overtly.

[3] Among standard sources familiar to political scientists are *America Votes, City and County Data Book, Historical Statistics of the United States Since Colonial Times,* and, of course, the U.S. *Census.*

Again, as Webb and most modern social scientists emphasize, the need is for ingenuity and multiple measures of confirmation. Alone, most of these measures are insufficient.

IDEAL TYPES, PROPERTY SPACE, AND CODING

Ideal Types

A term originated by Max Weber, ideal types are hypothetically concrete units (such as role types, personality types, social classes, types of buildings) constructed by the researcher from relevant associated traits. They are thus a special form of classification, not intended to be exhaustive or even descriptive of reality, but rather to aid analysis by enabling strong contrasts. Ideal types may be thought of as poles of a continuum along which reality lies. Ideal types may then be used as standards against which observed cases may be measured and compared.

For example, Weber distinguished traditional, charismatic, and rational-legal types of organization. Amitai Etzioni, a well-known organization theorist, has typed organizations according to their mode of control—coercive, utilitarian, or normative. In any particular case the researcher would have to choose which organization typology is more useful for his purposes. And in any particular case he would probably find that coercive, utilitarian, and normative elements were all present, although he would presumably class the organization by its dominant trait.

Example

To return to the example of riots, one could employ a set of ideal-typical explanations of riots: human drives, cultural character, social conditions, and pragmatic goals. Human drives explanations of rioting may be broken into three types—biogenetic, medical, and psychological; e.g., riots are caused by man's instinct toward aggression. Cultural character explanations can be separated into racial, class, age, sex, and cultural conjunction types; e.g., riots are caused by youthfulness. Social conditions explanations divide into absolute, relative, and changing deprivation; e.g., riots are caused by economic reversals.

Finally, the pragmatic goals explanations are divided into economic and political goals, and these into popular and conspiratorial theories; e.g., riots are caused by subversives.

The very fact that various authors writing on why riots happen use a great many sometimes conflicting, often ambiguous explanations hinders consideration of the issue. By constructing ideal-type explanations one is able to avoid the problem of "What did Smith *really* mean?" and instead focus first on the simply ideal-typical explanations, and then upon various combinations of them, until a sufficiently sophisticated theoretical explanation is elaborated.

Property Space

Property space is simply one of two basic forms of data representation. Ordinarily it is equated with tabular property space, whereby one property (e.g., family income) of n levels (low, medium, high) is crosstabulated against another property (e.g., party identification) of m levels (Republican or Democrat), resulting in an n-by-m table (in this case 3 by 2).

Property space may also refer to graphic property space, where one property is represented as an x axis (usually the dependent variable) and the other as a y axis. Any given data observation then has a set of x and y property space coordinates. This form of property space thus results in a *scatter diagram* of the data points.

Figure 5.1 (a)   Graphic Representation of Property Space

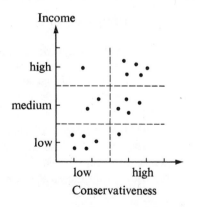

Coding

Coding is the classifying of properties. That is, any property or variable (e.g., income) may be classed or coded into a number of classes or ranges (high, medium, and low incomes) for purposes of analysis. These ranges then become the rows and columns of tabular property space, that is, of tables. All of this is extremely elementary in conception, but in practice becomes problematic. It is easy to set ranges to properties—to code variables, but it is difficult to do this well.

Figure 5.1 (b)   Tabular Representation

		Income			
		Low	Medium	High	
Conservativeness	Low	5	2	1	8
	High	1	4	5	10
		6	6	6	18

There are several general criteria for good coding. The first is that *the code must serve the purposes of the researcher;* this criterion overrides the others. But beyond this, generally speaking, coded variables should have ranges that:

1. Avoid having too large a proportion of the observations fall in any one class.
2. Are comprehensive, so that all observations will fall into some class.
3. Have classes that do not overlap, so that any observation will fall into only one class.

In addition, provision must be made for the handling of all data, including "no response," "no data," "refuse to answer," and ambiguous or irrelevant responses or observations. As the number of variables and the number of observations increase, there is greater need to handle data in quantitative ways through data processing machines; here the problems of coding become paramount.

Examples

Some examples of coding problems may clarify this point. First, to code income one might set three ranges: below $5000, $5000–10,000, and $10,000 and above. This would meet the distribution-of-respondents criterion above in the case of an average suburb, but for a slum neighborhood it would not, since the great majority of respondents would fall in the first category. Thus some *prior knowledge* of the distribution of the variable is essential to setting good ranges. Second, it is often difficult to get *comprehensive* ranges. One item used in coding newspaper riot reports might be "predominant mode of dispersal of crowd," divided into eight ranges: police force, troops force, appeal, negotiation, spontaneous, other, not reported or uncertain, and not dispersed. Even this formulation results in many events being classed as "other," and it is not always easy to determine which mode is "predominant," resulting in "ambiguous" (uncertain) responses. Third, avoiding *overlap* is also difficult. For example, the variable "type of police action in a particular riot sequence" may require over two dozen ranges. To take another example, the variable "physical setting of first violence" cannot be broken into mutually exclusive categories (a riot might simultaneously be in "a street outside a school" and in "a street in a predominantly shopping area") — yet to have mutually exclusive variables would mean having not one variable (physical setting), but a great many, one for each setting. Thus, especially for nominal data, coding becomes difficult; often it is impossible to meet the criteria for a good code given above.

Levels of Data

Levels of data include the nominal, ordinal, interval, and ratio. *Ratio scale* data have a true zero point and equal intervals; they can be used for any arithmetic operation. For example, data on income are ratio data—having a measurement of zero income really means no income, and the distance from $0 to $1000 is the same as the distance from $1000 to $2000. *Interval data* lack a true zero point but have equal intervals; addition and subtraction are possible, but not multiplication or division. For example, degrees Farenheit is an interval measure—the distance from zero degrees to 10 degrees is the same as from 10 to 20 degrees, but 20 degrees is *not* twice as high as 10 degrees because there is no true zero point (zero degrees is not really "no temperature").

Ordinal data lack both a true zero point and equal intervals; adding, dividing, multiplying, and subtracting are not possible. For example, the class rank of students is of this type. Assuming class rank is supposed to measure achievement validly (a debatable proposition!), it is still not possible in a class of 100 to say that rank 50 represents twice the achievement of rank 25 (intervals may well be not equal). Nor does any adding or subtracting operation make sense with ordinal data. The only possible operations involve less than, equal to, and more than concepts. *Nominal data* do not even meet the requirement of order met by all "higher" forms of data. For example, the various physical settings discussed under coding are nominal data—even though the settings may be numbered 1 through 35, these numbers are arbitrary; a particular setting might just as well be numbered 6 as 22, for example. There is no logical basis for adding or multiplying such numbers.

Multivariate Table Analysis

Multivariate table analysis is an example of the kind of research procedure used in connection with the concepts discussed in this section. This is a subtabling method used to uncover *spurious relationships.* Table 5.1 contains an example that suggests being Protestant is associated with a high education; introducing the third variable, social class, in the subtables shows no effect of education once class is considered. This hypothetical case suggests the hypothesized relationship between religion and education was spurious.

The subtables in Table 5.1 show that if a person is in the "upper half" by class, he tends to be highly educated whether he is Protestant or Catholic. Similarly, if the person is in the "lower half" by class, then he tends to be poorly educated regardless of whether he is Protestant or Catholic. This suggests that the assumed relationship of religion to education is false by virtue of controlling for a third variable, social class.

Table 5.1   Example of Multivariate Analysis

Original Table

Education

		High	Low	Total
	Protestant	55	35	90
Religion	Catholic	35	55	90
	Total	90	90	180

"Upper Half" Class Subtable

	High	Low	Total
Protestant	50	10	60
Catholic	25	5	30
Total	75	15	90

"Lower Half" Class Subtable

	High	Low	Total
Protestant	5	25	30
Catholic	10	50	60
Total	15	75	90

CONTENT ANALYSIS

Content analysis is one of the quantitative methods that could be a course in itself. It is used as a way of coding and thereby quantifying written material such as newspapers and speeches or other communications such as broadcasts. A simple form of content analysis might be to count the number of newspaper editorials for or against a particular policy, or for the president's position as an index of policy of presidential support. One researcher used fiction stories to classify characters by ethnicity and treatment in the story; by this method he showed that Anglo-Saxons appear in more socially-approved character roles.

A better-known example is Frederick Mosteller's work on the identification of the *Federalist Papers*. Mosteller started with four sets of papers: those known to have been written by Hamilton, those known to have been written by Madison, those which were thought to have been written by one or the other, and those thought to have been written by both. One of the initial steps was to feed into a computer the text of the known sets of papers, programming it to tabulate word frequencies and select out words that differentiated between the two men. Table 5.2 shows that the word "enough" tended to be used by Hamilton but not by Madison. These key differentiating words were then used in combination to attribute authorship of the disputed papers.

Table 5.2   Example of Content Analysis on the Federalist Papers

Key Word Rate per 1000 Words

Key Word	enough	while	whilst	upon	Total words included (1000's)
Hamilton known set	0.59	0.26	0.00	2.94	45.7
Madison known set	0.00	0.00	0.47	0.16	51.1
Disputed set	0.00	0.00	0.34	0.08	23.8
Both set	0.18	0.00	0.36	0.36	5.6

A non-mathematical solution of the authorship problem would be to attribute papers with "whiles" and no "whilsts" to Hamilton, and the reverse to Madison. This would be checked by a high or low rate on "enoughs" and "upons." In social science the solution is somewhat more complex, involving the application of tests of significance. Since this requires an understanding of materials to be treated in later chapters, detailed content analysis tests are not treated here, although the texts listed in the readings may be consulted once the student has gained a deeper knowledge of statistics.

INTERACTION ANALYSIS

Interaction analysis is to behavior what content analysis is to communications. That is, interaction analysis is a way of classifying types of behavior. It was designed for the general study of the small group by Robert Bales, who developed a typology with twelve ranges to classify observed behavior:[4]

[4] Robert F. Bales, *Interaction Process Analysis: A Method for the Study of Small Groups* (Reading, Mass.: Addison-Wesley, 1950), p. 486.

Observation Categories in Bales' Typology

I. Positive Reactions: expressive-integrative social-emotional area
   A. Shows solidarity; raises status of others, gives help
   B. Shows tension release; laughs, shows satisfaction
   C. Agrees; shows passive acceptance, understands, complies

II. Attempted Answers: instrumental-adaptive task area
   A. Gives suggestions; direction, implies autonomy for other
   B. Gives opinion; evaluation, expresses feeling, wish
   C. Gives orientation; information, repeats, clarifies

III. Questions: Instrumental-adaptive task area
   A. Asks for orientation; information, repetition, confirmation
   B. Asks for opinion; evaluation, analysis, expression of feeling
   C. Asks for suggestion; direction, possible ways to act

IV. Negative Reactions: expressive-integrations, social-emotional area
   A. Disagrees; shows passive rejection, witholds help
   B. Shows tension; asks for help, withdraws from field
   C. Shows antagonism; deflates status of others, defends or asserts self.

Bales then used these categories, which have since become somewhat standard, to observe the behavior of an experimental group which was given an artificial task. He observed, for example, that groups of three or four tend to have more even distribution of participation, whereas in larger groups participation is more concentrated in a "number one man." In examining the Borgatta and Crowther text mentioned in the readings, however, it is apparent there are many alternatives to Bales' exact typology. Which typology is chosen depends upon the purposes of the researcher. Such analyses are often confined to experimental small group situations, but in general the researcher may develop his own set of categories to classify any type of observable behavior, just as he can devise any set of categories to classify words or concepts in content analysis. These observation categories may be used to note the pattern of interactions at one point in time *(static analysis)* or over several points in time *(dynamic analysis)*, both to focus on general patterns of interaction of particular *individuals* in a variety of contexts and on differences in such *patterns* when contexts vary.

SOCIOMETRY

In its broadest definition, sociometry is equated with all research involving quantitative scales. More narrowly speaking, it is ordinarily equated with sociography, which was devised as a system for examining group behavior as a totality. The focus, as in interaction analysis, is ordinarily on the small group, although it has, as in Hunter's *Top Leadership, U.S.A.*, been applied to national studies as well. This method provides a pictorial means of presenting data about complex inter-individual relationships.

For example, if individuals are thought of as points on a blank piece of paper, we might employ certain conventions of sociometry, as shown in Figure 5.2, to illustrate various typical relationships. Thus, the "star" is made up of several lines pointing toward or away from a central point, representing an individual who attracts many and who in turn reciprocates, ignores, or rejects. Other typical formations are the "chain," or series of unreciprocated relationships; the "mutual first choice"—the pair; and the "power behind the throne"—the object of attraction of a few very attractive individuals. Finally, of course, there is the "isolate," not chosen by anyone.

Figure 5.2   Some Typical Sociometric Representations

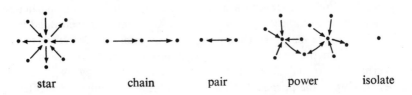

star   chain   pair   power   isolate

Sociometry is a method used to map informal groups. Sociometric *tests* are administered to the participants to determine direction of relationships, although sometimes this is determined by *observation*. For example, a sociometric test might ask members of a political group which other members they like best and least personally, whom they like best and least as someone to work with, or whom they hold in most and least esteem. Using responses to such questions relationships among group members could be mapped, as shown in Figure 5.3.

Figure 5.3   Sociometrically-mapped Diagrams

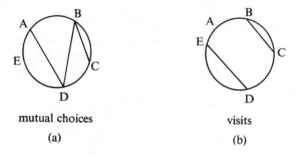

mutual choices   visits

(a)   (b)

Sociometric diagrams may represent either *attitudinally*-based or *observationally*-based relationships, such as mutual choices or mutual visits, respectively. Attitudinally-based measures may rely on *ideal* (who do you want to work with?) and *actual* (who do you in fact work with?) subject orientations. Thus, the question of reputation for power—"Who do you think has the most power in this group, if anyone?"—could be an attitudinal-actual criterion in a sociometric test of a power relationship.

Criticisms

This method, like any other, has several problems: it tends not to record illicit or subconscious relationships; it is apt to record attractions more than dislikes because respondents are more willing to reveal their attractions; and it is a static measure for one point in time. Sociometry is difficult to apply to larger, more complex groups. Also, it is liable not to record or compensate for subjects' tendency to confine choices to their own general class range and it usually (but not inevitably) relies on subjective data.

On the other hand, sociometric testing and presentation can be much more varied and complex than it is possible to present here. Not only are objective as well as subjective measures of relationships possible, and affective as well as instrumental, but it can also be applied at several points in time and for more than dichotomous relationships (such as attraction and repulsion). In more complex treatments, presentation of data becomes elaborate, sometimes necessitating representation of data in a *sociometric matrix* rather than a pictorial diagram. The matrix is an *n*-by-*n* table (square table) representing individuals across the top and the same individuals in the same order down the side. For each possible pair the range of the criterion is shown; for example, for the criterion "Whom do you like most?" the ranges might be: attraction = plus one, indifference = zero, repulsion = minus one. Moreover, such sociometric information may be used as an index of abstract relationship variables. For instance, the general level of "popularity" in one group might be compared with the level in a second group by comparing the proportion of members chosen as "liked" in the former with the proportion in the latter.

Some generality may be attained by securing data for many incumbents of each of several roles or positions, averaging, and using averages to map relationships between positions rather than between individuals. Thus, if analogous political groups exist, the researcher may use averaged sociometric data to indicate general relationships between, for example, a group's president and his executive secretary and other roles. This general procedure may be used to relate occupational categories, social classes, age cohorts, and the like. The researcher must be aware, however, that this procedure involves transforming the data by classifying, measuring, and averaging; like any indirect method of measurement, information is lost at each step. Furthermore, there is the general question of validity, the question of whether the indices really do measure the variables they are supposed to.

PANEL STUDIES AND COHORT ANALYSIS

In several of the methods discussed above it is possible to apply static measures such as sociometric tests at various intervals in time to the same subjects in order to gain a "dynamic" perspective. The **panel method** involves the problem of possible *sensitization* of subjects. That is, persons given a test may react differently to a later similar test simply due to the experience of the first test itself. Checking for sensitization effects involves administering the test to a control group (one chosen in the same way and apparently similar to the test group) as well as the retesting the test group to see if both groups respond similarly. Sensitization may occur not only in testing and questionnaires but also in studies involving observation.

Cohort analysis is similar to panel study analysis. It traces changes in attitudes of the same group over time, although not for the same individuals. Age cohorts (age groups) from different time periods on similar survey questions can be used to simulate panel studies. For example, if survey question X is asked in both 1945 and 1965, and if in both cases data are available by age groups, then the researcher can look at the age 20–29 cohort in 1945 and compare responses with the age 40–49 cohort for 1965. Conceivably one could look at both age groups at the same point in time but only if all other relevant variables except age can be held constant.

6

Survey Research and Sampling

The classic work in the field of survey research remains Herbert Hyman's *Survey Design and Analysis* (Free Press, 1955); however, beginning students may prefer the excellent handbook by Charles Backstrom and Gerald Hursh, *Survey Research* (Northwestern University paperback, 1963). A. N. Oppenheim's *Questionnaire Design and Attitude Measurement* (Basic Books, 1966) is a general treatment of the subject containing highly useful chapters on attitude scaling and projective techniques.

Since these books mention sampling statistics only briefly, any of several standard statistics books should also be consulted, such as K. A. Yeomans, "Statistical Sampling Practice," Chapter 3 in *Applied Statistics: Statistics for the Social Scientist*, Vol. II (Penguin paperback, 1968). The beginning student may prefer Morris J. Slonim's amusing and informative short paperback *Sampling in a Nutshell* (Simon and Schuster, 1966).

For many years, especially since World War II, the sample survey has been a common means of data gathering in political science. Vast amounts of electoral, opinion, and general social data are now available on a host of topics for anyone who wishes to take advantage of it. To utilize the information stored in "data banks" at various universities or to undertake similar studies of one's own it is necessary to understand the rudiments of how interview and questionnaire schedules are framed (survey design), how people are selected (sampling), and how the significance of the results can be appraised (sampling statistics). The last factor, sampling statistics, is particularly important since it raises the concept of a "normal distribution" which, as later chapters demonstrate, is the basis of several other areas of political science methods.

SURVEY DESIGN

Interviews (oral) and questionnaires (written) are often used in the social sciences to gain both attitudinal and factual data. Despite the great time and expense that this method entails, it may be selected over case studies, participant observation, or small group sociometric testing because it provides greater breadth. Thus, while the participant observer may immerse himself more deeply in the subject matter, the sample surveyor takes much shallower but far more representative observations. Surveyors argue that it is better to generalize on the basis of less but representative information than on the basis of more information about cases of unknown representativeness.

Writing the Questions

The surveyor limits himself at the outset to asking questions to gain specific information that he needs to test his hypotheses. This implies, of course, that the researcher must also formulate his central hypotheses in advance—he must have the hypothesis-generating skills discussed in the initial chapters. In this the researcher is usually aided by several weeks or more spent consulting related literature and studies, by talking with colleagues who may have done similar work, and perhaps attempting to make his own study comparable to previous studies. The consideration here is not to imitate previous researchers but to formulate questions in a way that analogous results will ensue, enabling comparison of one's own studies with previous research.

The interview or questionnaire usually starts off with simple identification questions, such as age, sex, race, occupation, education, income and the like. Part of the identification can be done by a trained interviewer without the need to ask questions. Sometimes, for example, the interviewer rates "life style" by the nature of living room furnishings (the Chapin Social Status Scale). Identification may also include matters relating to the respondent's *role* (club and religious affiliations, friendship patterns, leadership positions) and *level of information* (sources of information, frequency of exposure). *Entrapment questions,* such as asking if the respondent has recently read a nonexistent magazine, may be used to weed out unreliable respondents.

In formulating the *attitude questions,* including questions involving *self-evaluation* (e.g., Are you very/average/not very popular?), a whole series of considerations arises:

1. Are all terms well-defined and unambiguous? In the above example, for instance, popular with whom? In the question, "Do you know anyone who participated in the riot?" the word "participate" is ambiguous; it could apply only to those who actually engaged in violence or also include onlookers who followed the crowds.

2. Are emotionally-toned words and leading questions avoided? For example, the researcher should never put words into the respondent's mouth, as by asking, "You weren't involved in the riot, were you?" A variant of this is giving the respondent unfair alternatives, or simply failing to inform him of the alternatives. The respondent who favors policy A, even knowing that alternative B is available, gives a quite different response from one who favors A not given any alternative.

3. Are all terms specific? For example, in the question, "Do you approve of government policy?" does "government" refer to local, state, or federal levels? Is the time period about which the question is asked clear? If value judgments are called for, is the value comparison made clear? That is, if the respondent is asked to rank town officials' performance as above average/average/below average, is the criterion of comparison—what is considered "average performance"—made clear?

4. Is enough information provided in a readily understandable way? Complicated terms like "sovereignty" should not be used, nor should technical social science jargon. On the other hand, enough background information should be provided to assure that the respondent understands the context of the question, yet not so much that he may fail to follow it. For example, if a

respondent's attitudes toward the Voting Rights Act of 1965 is called for, a brief explanation of the provisions of the act is necessary.

5. Other considerations: Is the question too "folksy?" Does the question involve just one point, or does it call for several possible responses to different parts of the question? Are double negatives used? If the question is answered by multiple choice, are the questions mutually exclusive or is more than one response permitted?

Structuring the Interview

One of the first decisions is that of **format.** Is direct interview possible, or do cost and time considerations force resort to the less reliable mail or telephone formats? Is the interview going to be intensive, covering a subject in depth, or extensive, covering a broader range of topics? Will it be long or short? Some of these considerations are related, of course. Mail questionnaires call for shorter schedules. The impersonality of the telephone format makes intensive interviewing difficult.

A second consideration is that of **response structure.** Will the respondent be allowed to frame his answer in his own words ("open-ended responses") or must he select from among predetermined alternatives ("structured responses," such as multiple choice or ranking scales). Or is a combination to be used, with the interviewer asking a structured question and then following it up with an open-ended question for greater depth? The researcher should not assume that open-ended questions are a substitute for "depth" studies used in motivational psychology, for example. These techniques include various "projective" items, such as having the respondent interpret inkblots or give a short story about an ambiguous picture; their purpose is to get around the psychological inhibitions that may thwart even open-ended questions.

A third consideration relates to the **sequence** of items on the questionnaire or interview schedule. The interviewer should begin with a brief, natural introduction identifying the auspices under which the study is conducted. Assurance of anonymity should be given, and the initial questions should be neutral and non-threatening, including if possible questions that arouse the respondent's interest. Entrapment or filter questions may be used to weed out undesirable respondents (e.g., non-citizens or non-voters, in some studies). Then questions of a general nature about the subject of the study may be asked, working toward the more specific and more controversial questions.

Finally, internal and external **checks** must be considered. Items should be scattered throughout the interview, enabling the researcher to check the consistency of responses. Internal checks spot the consistency of one response with another; for example, age asked directly on one item and compared with date of graduation from high school asked on another would be an internal check. Structured responses may be compared with follow-up open-ended responses. Or the same respondent may be reinterviewed at a later date and responses compared. External checks involve comparison of responses with interviewer's observations or with answers in previous surveys, archival data, or interviews with related others. For instance, a man's responses may be compared with his wife's. Or a split-form interview —two similar interviews with corresponding questions differing slightly in wording—may be used to check whether specific wording is having an unforeseen effect.

Mechanics of Interviewing

The survey researcher exists at the mercy of his interviewers. Therefore, careful instruction of interviewers is essential. Ideally, mature women have been found to be the best interviewers, eliciting highest response rates. The interviewer should be instructed in the importance of objectivity, understand the purpose of each question, never suggest answers, should interview alone, be friendly and naturally sociable yet firm and neutral, and have a neat, not formidable appearance. Interviewers should be paid by the hour, not by the interview, as this might give incentive for quick, slipshod techniques. Preparation of interviewers should include role-playing and if possible supervised field experience. In addition, the interviewer must be provided with the material paraphernalia of his trade—an easy-to-read schedule, notebook, letter of introduction, a manual, etc.

Sources of error include faults in coding, tabulating, and processing data, or errors of judgment in interpreting the data, including those due to interviewer or researcher bias. In addition, error can occur because of bad timing: a sample of rainy-day bus riders will be different from fair weather riders, for example. Or the sample itself may be non-random, unrepresentative of the target universe (the population group relevant to the hypotheses).

Pretesting the interview or questionnaire is also an essential step. No matter how careful the advance preparation, the initial interview usually contains words people do not understand, has confusing terms and phrases, asks for information too bluntly, or contains some other problem. Pretesting is simply trying out the interview in draft form on a population group in the field, preferably a small random sample taken in the manner projected for the final sample. Respondents' reactions to the questions and difficulties encountered by the interviewer provide an invaluable guide to revising the draft interview.

SAMPLING METHODS

Ideally researchers would not take samples at all; instead they would take *enumerations*—gather information from everybody. The idea behind sampling is simply that because it is too expensive in time and money to interview everyone, it is the second-best thing to interview a smaller number of representative people. Sampling methods have been devised to help the researcher find representative people to interview.

Non-random Sampling

Most sampling is **probability** or **random sampling,** but other kinds of samples are sometimes used. Newspapers often use *haphazard samples* in their man-on-the-street interview columns. This is one form of **availability sample,** in which the researcher selects his sample from among those who volunteer or are otherwise available. Naturally, such a sample cannot be presumed to be representative. The well-known *Kinsey Report* on sexual behavior of females has often been criticized for including a large number of female inmates of prisons in the sample simply because they were available for interview.

Other forms of non-random sampling methods include the **judgment sample,** in which the researcher asks an arbitrary list of "experts" to select representative men. Or a **chain sample** may be used, starting with one respondent selected by any means who meets some basic criterion (in a sample of draft resisters, for example, someone who had turned in his draft card); this respondent is then asked to name other individuals like himself with regard to the criterion. These reference individuals are then interviewed and further references acquired in a snowballing or chain process. The non-random sampling methods have the advantage of being quicker and cheaper, but it cannot be assumed that they result in a representative sample. In fact, many researchers believe it is best to assume that a sample selected by any non-random method will be significantly different on items of interest to the researcher from a random sample.

Random Sampling

The basic idea behind **simple random sampling** is to make a list of all members of the target population and then select respondents from this list in a way such that every member has an equal chance of being selected. This is usually done by using a table of random numbers generated by a computer. For example, the researcher might arbitrarily determine in advance that he will start with the first page, fifth row, second column of the table of random numbers. He finds this number and selects that individual from the list of all members. He may continue in this manner or may use **interval sampling;** that is, the researcher may start with the individual selected above and then take every fifth, every ninth, or whatever interval is appropriate to generate the desired number of respondents.

Although these methods may be used on small populations, such as the universe of students at a college, it is impossible to list all the residents of a country or even of a large city. Sometimes surrogate lists are used, such as telephone and city directories, police, utility company, voter registration, school census, auto owners, or marriage-divorce lists, or some combination. None of these surrogates can be considered highly reliable. Telephone directories, for example, are biased against inclusion of the poor, who cannot afford telephones or share them among several families, and the well-to-do, who often have unlisted numbers.

For larger population groups some form of **multi-stage sampling** is generally used—either **cluster sampling** (sample of groups) or **area sampling** (sample of territorial units). Here the researcher makes a list of all states, takes a simple random sample of states, then for these states makes a list of all counties, takes a random sample of counties, then a sample of census tracts, then a sample of tract blocks (or the equivalent units for rural areas). Next a list is made, in the field or from city directories, of the dwelling units in the final sample blocks—or of all families or even all individuals living on the block —and finally a random interval sample is taken of these families or individuals. This is an extremely laborious and complicated procedure dealt with at length in the Backstrom and Hursh reading. Large national samples, when desired by political scientists, are usually taken by professional polling companies such as the famous Gallup or Harris poll groups.

Random sampling alone does not guarantee representativeness of the sample. Therefore, some researchers use **stratified sampling** to assure that all important groups will be represented according to their known proportion in the population. This method, often used in conjunction with area sampling, simply breaks the overall sample into several samples. For example, an overall sample of 2000 might be divided into two subsamples: 1000 men and 1000 women. These subsamples might in turn be broken down several times by such criteria as age, region, city size, socio-economic status, and race. These are then used as the target populations of random sampling methods such as cluster or area sampling.

Sampling Error

Finally, there is always the danger of unexpected sampling error. Interviewer bias, bad timing, or poorly-worded interviews have already been mentioned. In addition there is the danger of "systematic sampling": the researcher may use the random interval method without realizing that the list from which he is sampling is not haphazard but instead has a systematic pattern. For example, sampling every other U.S. senator on the *Congressional Quarterly* list will either result in all senior or all junior senators, since there are two per state and senators are listed by state with the senior senator first. Or a sample that always starts with the corner house in a block would oversample corner houses, which usually are more valuable and have occupants with above average income. Samples during the day are likely to oversample women and the unemployed. All samples tend to undersample transient members of the population. Persons living in institutions such as nursing homes or prisons must be considered.

Interviewing more than one person in the same household will exaggerate any sampling bias that exists.

The greatest problem for the survey researcher is dealing with those who are not at home or refuse to answer. He must plan in advance that a certain proportion of his sample will be in this category. It is therefore necessary to take a sample some percentage higher (ordinarily 10%, sometimes more in neighborhoods with high transiency and many vacancies) than would otherwise be taken. In a random sample substitutions should never be made. If a selected house is vacant, the interview is so marked and is processed as such; it is not thrown out since it does represent real information. This is even more true of persons refusing to answer questions or not locatable. The researcher must assume that nonrespondents are significantly different from first responders. Nonrespondents are never thrown out of the sample, but like vacancies are processed as such along with the rest of the sample. Nonrespondents may be handled by setting aside those interviews secured initially and then making *call-backs* to again try to interview those not contacted the first time. Interviews obtained the second time are set aside, as are those obtained the third time. By comparing answers to a given item among the initial, second, and third sets, some extrapolation estimate may be made about the nature of the responses of the final nonresponse set.

SAMPLING STATISTICS

One necessary prerequisite to sampling is being able to compute how large a sample must be taken. While it is possible in many applications to simply look this up in a table, such as "Simple Random Sample Size for Several Degrees of Precision" given in the Backstrom and Hursh reading, the researcher may also be led astray if he does not understand the criteria involved. The sample size required depends on what is to be done with the data obtained. Therefore, it is necessary to drop the subject of sampling for a moment and consider some possible ways of using survey answers.

Measures of Central Tendency

The purpose of all statistics is to make complex things understandable through simplification. And simplification always involves loss of information. Thus, if we have a list of one hundred people and their corresponding ages, a perceptive mind could understand everything about this information on ages without using statistics. But suppose there were fifty such lists! No one could directly absorb fifty lists of information on one hundred units each. Instead we would be aided by knowing the average age in each of the fifty lists, and perhaps the grand average age in all fifty lists together. By looking only at averages information has been lost, yet in spite of this we may understand more for the time invested. This is all very obvious, but the beginning statistician should keep in mind that the purpose of all statistics is to make complex things simple by losing information.

Measures of central tendency include various kinds of *averages,* the most common of which is the mean. The **mean** is the sum of measures divided by the number of units; one would add up all the ages of 100 people and then divide by 100 to get the mean age. However, recall from the last chapter that one can add and subtract measures only if the data are interval or metric data (e.g., if the distance from a measure of 2 to 3 is the same as from 4 to 5).

If the data are ordinal (for example, if people are ranked one to one hundred according to liberalism, from 1 = most liberal to 100 = most conservative), then it is necessary to use the **median,** the measure of the unit (person in this case) in the middle. For nominal data where not even order is known the average used is the **mode,** the measure of the category with the largest number of units (or people).

Measures of Variation

In addition to central tendency, another convenient summary statistic is one that measures how much spread there is around the central tendency. For example, are most people very close to the average age—is the group homogenous? or is there a wide spread of ages from young to old with not very many within a year of the average age? Thus **variance,** the measure of this spread around the central tendency, is based on how much each unit (each person's age, for example) deviates from the mean (the mean age, for example). Since this involves subtracting, *deviation measures of variance can only be used with interval or metric data.* Although often ignored in political science, this is especially important since much survey data are nominal or ordinal (e.g., attitudes rated from "very favorable" to "very unfavorable"); *Q* dispersion, discussed in Chapter 7, measures ordinal variance.

The difference between the unit score *x* (a given person's age), and the average score $\bar{x}$ (the mean age for a list of people), is called a **deviation.** The mean deviation is simply the absolute values of all the *x* scores on a list added up and divided by the number on the list, *n*. Absolute values means ignoring the plus or minus sign; if raw values of the deviations were added the sum would be zero, by definition of the mean. Unfortunately, taking absolute values interferes with later statistical inferences one may want to make. Instead, it is possible to get rid of the signs by squaring the *x*-values, then adjusting by dividing through by *n*. That gives the formula for the *variance*, σ^2:[1]

$$\sigma^2 = \frac{\Sigma (x - \bar{x})^2}{n}$$

The *standard deviation,* σ, is simply the square root of the variance. Finally, when dealing with samples rather than complete enumerations the researcher divides by $(n-1)$ rather than *n;* this modification for *sample variance,* s^2, and *sample standard deviation, s,* serves to give a conservative estimate preferred by statisticians when dealing with samples.

There is one further statistic of variation that must be mentioned. In one sample of people's ages, the researcher could compute the mean age as a measure of central tendency, and also compute the standard deviation of age as a measure of the spread of sample ages around the mean. But if several samples were taken, then the researcher could compute several means; in fact, he could compute the mean of all the sample means, the *grand mean,* and also compute the spread of sample means around the grand mean. This measure of the variations of sample means from the grand mean of many samples (from the same population universe) is called the **standard error** (SE), and is approximated by dividing the sample standard deviation *s* by the square root of the sample size minus 1, or $\sqrt{n-1}$. This means that the standard error is always smaller than the standard deviation; the variation of the sample mean from a hypothetical grand mean will be less than the variation of sample scores from the sample mean.

---

[1] Note that "Σ" means "the sum of."

Example

| Explanation | Example |

Explanation

Begin with a list, in this case a list of labor riot frequencies by year for the 1930s in America.

For ten observations (years; $n=10$) a sum of 200 riots were recorded ($\Sigma x = 200$). This is an enumeration, not a sample. The x scores (riot frequencies) are metric data.

The sum of the squared deviations is 1322. To get the standard deviation this is divided by n (not $n-1$ as would be the case with a sample) and the square root is taken.

Standard error is computed by dividing the standard deviation by the square root of n (square root of 10 in this case). But note that since this is

Example

	x	$(x-\bar{x})^2$
1930	3	289
1931	28	64
1932	21	1
1933	17	9
1934	37	289
1935	30	100
1936	31	121
1937	22	4
1938	2	324
1939	9	121
$n=10$	$\Sigma x = 200$	1322

$$\bar{x} = 200/10 = 20$$
$$\sigma = \sqrt{1322/10} = 11.50$$
$$\text{SE} = 11.50/\sqrt{10} = 3.64$$

an enumeration and not a sample, standard error has no meaning in this case. The mean of an enumeration *is* the true mean; hence it makes no sense to talk about deviations of the computed mean from some grand mean.

Normal Distribution

The normal curve is one that approximates the distribution of heads and tails that one might obtain by flipping pennies. The standard normal curve occurs when the distribution represented by the normal curve has a mean of zero and when one standard deviation equals one measurement unit. For example, to express the riot frequencies in *standard scores* (z scores) rather than raw scores (x scores), one simply subtracts the mean, 20 in the previous example—this gives the distribution a mean of zero—and divides by the standard deviation, 11.5—this gives the distribution a standard deviation of one.

The standard normal curve, illustrated in Figure 6.1, has certain useful properties. If the distribution is normally distributed—and many political science variables are *not*, including dichotomous variables like sex and party, nominal variables like region—then a certain

Figure 6.1   Standard Normal Curve

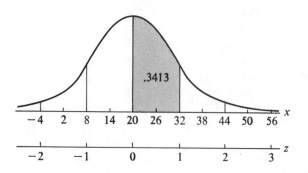

proportion of the universe will lie within one standard deviation of the mean (namely, 34.13% on one side or roughly ⅔ on both sides. Approximately 95% of the universe will lie within two standard deviations either way of the mean. About 99% will lie within three. The exact proportions can be easily read from Table II in the Appendix.

Applications to Sampling

Suppose one has taken a sample and computed the sample mean and sample standard deviation as 12 and 1.1, respectively. The normal table enables us to say that we can be about 95% sure that any given sample measurement will lie within two (actually 1.96) standard deviations of the mean; or any given sample measurement will lie within plus or minus 1.96 times 1.1 of the mean, 12.

More important, if the standard error in this sample is .20, then we can say that the sample mean (in this case 12) lies within plus or minus 1.96 (the number of standard errors one way or the other from the mean which mark off 95 percent of the area under the normal curve) times .20 of the real mean, with 95% confidence. These plus or minus limits are called **confidence limits.** The 95% confidence level is often considered the minimum acceptable level, meaning that in 100 samples from the same universe, in 95 percent of these the sample mean will fall within the stated confidence limits of the real mean. The 98%, 99%, and 99.9% levels are also used in more rigorous studies.

Tests of Hypotheses

These same sorts of inferences can be used to test **hypotheses about means.** A hypothesis of this type would be as follows:

Someone claims the average age of U.S. senators is 55, but you think it is higher. You take a sample of senators' ages and find the sample mean age is 61—but is 61 significantly different from 55? Or could this just be due to a chance sample when the real mean age was 55?

We could ask the same question this way: If we hypothesize a normal distribution around mean age of 55 and take samples from this distribution, what percent of the time would we get a sample mean age of

Figure 6.2

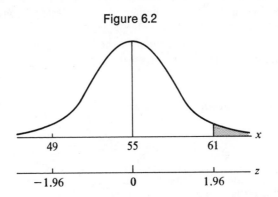

61 or higher? The shaded area to the right of the normal curve in Figure 6.2 represents that chance. The chance of getting a sample mean six units (years, in this case) away from the hypothesized real mean, 55, is equal to the area to the right of 61 and to the left of 49 on the normal curve. This would be a *two-tailed test* because it looks at both sides of the normal distribution.

Note that 1.96 *z* units (normal standard deviations or normal standard errors) corresponds to .4750 of the area under the normal curve.[2] Thus, if the distance from 55 to 61 and from 55 to 49 is equal

[2] This fraction is read directly from Table II.

to 1.96 or more, then the proportion under both tails would be .05 or less. This means that only .05 of the time would such a difference occur by chance.[3]

On the other hand, our original question calls for a *one-tailed test*, because we are not interested in the chance of getting a sample mean age six years *different* (greater or less, referring to both tails of the curve), but only the chance of getting a sample mean six years *greater* (referring to the right-side tail only) by chance. If 61 were 1.96 standard errors away from 55, then the proportion under *one tail* would be .025 (computed exactly as above), meaning that a sample mean 6 years higher or more would occur by chance only 2.5% of the time.

An easy formula for testing hypotheses about means simply involves taking the difference between the sample mean and the hypothesized real mean, between 61 and 55, and dividing by the standard error of the sample. But when the z score is computed this way, the researcher must be careful to decide whether he is interested in greater-or-less relationships (two tails) or only greater or only less relationships (one tail). The following examples show three sample formulas for computing z values in hypothesis testing.

Formula for z Values in Testing Hypotheses About Means

$$z = \frac{x - \mu_0}{s/\sqrt{n-1}}$$

Where x = the sample mean
μ_0 = the hypothesized real mean
s = the sample standard deviation (logically should be the real but unknown standard deviation)
n = the sample size

After z is computed, consult the normal table to see if the number of z units obtained mark off enough area under the normal curve, as in Figure 6.2. For instance, 1.96 z units either way mark off 95% of the area; if the sample mean is more than 1.96 z units away from the hypothesized real mean, then we can be 95% confident it is different from the

[3] Note that .05 is obtained by subtracting the proportion 1.96 from the mean, namely .4750, from half the curve, .5000, thus getting .025; the same is done for the other half of the curve, also getting .025—added together this gives .050.

hypothesized mean, and 97.5% confident it is more than the hypothesized mean (two- and one-tailed tests respectively).

Similar Formula for z Values in Testing Hypotheses About the Difference Between Two Independent Random Sample Means

Suppose that in similar samples taken in two cities the sample mean income is \$5500 for City 1 and \$6200 for City 2. We could test the *null hypothesis* that there is no statistically significant difference between these two sample means by computing a z value according to the formula below and following the same general procedures for testing hypotheses about means.

$$z = \frac{x_1 - x_2}{\sqrt{\dfrac{s_1^2}{n_1} + \dfrac{s_2^2}{n_2}}}$$

Similar Formula for z Values in Testing Hypotheses About the Difference Between Proportions ("Standard Error of a Proportion")

Suppose that similar samples taken in two cities show that the proportion of the population voting Democratic in a particular election was .60 in City 1 and .52 in City 2. We could test the null hypothesis that there is no statistically significant difference between the two cities in this regard by applying the following formula:

$$z = \sqrt{\frac{P_1 Q_1}{n_1} + \frac{P_2 Q_2}{n_2}}$$

where P_1 is the proportion in City 1 voting Democratic and Q_1 is the proportion voting non-Democratic.

Other Distributions

Normal distribution is appropriate when the units involved are normally distributed. A later chapter will give a way of testing to see if a variable is normally distributed; for now we should recognize that there are other distributions, such as those illustrated in Figure 6.3.

Figure 6.3

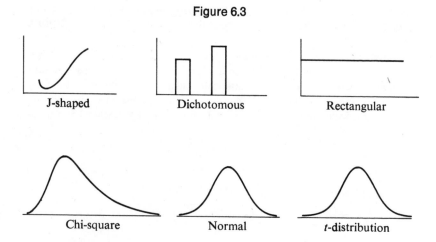

In the example just mentioned, one might think that the variable used (political party, divided into Democratic and non-Democratic) is a dichotomous variable and hence cannot be used in **parametric tests** —tests that assume a particular distribution as z tests assume a normal distribution. An important distinction must be made here. If we were working with the distribution of *parties* per se, then the z test could not be used. However, in the example we were working with the distribution of *voters,* which is quite a different matter. Similarly, party is a nominal-level variable and cannot be meaningfully added. Letting Democrat = 1 and non-Democrat = 2, it makes no sense to add to get 3. But voters is a metric-level variable and hence the arithmetic operations involved in z tests are permissible.

The beginning researcher should firmly understand that although an impressive array of statistics is built on the normal distribution as a parameter, there is nothing sacred about the normal distribution. Variables used in political analysis may very well *not* be normally distributed. It is even conceivable to make up one's own "ideal" distribution and work out a statistics based on that! The *t* **distribution** is a distribution similar but not identical to the normal distribution, and is used when sample size *n* is less than 30. The researcher simply uses a table of the *t* distribution instead of tables of the normal (*z*) distribution in an analogous manner. Finally, the **chi-square distribution** (χ^2), where

$$\chi^2 = \frac{(n-1)\,s^2}{\sigma^2},$$

based on sample and real standard deviations, is used in nonparametric tests of significance of tables (normal distribution not assumed), as discussed in a later chapter.

Computing Sample Size

Finally we are ready to come back to our original question, "How do we know in advance how large a sample we need to take?" *We need to take a sample big enough so that the variable with the largest standard deviation will still have a sample mean that falls within a tolerated limit of the real but unknown mean the desired percentage of the time.* For example, suppose the variable with the largest standard deviation is age. We then want a sample large enough so that some high percentage of the time (say 95% of the time), the sample mean of age would be within plus or minus the limit chosen, e.g., ±2 years of the real (population) mean age.

The formula for sample size is given below, where σ is the standard deviation of the variable with the largest variance, z is the number of normal standard deviations (z units) corresponding to the desired percentage of the area under the normal curve (1.96 z units to get 95% of the area either side of the mean, in this example), and T is the tolerated variation of the sample (2 in this case):

$$ss = (\sigma z/T)^2$$

Thus the bigger the standard deviation (the more variation) the larger the sample size. The higher the confidence level desired (the bigger the z), the larger the sample size needed. And the smaller the confidence limits desired (the smaller the T), the larger the sample size needed.

How does the survey researcher get the values to "plug into" this formula? He makes an educated guess. The z and T values are arbitrary, chosen by the researcher according to how rigorous he feels he must make his study. The σ value (sigma, the standard deviation) is the hard part; σ is not known at all, and the sample standard deviation s is not known either, prior to taking the sample. The best that can be done is to take a small pretest sample, mentioned earlier, and compute the pretest sample standard deviations for each variable. The largest pretest s is increased by some arbitrary amount (say 10%) to be on the conservative side and is used as an educated guess of σ in the sample size equation.

Note that if a sample is truly random the size of the real universe is irrelevant. Given the expected deviations, the desired confidence level, and limits, the same sample size would be appropriate whether the universe were a thousand or a million. Second, if the researcher plans on breaking his survey data down into subtables, each of which he hopes will be sensitive to (significant for) small relationships, the sample size must be even larger. This is dealt with by a chi-square method discussed in Chapter 8.

Extrapolating from a Sample to a Population Estimate

Suppose a sample of 20 out of the 120 months in a decade is taken and the number of riots for those sample months is determined to be 25. One might then want to estimate how many riots occurred during the whole decade, not just in the sample months. Since 120 months is six times 20 months, one could estimate that the entire decade had six times as many riots as the sample 20 months, $6 \times 25 = 150$ riots for the decade. This is called the simple **blow-up estimate.**

Having just one sample, the blow-up estimate is the only possible one. However, in a situation where a series of samples are taken different methods may be used. Suppose a researcher stood outside a polling place, asked a random sample of people how they voted, and made a blow-up estimate of the total vote for a particular party at that place. Later he might find out the actual vote and what his error was. The next time this survey is taken, knowledge of past error can be used to improve his estimate.

One way is to assume that the same % *error* will occur the second time. Thus, if the percent voting Democratic was overestimated by 10% the first time, compute the second simple blow-up and decrease it by 10% to get the **ratio estimate.** Or it could be assumed that the same absolute error will be made the second time. Thus, if the number voting Democratic is underestimated the first time by 800, then add 800 to the second blow-up to get the **difference estimate**. Or, a fraction of the absolute error could be added, that fraction being the regression coefficient, discussed in a later chapter, for the **regression estimate**. This topic is dealt with more fully in the Slonim reading.

Review: Taking a Sample of Legislators' Ages

Step 1. Estimate sample size. Set arbitrary desired confidence level (e.g., 95% level, z equals 1.96) and arbitrary limits (e.g., $T=6$). Take a small sample of, say, 10 legislators and compute the standard deviation as follows:

Pretest sample ages, x	$(x-\bar{x})^2$
49	27.0
38	262.4
59	23.0
81	718.2
44	104.0
64	96.0
59	23.0
49	27.0
38	262.4
61	46.2
$\Sigma x = 542$	$\Sigma(x-\bar{x})^2 = 1589.2$
$n = 10$	
$\bar{x} = 54.2$	

$$s = \sqrt{\frac{\Sigma(x-\bar{x})^2}{n-1}} = \sqrt{\frac{1589.2}{9}} = \sqrt{176.6} = 13.3$$

$$s' = 13.3 + .10(13.3) = 14.6$$

$$\text{sample size} = (\sigma z/T)^2 = 14.6 \times 1.96/6)^2 \cong 23$$

If we randomly sample 23 legislators from a real population of any number of normally distributed (by age) legislators, then 95% of the time our sample mean age would be within 6 years of the real mean age.

Step 2. Select the sample of 23 from a list of all legislators using a table of random numbers. Compute the measure of central tendency, mean, measure of variation, sample standard deviation, and standard error.

sample	$(x-\bar{x})$	$(x-\bar{x})^2$
57	5	25
53	1	1
50	-2	4
58	6	36
66	14	196
45	-7	49
48	-4	16
51	-1	1
53	1	1
61	9	81
60	8	64
44	-8	64
42	-10	100
69	17	289
42	-10	100
45	-7	49
54	2	4
46	-6	36
51	-1	1
50	-2	4
65	13	169
48	-4	16
45	-7	49
$\Sigma x = \overline{1203}$		$\overline{1355} = \Sigma(x-\bar{x})^2$

$$\text{mean} = 120/193 \cong 62$$

$$\text{standard deviation} = s = \sqrt{\frac{\Sigma(x-\bar{x})^2}{n-1}}$$

$$= \sqrt{\frac{1355}{22}} = \sqrt{61.6} \cong 7.8$$

$$\text{standard error} = s/\sqrt{n-1}$$

$$= 7.8/\sqrt{22}$$

$$\cong 1.7$$

7

Scaling

Any standard statistics text in social science will present a useful section on scaling. Among those texts mentioned in earlier chapters, the student might refer to Goode and Hatt, Chapters 15–17; Riley, Unit 9; or Simon, Chapter 20 (this last is a particularly basic introduction). A somewhat higher-level introductory treatment can be found in John T. Doby, ed., *An Introduction to Social Research* (Appleton-Century-Crofts, 1967), Chapter 8.

At a more specialized level, the political science student may find especially useful the excellent handbook on *Legislative Roll-Call Analysis* (Northwestern University paperback, 1966) by Anderson, Watts, and Wilcox. Another is that by Delbert C. Miller, *Handbook of Research Design and Social Measurement* (David McKay paperback, 1964). This work outlines in some detail three dozen scales in standard use by social scientists and gives an annotated list of many more. From it the student can gain deeper insight into the variety of applications of scaling to social research.

Scaling is a technique that addresses itself to the problem of measurement. Many concepts in political science cannot be measured by counting "natural" units such as votes. For example, power, welfare, and alienation are concepts important in political theory that cannot be easily quantified. Scales are a means of measuring important variables that cannot simply be counted in natural units. Figure 7.1 shows that the abstract variable "happiness," which lies along a continuum with no natural dividing points, may be measured by a scale made up of *items* (11 in this case) assumed to represent arbitrary points on the true continuum.

Figure 7.1   "Happiness Scale"

True Happiness in extreme									True Unhappiness in extreme	
			True Underlying Continuum							

				Scale						
1	2	3	4	5	6	7	8	9	10	11
Measured Happiness in extreme									Measured Unhappiness in extreme	

An individual who agrees with the statement, "I am truly happy" (item 1) might be ranked 1 on the happiness scale. Item 6 might be agreement with the statement, "I don't know if I'm happy or unhappy," while item 11 might be agreement with the statement, "I am truly unhappy." While this is not a "scientific" scale, it does bring out some of the important characteristics of scaling:

1. A scale is a series of ordered items. These items might be answers to questions, votes in a legislative body, or Supreme Court decisions—used to indicate some unmeasurable abstract variable, such as "conservativeness."
2. The items constitute an ordinal level of measurement. Point 2 on the happiness scale represents more happiness than point 3, but we cannot assume that the distance between points is equal in each case. Some researchers have sought to develop near-interval level scales. In better social science scales, intervals are less than equal but more than randomly unequal; such scales are somewhere between the ordinal and interval level of measurement.
3. The true underlying continuum assumed to be measured by the scale is represented by a single line. This is because the underlying continuum is presumed to be *unidimensional*. That is, hap-

piness is assumed to be a single concept and not an umbrella term encompassing many sometimes inconsistent sub-concepts.

4. Related to this, the scale is obviously assumed to measure the underlying continuum. Whether or not the "happiness scale" really measures true happiness is the question of *validity*. The ways of testing validity are discussed in Chapter 9.
5. It is also assumed that the scale is *reproducible,* that it could be reliably applied twice and get the same results, all other things equal.

There are many examples of simple, untested scales—scales with unknown validity and reproducibility. For example, one might ask a respondent directly, "From 1 equaling most liberal to 8 equaling least liberal, how liberal are you?" The respondent's answer would be his scale score. Of course such a direct method is too blunt a research instrument. Respondents would have difficulty, for example, in agreeing on the meaning of intermediate scale values like 6—is 6 "somewhat liberal" or "fairly liberal" or "rather liberal?"

Such direct "self-scaling" is not used in political science; instead, some more indirect measurement is used. For instance, in the sociometric tests discussed in Chapter 5, the number of times an individual is chosen by others can be used as a scale of "popularity." Another example is the widely-used "Bogardus Social Distance Scale," used to measure the "social distance" between groups.

The Bogardus Scale uses seven items, ranging from 1 = "Would admit blacks (or the name of some other group) to close kinship by marriage," through 4 = "Would admit blacks to employment in my occupation," to 7 = "Would exclude blacks from my country." The respondent's score is the lowest item he endorses. This scale might be administered to a cross-section of Americans, their scores averaged, and a "racial distance quotient" between blacks and the general population could be computed. Alternatively, this scale could be administered to a cross-section of blacks, asking them to respond to the scale for each of a number of other ethnic groups (English, Poles, Italians, etc.); this would be a second measure of "racial distance" between blacks and others, this time from the point of view of the black citizen. The Bogardus measure can be used in testing such hypotheses as "Groups characterized by higher social distance from others are more likely to be involved in rioting," or "Groups characterized by low social distance from others tend to occupy higher status roles."

THE CLUSTER BLOC TECHNIQUE

The cluster bloc was a technique commonly used before modern scaling techniques were developed, and is still widely used in legislative roll-call analysis, following procedures specified by Stuart Rice and Herman Beyle in the 1920s and early 1930s. Like modern scales, cluster bloc analysis enables the researcher to rank individuals according to some criterion and to group together those who are most alike by this criterion. For example, U.S. senators can be ranked according to their agreements on a set of votes and blocs of like-voting senators can be identified.

1. Selecting the Set of Votes

The first step is simply to decide which votes are relevant to the researcher's particular study. One study by David Truman looked at issues that divided political parties; "low cohesion" votes were selected by use of the Rice Index of Cohesion (R.I.C.). R.I.C. equals the percent of Democrats (or some other party) for an issue minus the percent against. Thus it varies from 0 (when 50% are for and 50% are opposed) to 100 (when 100% are for and none are opposed, or vice versa). R.I.C. takes absolute values, ignoring minus signs. A list of low cohesion votes could be those with a Rice Index below some arbitrary level, e.g., .40.

2. Computing Indices of Agreement

This step requires determining how much any given senator agrees with every other senator for the set of votes selected in the first step. A *simple* index of agreement would be the percent of times the aye votes of a given Senator match the aye votes of each other senator, but this has the unfortunate effect of treating absences as non-agreements. There are two ways of treating absences. First, in any pair if one or both senators were absent, that vote could be ignored; thus the index of agreement would be simply the percent of pairs of agreeing votes for those votes when both were present and voting. Alternatively, if the researcher believes absences or abstentions are not random but actually reflect "partial agreement" (because one senator may not agree, but may deliberately not oppose, by not voting), then the index of agreement could be the number of pairs of agreeing votes (full agreements) plus half, or some other arbitrary fraction, the number of votes where one senator did not vote (partial agreements) as a percentage of total number of pairs of votes.

In any given voting group the number of possible pairs is $n(n-1)/2$, where n is the size of the voting group. For 100 senators there thus could be 4,950 pairs! For a voting group of any considerable size, the data must be processed by a computer, as discussed in the Anderson, Watts and Wilcox handbook.

3. Forming the Cluster Bloc Matrix

The cluster bloc matrix in Table 7.1 is a square table showing the index of agreement for each senator with every other senator. It lists senators down the side and also across the top, in the same order; the intersection of these columns and rows contains the indices of agreement.

Table 7.1   A Cluster Bloc Matrix, Showing Two Blocs in Which the Index of Agreement is .50 or Higher for Any Pair

Senator

	1	2	3	4	5	6	7	8	9	10	11	12	13	14
1		81	59	62	43	44					40			
2	81		78	54	54		41							
3	59	78		60		40								
4	62	54	60		40									
5	43	54		40										
6	44		40											
7		41						68						
8							68							
9										40				
10									40		51	58	50	
11	40									51		68	63	71
12										58	68		80	
13										50	63	80		42
14											71		42	

Senator

Once indices of agreement are computed (step 2), formation of a cluster bloc matrix is relatively simple. The main problem is ordering the senators (in this case) in such a way that the largest number of blocs and the most inclusive blocs will be apparent. If in the example, senators 1, 2, 3, and 4 were instead listed as numbers 1, 5, 10, and 14, the bloc that appears in the upper left corner would not be readily apparent in the matrix.

The following procedure is used to order the members of a voting group in cluster bloc analysis:

1. Find the pair with the highest agreement score and list it first.
2. Find the next highest agreement score that includes a member of the first pair; the other member of this second pair is listed third.
3. Find the highest agreement score that includes one of the first three members and a fourth member, who is then listed fourth in the matrix. This process is continued until the matrix is complete.

Agreement scores that are high enough to be interesting to the researcher—.40 or higher in the example, but this is completely arbitrary and depends on the interests of the researcher—are then entered on the matrix.

Thus, the cluster bloc technique results in an ordering of senators according to their agreement on a set of votes of one type or another. The blocs that are identified for one set of votes can be compared to blocs existing for another set. For example, the bloc structure of Congress for race-related bills could be compared to the bloc structure for social security-related bills, to test the extent to which civil rights policy is related to domestic welfare policy. On the other hand, one must be careful not to assume that agreement is due to similar thinking—agreement can also be born of constituency pressures, bargaining ("log-rolling"), or party discipline.

THURSTONE EQUAL-APPEARING INTERVAL SCALES

The general idea of scaling, then, is to rank individuals (senators, for example) or groups of individuals (such as the Senate or several legislatures) according to some criterion (agreement on low cohesion votes, or agreement on social security issues). The Thurstone technique was developed to do this in a way so that the intervals between the rankings assigned by the scales would approximate equal intervals. This was considered important because interval-level statistical techniques (involving arithmetic manipulation of the data) could then be applied. Recent evidence suggests that less rigorous or less time-consuming scaling techniques may be sufficient in this regard. That is, deviation from normal distribution and interval-level data assumptions may not be as important as formerly assumed. Nevertheless, Thurstone scales are still in use and it is instructive to understand their construction.

The general procedure of the Thurstone technique is to have "judges" rank opinion statements into piles. The researcher then selects from these piles some statements to form his scale. Statements are selected from each of the ordered piles, giving preference to those statements the judges agreed on in ranking.

1.   Compiling Possible Scale Items

First the researcher writes on slips a large number of statements (say 100) about his subject, such as attitudes toward rioting. For example, these could include: "Rioting does more good than harm. Rioting encourages crime. Rioting helps focus needed attention on city problems." Each statement should:

1. Express only one idea (*not* "Rioting costs too much in moral and economic terms").
2. Avoid extremes that only a *small* minority could endorse (e.g., "Nearly all rioters are Communists").
3. Refer to the present, not the past (*not* "Riots have never done this country any good"). Referring to the past tends to ask the respondent for two responses, past effect of riots and effect of present riots.
4. Avoid unclear, ambiguous or slang words (e.g., any of the examples listed in Chapter 6 under "Writing the Questions").
5. Avoid *biasing response sets*. Biased response sets include the *agreeing response set*—since people tend to agree with statements regardless of content, statements should be worded positively and negatively in equal numbers—and *response sets related to format*—people tend to endorse items listed first more than last, for instance.

These comments apply to other types of scales and, for that matter, to questionnaire and interview items.

2. Having Judges Order the Possible Items

The second step is to have judges rank statements, written on slips of paper, into a number of piles according to how favorable or unfavorable the items are *to the variable* being studied—(here, rioting). Judges are *not* asked, and in fact are instructed *not* to rank the items according to how favorable or unfavorable their own feelings are toward the variable. The researcher must assemble a large number of judges and give them each a set of paper slips with the possible statements written on them. Thus, in our example each judge would have a set of 100 slips. Thurstone used 300 judges to rank 130 items. Theoretically the best judges would be selected by a random sample of the population to be scaled. Empirical studies have shown, however, that even white Southerners do not rank civil rights items much differently from blacks. The judges, usually college students because of their availability, rank the slips according to favorableness of the statement on each slip to the subject, on a "scale" from one to eleven (or some other arbitrary scale). Thus the statement "Rioting does more good than harm" might be ranked in the ninth pile by one judge, in the seventh pile by another, and in the tenth pile by a third (where the eleventh pile represents the most favorable).

3. Computing the Average Value for Each Statement

Each judge thus has made eleven piles; these are combined into one master set of eleven piles (all slips in pile one for each judge are placed in master pile one, etc.). The number of the pile determines the number given to each slip. Thus every slip in master pile one is numbered 1, every slip in master pile two is numbered 2, etc.

Once this is done, the slips are regrouped by *statement*. Suppose the statement "Rioting does more good than harm" had slips in piles 7, 9, 10 and perhaps others; all of the slips corresponding to this statement are collected and put aside, and this is done for each statement. Each statement will then have a pile of slips corresponding to the number of judges. For each statement the *median* value is found; median, as discussed earlier, is the measure of central tendency appropriate for ordinal data.

To complete step 3, all statements with a median of 1 are placed in the 1 pile, all those with a median of 2 are placed in the 2 pile, and so on up to 11.

4. Selecting the Specific Scale Items

Two criteria are used to select which specific statements (items) out of the 100 possible items are to be used in the final scale. First, the full range of the scale should be represented. This is accomplished by making sure that at least one item (statement) is selected from each of the final eleven piles in step three. Second, in each pile items are selected according to how much agreement there was among judges that the item belonged in that pile; the items thus chosen are characterized by having the least **dispersion**—where judges' placements are spread out the least.

One could identify the items with the least dispersion as those with the lowest standard deviation, but this would require treating the item rank numbers (one to eleven) as if they were interval-level data, which they are not. Therefore, Thurstone used the Q **Value** method. Q values are measures of dispersion, akin to standard deviations in their general purpose but suitable for ordinal data. They are based on computing *graphic medians* and *ogive values* (cumulative percentage values) as shown in Figure 7.2.

Figure 7.2   Graph of Q Values for One Item

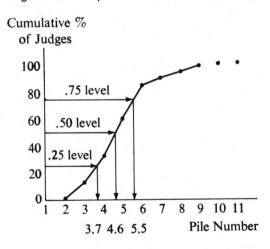

4(a).   Computing Q Values

First a graph is constructed, with the cumulative percentage of
judges on the y axis and pile number on the x axis; such a graph is
constructed for each statement. Sample data for this graph are given
in Table 7.2.

Table 7.2   Sample Data for Graph of Figure 7.2

Pile Number	Number of Judges	Cumulative %
1	0	0 %
2	3	2.5
3	12	12.5
4	21	30.0
5	36	60.0
6	24	80.0
7	12	90.0
8	9	97.5
9	3	100.0
10	0	100.0
11	0	100.0
	$N=120$	

Thus, Figure 7.2 shows that 60% of the judges ranked this particular item in pile 5 or lower; 97.5% ranked it in pile 8 or lower. The
.60, .975, etc. levels are the **ogive** levels. The **graphic median** can be
determined by reading the pile number that corresponds to the .50
level—4.6 in this example.

Q dispersion is the difference between the pile number corresponding to the .75 level and the .25 level (Q thus stands for quartile). In
this case Q dispersion equals 5.5 minus 3.7 or 1.8. The Q value for
this item is 1.8. If that is the lowest Q value for any statement in that
particular pile (reflecting highest judges' agreement) it will be
selected for the final scale.[1]

[1] Note that the .75 and .25 levels are arbitrary and could be changed to suit
particular research needs. Similarly, when dispersion is "low enough" is an
arbitrary choice.

5. Testing the Reliability of the Thurstone Scale

The four previous steps should result in a set of scale items that can be used to rank subjects into 11 groups according to their favorableness or unfavorableness toward rioting. Note that unlike the judges, subjects are asked to rank items according to how favorable their *own feelings* are toward the statement, *not* how favorable the statement is toward the variable being studied. The subject's **scale score** is the average (usually the mean, sometimes the median) of the scale values of the items (statements) he endorses.

The scale is said to be **reliable** if the same individuals would get the same scores for similar Thurstone scales. To test reliability, enough items are selected in step 4 to form two scales from the same group of possible items (devised in step 1). The two similar scales are administered to the same individuals and the average percent difference in scale scores is taken as a measure of unreliability; reliability is 1 minus this average. Thus, if for a group of fifty subjects, the scale scores on the first test were an average of 8.2% different from the scale scores on a second similar test, then the *split-halves reliability* (i.e., reliability measured by using two similar tests) would be 91.8%. How high reliability must be before the scale is "good enough" is arbitrary, although the 90% level is ordinarily considered acceptable.

LIKERT SCALES

Likert scales are much simpler than Thurstone scales, and although in Likert scales there is no specific attempt to attain a near-interval level of measurement, it has not been proved that Thurstone scales are much different in this regard. In the Likert method judges are asked to score statement items according to the degree to which they themselves agree or disagree with the statement. Ordinarily there are five choices for each statement: strongly agree/agree/uncertain/disagree/strongly disagree. Items are selected according to the degree to which they are sensitive to differences in the judges' feelings about the variable being examined.

1. Compiling Possible Scale Items

This step is the same as step 1 in the Thurstone method.

2. Having Judges Rank the Possible Items

Each judge is given a list of all the possible statement items compiled in the first step. Each is then asked to strongly agree, agree, etc., and assign point values to each choice (e.g., strongly agree=1, agree =2, and so on).

3. Computing the Average Value for Each Statement

Each statement item is then given a score equal to the average response, 1 to 5, given by the judges.[2] The standard deviation of these item scores can then be computed, ignoring the fact that the data are ordinal, not interval, and normal tables can be used to weight the statement items according to how far they deviate from the average item score for all items. Thus these weights constitute criteria for weighting a 1 ("strongly agree") response on an extreme item *more* than a 1 response on a less extreme item. However, it has been found that this refinement gives results only 1% or 2% different than if no weights are computed; therefore, *this step is usually omitted.*

4. Selecting the Scale Items

Each judge is given a score equal to the average, 1 to 5, of all his responses—again, after items have been reordered so that a 1 response always represents strong favorability toward the variable, even when the statement is negatively worded. Judges are then ranked by this

[2] Statements are first renumbered, of course, so that a 1 response is always favorable to the variable being studied, whether that statement is worded positively or negatively; this involves making "strongly disagree" equal 1 for items worded negatively.

score and the top and bottom 25% (or some other arbitrary fraction) of the judges are identified. The top 25% represents those judges least favorable toward the variable being studied (for example, least favorable toward rioting) and the bottom 25% the most favorable (since they tended to give 1 and 2 responses to statements such as "Riots help focus needed attention on city problems"). The items to select are those that best distinguish between the top 25% of judges on the one hand and the bottom 25% on the other.

Items that meet this criterion are identified by the **discriminative power (DP) method.** For any given statement, the DP measure is the weighted mean response of the top 25% minus the weighted mean response of the bottom 25% of the judges, as illustrated in Table 7.3.

Table 7.3   DP Computing Table for One Scale Item

(1) Group	(2) Number in Group	(3) Item Responses 1 2 3 4 5	(4) Weighted Total (response value times frequency)	(5) Weighted Mean (4) / (2)
Top 25%	30	0 2 10 9 9	0+4+30+ 36+45=115	115/30=3.83
Low 25%	30	6 24 0 0 0	6+48+0+ 0+0=54	54/30 =1.80
(6) Discriminative Power of a particular item			DP=3.83−1.80=2.03	

The DP index must be computed for each of the possible scale items, and those items with the largest DP indices will be selected. These are the items that best discriminate among judges holding differing attitudes toward the test variable. The *number of items* in a "good" scale is arbitrary, most Likert scales ranging between 50 and a few hundred statement items. The number should be large enough to give stability to the scale yet not so great that the respondent becomes bored or tired with the study; these factors will be different according to the research task. Note also that there is nothing absolute about having five responses, although this is common. Ofter the "uncertain" category is left out, forcing respondents to take a position, on the assumption that "true neutrals" will be forced one direction or the other at random. Few Likert scales have less than four or more than seven response categories, however.

5. Testing the Reliability of the Scale

When a Likert test is administered, by asking a respondent to rank 50 or more statement items from 1 = strongly agree to 5 = strongly disagree, the respondent's *scale score* is simply the average score, 1 to 5, for his responses to all the items, again, after negatively-worded statements have been renumbered. The Likert scale thus provides a mechanism for ranking individuals according to their position on a test variable.

Reliability of the scale can be tested in much the same manner as in the Thurstone method, simply by selecting enough items for two scales (usually at least one hundred) and randomly dividing them into two sets, constituting two scales. The test of *split-halves reliability* is administered as described for the Thurstone technique.

The Likert scale, finally, involves several additional features. First, unlike the Thurstone method, no attempt is made by the judges (or anyone) to evaluate the meaning or affective content of the items. Although the items do differentiate quite clearly between high- and low-scoring judges, there is absolutely no guarantee that the scale items selected will be representative of statements (items) about the test variable (such as rioting) in general. Hence there may be some danger, as Harry Upshaw has noted, that the items appropriate to one set of judges may not be appropriate to another. Upshaw suggests selecting judges at random from the population eventually to be tested as a precautionary measure. Moreover, the Likert method tends toward selection of items reflecting extreme statements, since the criterion for item selection is ability to differentiate between judges in the extreme quartiles, and may be less sensitive in distinguishing among "moderate" respondents.

GUTTMAN SCALES (SCALOGRAM ANALYSIS)

The Guttman scale, often used in more rigorous social science research, aims for **unidimensionality**. That is, it attempts to assure that the scale measures only one underlying dimension—in the "happiness" example given initially, that only one of the many meanings of happiness is measured. It does this not simply by evaluating a number of scale item responses, but by looking at each response in relation to every other response. Specifically, the items on a Guttman scale may be arranged so that an endorsement of one implies endorsement of all previous items. In a Guttman scale, if a respondent agrees with statement 3, he will also agree with statements 2 and 1; if a senator votes for bill 3, he will also vote for bills 2 and 1; if a city experiences riot behavior type 3, it will have also experienced riot behavior types 2 and 1.

1. Selecting the Scale Items

As implied in the preceding paragraph, the items scaled can be statement items, calling for agreement or disagreement; legislative votes, pro or not pro; or even political events, it happened or did not happen. Although more complex Guttman scaling may be undertaken, this section will deal only with the case where each item has two response values, such as agree or not agree.

2. Forming the Initial Guttman Table

Once selected according to the particular researcher's needs, possible scale items are then presented to a large number of judges for their evaluation. Thus a table could be made listing judges down the side and items across the top, with Xs in the appropriate spaces to indicate agreement with the item.

Table 7.4   Perfect Guttman Scale

Item

		1	2	3	4	5	6	7	8	9	10
	1	X	X								
	2	X	X	X							
	3	X	X	X	X	X					
Judge	4	X	X	X	X	X	X	X			
	5	X	X	X	X	X	X	X	X		
	6	X	X	X	X	X	X	X	X	X	
	7	X	X	X	X	X	X	X	X	X	X

A perfect Guttman scale would look like Table 7.4, resembling right triangle with no blanks (non-agreements) inside the triangle and no Xs outside it; if blanks or deviant Xs occur they would be *scale errors.*

The problem of how to know which item to put first, second, etc., and the parallel problem of which judge to put first, second, etc., is the problem of *arrangement.* First, relying on his own judgment, the researcher orders the items according to their extremism. Then the respondent who endorsed the fewest items is placed first, and so on down to the last person, who endorsed the most items.

3. Selecting the Final Scale Items

The initial table may be refined by inspection or by applying Yule's Q test. By *inspection* of the initial table, judges may be rearranged to reduce scale errors. For example, in Table 7.4 if the third judge responded "X, X, blank, blank, X," the number of errors (2, for the two internal blanks) could be reduced to 1 by making him the second judge (1 error for the 1 external X). Also by inspection, items may be rearranged to form a more perfect triangle. Similarly, items in whose columns appear many errors may be omitted entirely. Finally, if desired, redundant items may also be omitted. Redundant items are those whose presence does not lead to greater differentiation among the judges. In Table 7.4, items 1 or 2, 4 or 5, and 6 or 7 are redundant.

By the Q test scalable items may be identified and non-scalable items thrown out. This will not refine the table for redundant items, nor will it deal with minimizing scale errors due to poor ordering of judges, however. Research on legislative roll-call analysis by Duncan MacRea has shown that items having a Yule's Q of .80 or higher with each other are scalable. Yule's Q is equal to the main diagonal product, minus the off diagonal product, divided by the sum of both, for

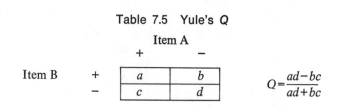

Table 7.5   Yule's Q

the 2-by-2 table formed by any two items. It is a measure of "asso-ciation" further discussed in Chapter 9. Each item in the scale should have a Q of .80 or higher when paired with any item previous to it on the scale. For instance, in Table 7.4, item 5 should be asso-ciated at the .80 level or better with items 4, 3, 2, and 1. Item 10 should be associated with all the other items, since all precede it on the scale. Note that this method will lead to omitting items like 1 and 2 in the example—items on which *all* judges agree. This is because in the 2-by-2 table formed by items 1 or 2 with any of the others, the *b* and *d* boxes will be zero, leading Yule's Q to be zero as well. The main reason for emphasis on the Q test is that the inspection method becomes extremely unwieldy when the number of judges and items is large. The Q test method can be used on computer programs in these situations.

4. Testing the Scale

Once final scale items have been selected in step 3, the test scale can be administered to the population (of people or of events) to be studied, and a Guttman table ("scalogram") constructed. Unlike Table 7.4, this table will undoubtedly have errors (interior blanks and exterior Xs). How many errors are permissible before a scale is regarded as inadequate for the population under study? Two tests have been devised to answer this question: the test of reproducibility and the test of scalability. (In some studies the judges *are* the popu-lation to be studied, so step 4 proceeds immediately to these tests).

The coefficient of reproducibility method has been a standard test. It is equal to 1 minus the number of errors divided by the number of choices:

$$C_r = 1 - e/n$$

where e = number of errors = either interior blanks or exterior Xs,

and n = number of choices = number of items times the number of judges or subjects.

A scale is arbitrarily but commonly considered adequate if the coeffi-cient of reproducibility is .90 or higher.

Unfortunately, the coefficient of reproducibility has some problems as a statistic. If Xs and blanks are considered response categories, then by definition the number of errors for any item cannot be greater than the number of responses in the least numerous category. If the percent of responses in the most numerous category is 90%, then the coefficient of reproducibility *must* be at least .90! C_r is never below .50.[3]

The coefficient of scalability is a statistic that varies between zero and one and is not affected by response category (Xs or blanks) frequencies. It is equal to 1 minus the number of errors divided by the number of errors expected by chance:

$$C_s = 1 - e/x$$

where e = number of errors = interior blanks plus exterior Xs,

           x = errors expected by chance = $c(n - T_n)$,

           c = chance of getting any choice right by chance alone (.5 if there are only two response categories),

           n = number of choices of any type,

and T_n = number of choices in the most numerous response category for each item.

While this seems complex, the following examples will illustrate its simplicity.

Example 1

A Guttman Scale such as that shown in Table 7.6 might be developed for fifteen senators on a committee, voting on ten issues (Xs denote aye votes, blanks denote nay). Is this scale good enough? By counting interior blanks and exterior Xs we see there are 16 errors, but is this too many?

---

[3] If the number of errors for any item *were* larger than the number of responses in the least numerous category for that item, the item could be rearranged on the scale so that the number of errors would be no more than the number of responses in the least numerous category.

Table 7.6

Vote

Senator	1	2	3	4	5	6	7	8	9	10
1	X	X				X				
2		X	X							
3	X	X	X							
4	X	X	X							
5	X	X		X					X	
6	X	X	X	X			X		X	
7	X	X		X						
8		X	X	X	X				X	
9	X		X	X	X					
10	X	X			X	X	X			
11	X	X	X	X	X	X	X			
12	X	X	X	X	X	X	X	X		
13	X		X	X		X	X	X	X	
14	X	X	X		X	X	X	X	X	
15	X		X	X	X	X	X	X	X	X

$$e= \quad 2 \quad 3 \quad 3 \quad 2 \quad 1 \quad 1 \quad 1 \quad 0 \quad 3 \qquad 0= 16$$
$$T_n=13 \quad 12 \quad 11 \quad 9 \quad 8 \quad 8 \quad 8 \quad 11 \quad 9 \qquad 14=103$$
$$n=15\times10=150 \qquad\qquad\qquad\qquad\qquad c= .5$$

The answer depends on how many errors we would expect by chance, given the total aye and nay count for each vote. Knowing that 13 senators out of 15 voted aye on vote 1, for example, tells us that there could not possibly be more than $15-13=2$ errors. Knowing that 9 of 15 senators voted nay (unlike vote 1, here the nay votes are the most numerous response category) on vote 9 tells us that there could not be more than $15-9=6$ errors.

That is, the most errors there could be, given the total count for each vote, is the number of choices ($n=150$) minus the total in the most numerous category of each item ($T_n=103$). In this case the maximum possible errors would be $150-103=47$. Since in this example a senator could vote two ways (aye or nay), the number of errors expected by chance is $\frac{1}{2}(47)=23.5$.

The question now becomes, "Is a scale that reduces chance errors from 23.5 to observed errors of 16 good enough?" The coefficient of scalability is an index used to answer this question; the scale is commonly but arbitrarily judged "good enough" if C_s is .60 or better. C_s is 1 minus observed errors divided by errors by chance. In this example, $C_s = 1 - (16/23.5) = 1 - .68 = .32$; hence the scale is judged an inadequate tool for ranking senators.

Example 2

Guttman scales need not be limited to ranking people by attitudes or votes; they may also be used to rank events. Jules Wanderer,[4] for example, recently developed an 8-item scale of riot severity which met Guttman criteria and had a C_r of .92.

Table 7.7   Wanderer's Guttman Scale of Riot Severity

Scale Type	% Cities ($n=75$)	Items Reported	Scale Errors
8	4	No scale items	2
7	19	"Vandalism"	10
6	13	All of the above & "interference with firemen"	3
5	16	All of the above & "looting"	3
4	13	All of the above & "sniping"	7
3	7	All of the above & "called state police"	4
2	17	All of the above & "called National Guard"	11
1	11	All of the above & "law officer or civilian killed"	2
Total	100%		42

Source: Jules J. Wanderer, "An Index of Riot Severity and Some Correlates," *American Journal of Sociology* 74:5 (March, 1969), Table 1, page 503. Copyright © The University of Chicago Press, by permission of the author and publisher.

Additional Considerations

Since Guttman scales were developed, many refinements and criticisms have been made. **Stouffer's H technique,** for example, is a proposal to give greater stability to Guttman scales by basing each scale item on three or more sub-items. Thus item 1 might reflect sub-items 1 (a), 1 (b), and 1 (c); if a respondent endorsed at least 2 out of the

---

[4] Jules J. Wanderer, "An Index of Riot Severity and Some Correlates," *American Journal of Sociology* 74:5 (March, 1969), p. 503.

3 sub-items he would be listed on item 1 as endorsing item 1. That is, the *H* technique is a method that reduces the effect of random errors on the Guttman scale by making each item a summary of three or more similar sub-items.

It is somewhat misleading simply to present a coefficient of reproducibility without indicating the level of confidence one may have in it. Guttman therefore suggested computing the *standard error of reproducibility* when scale data are based on a sample. Recall from the previous chapter that when data are based on enumeration rather than sample, the coefficient of reproducibility is the true one and there is no point in computing standard error. The formula

$$\text{SE Rep} \approx \sqrt{(1 - C_r)(C_r)/n}$$

gives a close approximation to standard error of reproducibility, which in Example 1 would equal the square root of $[(1 - .89)(.89)/150]$, or .026. Since two standard errors corresponds to roughly 95% of a normal distribution, one may be 95% confident that the real coefficient of reproducibility lies within plus or minus $2(.026) = .052$ of the scale coefficient of .89.[5]

Harry Upshaw has suggested a **chi-square test of scale significance.** Using this method, the researcher would first determine his observed Guttman scale data in the usual manner, noting the proportion of respondents endorsing each item. In Example 1, for instance, item 1 was endorsed by 13 out of 15, or about 87% of respondents; item 2 by 80%, etc. Then, using a table of random numbers the researcher can generate a hypothetical chance scale. For item 1, if the first two random numbers encountered (found in a random number table) are 87 or less, the first respondent is listed as endorsing item 1; if the first two random numbers are from 88 to 00, then he is listed as not endorsing item 1. The same procedure is applied to respondents 2 through 15 for each item. For item 2, 01 through 80 correspond to endorsements and 81 through 00 correspond to non-endorsements, etc. In this way a hypothetical chance table can be constructed. Finally, a list can be made for number of respondents with no errors, number with one error, number with two errors, etc. This list can be made for both the observed data and the expected (hypothetical,

[5] For more advanced tests of scale significance, see Roland Chilton, "A Review and Comparison of Simple Statistical Tests for Scalogram Analysis," *American Sociological Review* 34:2 (April, 1969), p. 237.

chance) data. Chi-square, discussed in the next chapter, is a measure of the significance of the difference between observed and expected (chance) data.

Finally, it must be emphasized that Guttman scales do not guarantee unidimensionality, although scales not meeting Guttman criteria are very probably multidimensional. That is, Guttman scaling is not a foolproof test of the claim that a particular scale measures only one underlying continuum. Even if the reproducibility of the scale is significantly better than chance, some of the scale items may still measure underlying dimensions. In a fully homogeneous scale there will be no cases in which a respondent does not endorse one item but nevertheless endorses another less frequently endorsed item. That is, for every pair of items (arranged in a 2-by-2 table with the more endorsed item to the side and the less endorsed on top, as shown in Table 7.8) the c cell will tend to be zero except for random errors.

Table 7.8

		Less Endorsed Item	
		Aye	Nay
More Endorsed Item	Aye	a	b
	Nay	c	d

Thus in a perfect scale—one that is fully homogeneous—every pair of items will have $Q = 1.0$. The Q test must be used as a check on the full unidimensionality of Guttman scales.[6]

---

[6] A review of the problem of checking unidimensionality is contained in Carmi Schooler, "A Note of Exteme Caution in the Use of Guttman Scales," *American Journal of Sociology* 74:3 (November, 1968), p. 296.

8

Significance and Analysis of Tables

Of the many texts that present good treatments of measures of significance and association, Robert S. Weiss's *Statistics in Social Research* (Wiley, 1968; especially Chapters 10, 11, 14, 15) is among the best. Another highly useful book is Sidney Siegel, *Nonparametric Statistics for the Behavioral Sciences* (McGraw-Hill, 1965). William Kruskal, "Significance, Tests of," in the *International Encyclopedia of the Social Sciences* might also be referred to.

In addition, many of the texts mentioned in earlier chapters present competent discussions of this topic.

After the researcher's hypotheses have been creatively formed and data collected, perhaps using survey or scaling techniques previously discussed, he must still answer four crucial methodological questions:

1. Do the data show any relationship at all?
2. Is the relationship strong?
3. Is the relationship really what the researcher thinks it is?
4. Does it matter?

The first three questions relate to *significance, association,* and *validity,* respectively. The fourth question, the *substantive importance of the research,* while absolutely essential, relates to creativity and a sensitivity for relevant scholarship, which cannot be taught.

Significance deals with the question of whether the observed results are very likely to be different from chance. If in a sample of six we found that the three men were Democrats and the three women were Republicans, we might think this was just chance. But if the sample were of 600 and the same proportions held, all men being Democrats and all women Republicans, we would not attribute this to mere chance.

Association, in contrast, deals with the strength of the relationship. The above examples both have the same strength, because the proportion of men being Democratic and women being Republican is the same, whether the sample size is six or six hundred.

Validity is the question of whether the researcher is truly measuring party affiliation or whether he is really measuring something else; whether the data were gathered properly; whether the relationship would hold for a future set of data; and whether the relationship would hold if other variables were controlled for.

SIGNIFICANCE AND USES OF THE CHI-SQUARE STATISTIC

To facilitate easy communication, social scientists use certain (arbitrary) standard ways of presenting data in tables. First, when data are presented in percentages, the researcher must also present the sample size on which the percentages are based. Second, the independent variable is usually placed at the top of the table, the dependent variable to the side, and percentages are computed down the columns. For example, in Table 8.1 political party is the independent (causal) variable presumed to "cause" voting or non-voting.

Table 8.1

	Democrat	Republican	
Voted	72%	58%	
Didn't Vote	28%	42%	
	100%	100%	$N=150$

Hence it is placed at the top of the table. Having percentages add to 100% by columns rather than rows enables the researcher to quickly see what he is most interested in, the differential effect of the independent variable on the dependent variable. The sample size, 150, is stated at the side to indicate that this relationship is based on 150 individuals.

Using Chi-square for Significance Tests

A table is considered significant if it is "sufficiently" different from what would occur by chance. This implies that two tables are needed for comparison: a table of observed (real) data and a table of expected (chance) data.

1. Computing the Expected Frequencies

If Table 8.2 were the result of a sample survey, for example, the next step would be to compute the expected cell frequencies, *given*

Table 8.2   Observed Data

	Male	Female	row marginals
Republican	15	10	25
Democrat	5	20	25
column marginals	20	30	$N = 50$

the marginals—that is, given that half of the sample is Republican and half Democrat, and that its male–female ratio is 2:3. The expected frequency for any cell is the product of its row marginal times its column marginal divided by N, the sample size. Thus by chance, given the marginals, one would expect the number of male Republicans to be not 15 (the observed frequency) but rather the marginal of the cell's row (25), times the marginal of the cell's column (20), divided by N (50), which equals 10. (To check: the marginal products divided by N should be the same as the proportion of Republicans [1/2] times the proportion of males [2/5] times N. Both give the expected frequency given the marginals.) Note that this procedure necessarily results in an "expected" table that has marginals identical to the "observed" table.

Table 8.3   Expected Data

	Male	Female	row marginals
Republican	10	15	25
Democrat	10	15	25
column marginals	20	30	50

2. Computing Chi-square (χ^2)

Chi-square is a statistic designed to summarize the extent of difference of observed data from expected data. The expected data need *not* be normally distributed; therefore chi-square, unlike the normal z tests discussed in Chapter 6, is **nonparametric.** The data need not conform to any particular distribution parameters, such as the normal distribution, for chi-square to be used. Chi-square,

$$\chi^2 = \sum \frac{(0-E)^2}{E}$$

is the sum equal to the square of the *observed* first cell frequency minus the *expected* first cell frequency, divided by the expected first cell frequency, plus the same for the second cell, and so on for as many cells as the table contains.

From Tables 8.2 and 8.3 in the example, chi-square equals 8.33:

$$\chi^2 = \sum \frac{(15-10)^2}{10} + \frac{(10-15)^2}{15} + \frac{(5-10)^2}{10} + \frac{(20-15)^2}{15}$$

$$= 2.5 + 1.67 + 2.5 + 1.67$$

$$= 8.33$$

3. Computing Degrees of Freedom

One more step is necessary before the researcher can use a chi-square statistics table to determine if his observed table is significant. The more cells there are in a table, the bigger the chi-square value has to be for the same level of significance. For example, a chi-square of 8.33 is significant at the .05 level for a 2-by-2 table, but this would not be enough for a 3-by-3 table.

Degrees of freedom equals number of rows minus 1, times number of columns minus 1:

$$d.f. = (r-1)(c-1)$$

Thus a 2-by-2 table has 1 degree of freedom. This refers to the fact that given the marginals and the frequency of one cell in a 2-by-2 table, the rest of the cells may be filled out. Similarly, the last row and last column in a 3-by-3 (or any size) table can be filled out if the marginals and the other row and column entries are known.

4. Using the Chi-square Table

Once the researcher has presented his observed table, computed the expected table and the chi-square value, and after he has determined the number of degrees of freedom associated with that size table, he then simply looks at a table of chi-square values such as that shown in Table 8.4.

Table 8.4   Table of Distribution of χ^2

		Probability		
d.f.	.99	.98	.95	.90
1	.000157	.000628	.00393	.0158
2	.0201	.0404	.103	.211
3	.115	.185	.352	.584
4	.297	.429	.711	1.064
⋮				
30	14.053	16.306	18.493	20.599

d.f.	.10	.05	.02	.01	.001
1	2.706	3.841	5.412	6.635	10.827
2	4.605	5.991	7.824	9.210	13.815
3	6.251	7.815	9.837	11.345	16.268
4	7.779	9.488	11.668	13.277	18.465
⋮	⋮				
30	40.256	43.773	47.962	50.892	59.703

Thus, for 1 d.f. the researcher finds that his chi-square value, 8.33, lies between the .01 and .001 probability levels. This means that a table as or more different from the expected table would occur by chance, given the marginal distribution of the variables, only one time in a hundred to one time in a thousand. The .05 level is usually considered the minimum level of acceptable significance—even then the researcher will be wrong five times out of a hundred in thinking his table is significant when it is not. Similarly, the computed chi-square value must be below the .95 level for the researcher to conclude that the table is significantly *not* different from chance. Actually, the researcher should determine *in advance* what level of significance (e.g., .05, .02, .01, .001) is appropriate to the needs of his research; he should *not*, for example, start with the decision that the .01 level is required and then make "exceptions" for relationships that only meet the .05 level.

The foregoing procedure may be used to compute chi-square under certain conditions:

1. *If* sample size, N, is 20 or more; if not, the Fisher Exact Test of significance discussed below should be used instead, *and*
2. *If* all expected cell frequencies are 5 or more, in a 2-by-2 table; if not, Yates' Correction for chi-square should be used.
3. *Or* if 80% of the expected cell frequencies in a larger table are 5 or more; if not, rows and/or columns *must* be omitted and/or combined to get a table that satisfies this condition.
4. Finally, no cell may have a frequency of less than 1.

Enumerations and Significance

It is especially important to note that when the observed data are based on a study of an entire population (an enumeration of every member) rather than a sample, significance tests are irrelevant. Whatever relationship is shown in the table is necessarily the true relationship, and there is *no* chance that the relationship is mere chance. If the researcher is dealing with *enumerated* rather than *sampled* data, he should skip tests of significance and instead proceed directly to measures of association (strength of relationship). Moreover, tests of significance assume not only a sample, but a *random* sample. If the researcher's data are based on a non-random sample he has violated the assumptions of significance tests, and the significance statistics he presents should be used for exploratory purposes only; some in fact argue that they should not be used at all.

Yates' Correction for Continuity

If sample size is 20 or more in a 2-by-2 table but a cell frequency is less than 5, then Yates' Correction may be used. This is done by simply replacing the regular chi-square formula in step 2 above with the following formula:

$$\chi^2 = \sum \frac{(|0 - E| - .5)^2}{E}$$

That is, for each cell, .5 is subtracted from the difference of observed minus expected frequencies before squaring and dividing by E. The other steps remain the same.

OTHER USES OF CHI-SQUARE

Chi-square techniques, as mentioned in previous chapters, are used to test scale significance and to estimate needed sample size. In addition, the chi-square "goodness of fit" test is used to determine whether a particular variable is normally distributed (or conforms to some other desired distribution) and hence would be appropriate for statistics requiring this assumption. Finally, Chapter 9 will show how chi-square is the base for several measures of association (strength).

Chi-square and Scale Significance

At the end of Chapter 8, Upshaw's method of testing Guttman scales was mentioned. In this method the researcher constructs his observed scale in the usual way and then constructs a chance, expected scale using random numbers. Two lists are then made, one for the observed and one for the expected data, listing the number of respondents with no scale errors, with one error, and so on, up to N respondents. These observed and expected frequencies can then be substituted in the regular chi-square formula (step 2) and the resulting chi-square statistic can be used to check significance levels. Degrees of freedom in this test is $N - 1$. This enables the researcher to present a Guttman scale, state that it is scalable at least at the .60 level and is significant at least at the .05 level, for example.

Chi-square and Sample Size

Chi-square can also help the researcher determine sample size needed, before he makes his study. He needs a sample big enough to reasonably assure that specified differences from chance will be found significant, as the following example illustrates.

1. Determining Desired Significance and Difference Levels

The researcher simply specifies the level of significance he feels appropriate for his study (.05 for most social science research, .001 for medical research, for example), and what is the *least* difference he wants to be detected as significant. For example, in the simple example of sex and political party affiliation cited earlier, the researcher might specify that he wants a 10% difference found significant at the .05 level. This step is purely arbitrary, depending on research needs.

2. Specifying Expected and Least-difference Tables

To specify the expected table, the researcher must have some way of estimating the marginal frequencies. That is, through some method —census data, small sample, expert opinion, sheer guess—he must make an estimate; once this is done the expected cell frequencies are computed as discussed earlier—marginal products divided by N, or as in Table 8.5, expressed in terms of percentages.

Table 8.5

	Male	Female	
Republican	$.20N$	$.30N$	$.50N$
Democrat	$.20N$	$.30N$	$.50N$
	$.40N$	$.60N$	$1.00N$

(a)   Expected Table

	Male	Female	
Republican	$.25N$	$.25N$	$.50N$
Democrat	$.15N$	$.35N$	$.50N$
	$.40N$	$.60N$	$1.00N$

(b)   Least-difference Table

If the researcher knows that half the population is Democrat and half Republican, and if he also knows 40% is male and 60% female, he can construct an expected table as shown in Table 8.5(a). By placing 10% more of the relationship on the diagonal which he expects will show a relationship—here, the Male-Republican, Female-Democrat diagonal—and 10% less on the other diagonal, the researcher can specify the 10% difference table he chose in step 1.[1]

3. Solve for N

The researcher then substitutes the least-difference proportions (using them as the observed frequencies) and also the expected frequencies in the chi-square formula and solves for N, first setting χ^2 equal to 3.841, which is the chi-square value for 1 d.f. at the .05 level:

$$\chi^2 = 3.841 = \sum \frac{(.25N - .20N)^2}{.20N} + \frac{(.25N - .30N)^2}{.30N}$$
$$+ \frac{(.15N - .20N)^2}{.20N} + \frac{(.35N - .30N)^2}{.30N}$$
$$= \frac{.0025N^2}{.20} + \frac{.0025N^2}{.30} + \frac{.0025N^2}{.20} + \frac{.0025N^2}{.30}$$
$$= .0125N^2 + .0083N^2 + .0125N^2 + .0083N^2$$
$$3.841 = .0416N^2$$
$$N = \sqrt{3.841/.0416} = \sqrt{92.3} = 9.6$$

Thus the researcher needs to take a sample of at least 10 individuals to be 95% sure of detecting a 10% difference from chance. Note that this is for one table only. If the table is to be subtabled, as in multivariate analysis discussed earlier, an even larger sample will be needed to detect a 10% difference in the subtables. If the subtable divides the main table into two equal subtables, then twice as large a sample will be needed; if it splits the main table 3/4 in one subtable and 1/4 the other, then a sample 4 times as large is needed. For subtables, the computed sample size is multiplied by the reciprocal of the

---

[1] The least-difference table is arbitrary and may be specified in any manner the researcher desires, as long as that is the least strong difference to be detected.

smallest fraction of the main table received by any subtable, in this case by 4, the reciprocal of 1/4.

This method does not eliminate the need to compute sample size by the binomial (normal table) method presented earlier. Whichever method results in the *higher* sample size is used.[2]

Chi-square and Goodness of Fit

The researcher often desires to know if the frequencies associated with a particular variable conform to his expectations. For example, a researcher dealing with the Guttman scale of riot severity may wish to know if the distribution of numbers of riots (frequencies) on this scale of severity (the variable) is normally distributed (a hypothesized expectation). The chi-square goodness-of-fit test is used to determine if results for a particular variable are normally distributed, are the same as another known distribution of data, or conform to any other particular distribution specified in advance.

Chi-square, as mentioned earlier, is a nonparametric statistic because it can be used to test whether *any* observed distribution is significantly different from any given hypothetical distribution. Most often the hypothetical ("expected") distribution is the normal distribution; the researcher wishes to see if it is technically valid to use **parametric tests**—tests that assume the variable is normally distributed in the "real world," although not *necessarily* in a given sample.

The previous chapter presented an index of riot severity; Table 8.6 shows a way of testing to see if the index is normally distributed. The scale in Chapter 7 had 8 scale types (column 1). In addition, data were presented showing the number of cities in each scale category (column 2). The question is, "Is the distribution shown in column 2 what would be expected if riot severity were normally distributed?"

To answer this we must compute the normally-expected frequencies for each scale category (columns 3–7). In columns 3 and 4 we find the normalized frequency of riot scale intervals; this is obtained by subtracting the weighted mean frequency $f(\bar{x})$ from the scale intervals in column 1 (this gives column 3), and then by dividing the result in column 3 by the standard deviation of the observed frequencies, s (this yields column 4).

[2] Compute sample size for the smallest subtable; *then* estimate sample size needed overall.

Table 8.6 Chi-square Goodness-of-Fit Test for the Riot Severity Scale

(1) category interval	(2) observed frequency	(3) $(1) - f(\bar{x})$	(4) $(3)/s$ normalized frequency	(5) percent below	(6) percent within	(7) $(6) \times \Sigma(2)$ expected frequency	(8) $\lvert (2) - (7) \rvert$ absolute observed minus expected frequency	(9) $[(2) - (7)]^2/(7)$
8	4	3.6	.76	.78	.29	29	25	21.5
7	19	2.6	.55	.71	.08	8	11	15.1
6	13	1.6	.34	.63	.07	7	6	5.1
5	16	.6	.14	.56	.09	9	7	5.4
4	13	−.4	−.08	.47	.09	9	4	1.8
3	7	−1.4	−.30	.38	.07	7	0	0
2	17	−2.4	−.51	.31	.07	7	10	14.3
1	11	−3.4	−.72	.24	.24	24	13	7.0
	100							$\chi^2 = 70.2$

$$\Sigma x = 100$$
$$\bar{x} = 100/8$$
$$= 12.5$$

$$\Sigma f(x) = \Sigma(1)(2)$$
$$= 441$$

$$f(\bar{x}) = 441/100$$
$$= 4.41$$

$$s = \sqrt{\frac{\Sigma[(2) - \bar{x}]^2}{8}}$$
$$= \sqrt{180/8}$$
$$= 4.74$$

By subtracting the mean and dividing by the standard deviation we get a normal z distribution, as discussed in Chapter 7 on sampling. Simply by looking in a table of values for the normal curve found in any statistics text, we can derive the figures in column 5. Column 5 is the percent of cases which, in the normal table case, would fall in a particular category or lower. For example, 78% of the cases should fall to the left of $z = .76$ on a normal curve.

Column 6 shows the percentage of cases falling within a particular scale category. For the lowest case, scale category 1, the percent is the same as in column 5, namely 24%. Note that the lowest and highest category percentages include cases which, if the variable were truly normally distributed and if the normal case had the same mean and standard deviation as the observed data, would be in the extreme tails of the normal curve (would be outside the scale categories entirely). Often these "tails" make little difference since the percent of cases in them is so small; here, the standard deviation, 4.7 on an 8-point scale, is so large that the tails have a large effect. Thus, if riot severity were normally distributed, fully 24% of the cases would lie in category 1 or lower. The amount in category 2 is this proportion, .24, subtracted from the proportion listed in column 5 for category 2, namely .07. This subtracting process is continued on up the scale to the highest category, where the expected frequency is the other extreme "tail," in this case .29.

Expected frequency is the proportions in column 6 times the total number of cases (100 in this case), rounded to whole numbers. The expected frequencies, shown in column 7, are subtracted from the observed frequencies (column 2) to give column 8. Column 9 is the chi-square formula for the observed minus expected frequencies squared and divided by the expected frequencies. The sum of column 9 is the *chi-square value* for the observed distribution of riot severity. The number of *degrees of freedom* is the number of categories (8), minus the number of restrictions on the data (3; normal distribution with observed mean and observed standard deviation specified in advance), or 5 in this case.

Finally, we take the computed chi-square value, 70.2, and refer to the chi-square table found in the Appendix. For 5 d.f., the .95 level indicates how *small* chi-square must be for us to be 95% sure that the observed distribution is *not* significantly different from the normal distribution. The .05 level tells how large chi-square must be for us to be 95% sure the observed distribution *is* significantly different from chance. Since the chi-square value here of 70.2 is much larger than even the .001 level, we therefore conclude that the index of riot severity can *not* be treated as a normally-distributed variable.

FISHER EXACT TEST OF SIGNIFICANCE

When sample size is less than 20 for a 2-by-2 table, the Fisher Exact Test should be used. This method gives the exact chance of getting a particular table, given the marginals.

Table 8.7   General Case

a	b	r_1
c	d	r_2
c_1	c_2	n

$$p = \frac{r_1! r_2! c_1! c_2!}{n! a! b! c! d!}$$

1. Specify the Observed Table and All Stronger Tables

First the given table is presented, along with all stronger tables, as shown in Table 8.8. The stronger tables are specified by reducing the cell with the lowest count (the upper-right cell, 2, in this case) successively down to zero—since the marginals are known, the other cell frequencies follow automatically. The researcher must then compute p for each of these tables.

Table 8.8

7	2	9		8	1	9		9	0	9
5	6	11		4	7	11		3	8	11
12	8	20		12	8	20		12	8	20

observed table   next stronger   strongest table

2. Computing p

The probability of a table of a given strength is equal to the product of the marginal factorials divided by sample size factorial times the cell factorials, as shown in the following equation:[3]

---

[3] Factorial is a mathematical operation in which 1 is multiplied by 2 and this product in turn multiplied by 3, and so on up to n.

$$p_{\text{observed}} = \frac{9!\,11!\,12!\,8!}{20!\,7!\,2!\,5!\,6!} \qquad = .132$$

$$p_{\text{next stronger}} = \frac{9!\,11!\,12!\,8!}{20!\,8!\,1!\,4!\,7!} \qquad = .024$$

$$p_{\text{strongest}} = \frac{9!\,11!\,12!\,8!}{20!\,9!\,0!\,3!\,8!} \qquad = .001$$

$$p_{\text{total}} = .157$$

The result indicates that there is a 15.7% chance that, given the observed marginals, a table as strong or stronger than the observed table would occur by chance alone. Ordinarily social scientists consider a 5% chance the maximum acceptable level, so this observed table would not be considered significant.

3. Nondirectional Hypotheses

In the previous step we assumed that the researcher was only interested in the chance of getting a table as strong or stronger in the direction of the observed table (here, in the direction of the main or right-sloping diagonal). If the researcher were interested in a hypothesis about relationship as strong or stronger in *either* direction (either at least as many cases on the main diagonal, *or* as many on the off-diagonal), then p_{total} in step 2 must be doubled to give the appropriate statistic for a nondirectional hypothesis. For example, a unidirectional hypothesis might be that rioters are significantly younger than non-rioting residents of a disturbance area. A nondirectional hypothesis might be that rioters are significantly different from non-rioters in terms of ideological intensity.

OTHER TESTS OF SIGNIFICANCE

The chi-square and Fisher exact tests of significance may be used on all levels of data, even nominal data, no matter how they are distributed. Chi-square is used on larger samples and Fisher exact on smaller ones.[4] The *z* test and *t* test, discussed in the chapter on sam-

[4] For exact tests of tables other than 2-by-2, see W. L. Hays, ed., *Statistics for Psychologists* (New York: Holt, Rinehart & Winston, 1963), pp. 155–156 and 598–601 for examples.

pling, are also tests of significance, the former for larger samples and the latter for smaller samples. The z and t tests, however, may be validly used *only* on data that are normally distributed at the interval level.

As a further introduction to tests of significance, some of the nonparametric tests, useful with any distribution, will now be discussed.[5]

Nominal-level Nonparametric Tests

With nominal-level, nonparametric tests, the researcher could face one of three situations:

1. He might wish to see whether a specific sample is from an expected population (one-sample case; e.g., see if riot intensity is normally distributed).
2. He may wish to compare two samples (two-sample case; e.g., see if rioters in city A have same attributes as rioters in city B).
3. He may wish to compare among several samples (k-sample case; e.g., see if rioters have the same attributes in small, medium and large-size cities).

For the one-sample case, the chi-square goodness-of-fit test may be used, as may the **binomial test** if the population is divided into just two classes (as male-female, Republican-Democrat, or rioter-nonrioter). In the binomial test, for example, we may determine the probability of getting x observations in one category and $N-x$ in the other, given the expected chance of getting the first observation, P, and the chance of not getting it, Q (equals $1-P$):

$$p(x)_{\text{binomial}} = \frac{N! \, P^x Q^{N-x}}{x! \, (N-x)!}$$

Thus, if we know that a particular city is 60% Democrat ($P=.60$) and 40% Republican ($Q=.40$) and we sample a particular fraternal organization and find 70 Democrats ($x=70$) in our sample of 100 ($N=100$), using the formula above will show that the chance of getting 70 Democrats out of 100 persons sampled from a population split 60-40 is equal to

---

[5] These are presented in detail in the Siegel reading.

$$\frac{100! \; .60^{80}.40^{20}}{70!30!}$$

It can be seen that when N is large the binomial test requires computer application. Fortunately, when N is large the binomial distribution approximates the normal distribution.

If, when P is near $\frac{1}{2}$ and N is over 25, or when NPQ is at least 9, the researcher has an appropriate case, the normal tables may be used to determine the probability for the one-sample case, where the z value is:

$$z = \frac{(x \pm .5) - NP}{\sqrt{NPQ}} = \frac{69.5 - 60}{\sqrt{24}} = 1.94$$

(Note that .5 is added to x when x is smaller than NP, and subtracted when it is larger). From a normal table, we find that the area under a normal curve to the left of (as or more extreme than) 1.94 is .0262. Therefore, we can say that the hypothesis that the city has more Democrats is significant at the .026 level; for the two-tailed hypothesis, that the city is different by party, the level is doubled, .052.

For the nominal-level, two-sample case we may use the chi-square or Fisher exact tests discussed earlier when we want to see if one sample (e.g., the sample of city A for percent Democrat) is different from another independent sample (e.g., a sample of % Democratic in city B). The **McNemar test** is appropriate if the two samples are "related" rather than independent; that is, if

1. They are matched pairs, where every member of the first sample has a "partner" in the second sample, known in advance to have the same age, sex, educational level, or other relevant control-variable characteristics, *or*
2. The two samples are of the "before" and "after" type, where each individual serves as his own partner.

Table 8.9

		After Broadcast oppose	favor	
Before	favor	$a=6$	$b=20$	26
	oppose	$c=10$	$d=14$	24
		16	34	50

For example, the McNemar method might be used to test whether a television broadcast affected a group's political views. The McNemar method uses a variation of chi-square, emphasizing the difference between cells a and d:

$$\chi^2 = \frac{(|a-d|-1)^2}{a+d} = \frac{49}{20} = 2.45$$

Looking up this chi-square value in a chi-square table we find that a 2.45 value with d.f. $= 1$ (determined as before, $r-1$ times $c-1$) is not significant. Note that chi-square tables list significance levels for nondirectional hypotheses; for a directional hypothesis such as broadcast effects opinion, the significance found must be doubled—the .01 level becomes the .02 level, the .05 level becomes the .10 level, etc. Second, if the expected frequency of the a or d cells is less than 5, the binomial test should be used instead of the McNemar test. To do this the binomial formula is used, with $N=a+d$ and $x=a$ or d, whichever is smaller.

For nominal level, k-sample tests, chi-square is used if the samples are independent, and the **Cochran Q test** if they are related.[6]

Ordinal-level Nonparametric Tests of Significance

For the one-sample case, the **Kolmogorov-Smirnov D test** is used; as will be discussed, this can be extended to the two-sample ordinal case as well. Like chi-square, the D test is a goodness-of-fit significance test (one sample), but is considered a more powerful test and may be used when data are ordinal. Although chi-square may also be used on ordinal data for goodness of fit, the D test is preferred. To take the riot severity scale again, we might want to use the D test to see if the data are significantly different from the null hypothesis that riots are equally distributed by severity.

The **D value** is the largest absolute difference between the cumulative observed frequency and the cumulative expected frequency; when this is found (here .085), the researcher looks in a table of critical values of D to find the corresponding level of significance. By inspecting such a table we find that for $N=75$ (the number of riot

[6] The Cochran Q test is an extension of the McNemar two-sample test; it is discussed in the Siegel reading on pages 161–166.

Table 8.10   *D* Value Computing Table for Riot Severity

Rank Interval	1	2	3	4	5	6	7	8
$f(x)$ = number in category	8	13	5	10	12	10	14	3
$F_{cum}(x)$ = cumulative %	11	28	35	48	64	77	96	100
$f_{exp.\ cum}(x)$ = expected cumulative %	12.5	25	37.5	50	62.5	75	87.5	100
difference		1.5	3	2.5	2	1.5	2	8.5	—
D value								.085	

cities) at the .05 level (usually arbitrarily considered the minimum acceptable level), *D* must be at least .157. Since .085 is considerably less than that, we fail to reject the null hypothesis that riots are equally distributed by severity—this assumes, of course, that the data are based on good samples. The *D* test may be used even on small samples, unlike the chi-square test.

The **one-sample runs test** is also frequently used as a one-sample, nonparametric test of significance, appropriate when the population is divided into just two classes (male-female, Republican-Democrat, etc.). It is often used as a *test of randomness* of a sample. The idea is that a random sample will have at least a certain number of "runs." A run is a series of similar responses; in Figure 8.1 the first two R

Figure 8.1   Party Affiliations in Sample of 15

R R D D D D R D D R R R D R D

responses (indicating the first two persons sampled were Republican) constitute a run, the four Ds are a second run, etc., for 8 runs. Thus the number of runs, *r,* is 8; the number in the first category, n_1, is 7, and the number in the second category, n_2 is 8 (7 Rs and 8 Ds). Looking in a table of critical values for *r* in the runs test, for $n_1 = 7$ and $n_2 = 8$ we find that the number of runs, *r,* must be 4 or less, or 13 or more, for us to conclude that the sample is significantly different from random. Since our runs total, 8, is between 4 and 13, we fail to reject the null hypothesis that Republicans and Democrats were sampled by chance. That is, at the .05 level we may be confident that ours was indeed a random sample.

For a series of responses larger than 20, the normal z distribution approximates the r distribution:

$$z = \frac{r - \left(\dfrac{2n_1 n_2}{n_1 + n_2} + 1 \right)}{\sqrt{\dfrac{2n_1 n_2 (2n_1 n_2 - n_1 - n_2)}{(n_1 + n_2)^2 (n_1 + n_2 - 1)}}}$$

where the critical z value equals r reduced by a mean (the term after the minus sign in the numerator) and divided by a specified standard deviation (the term in the denominator).

For the two-sample, ordinal-level, nonparametric test of significance, extensions of the Kolmogorov-Smirnov test and the runs test have been devised.

Kolmogorov-Smirnov Two-sample Test, K_D

The K_D test is appropriate when samples are independent. It follows the same logic as the Kolmogorov-Smirnov one-sample D test, except instead of subtracting expected cumulative percentages from observed cumulative percentages, the observed cumulative percentages in one sample (e.g., cumulative percentage of cities in 1967 ranked by riot severity) are subtracted from the cumulative percentages for a second independent sample (e.g., the cumulative percentage of cities in 1969 ranked by riot severity). The D value is the largest difference in cumulative percentages for any given ordinal rank; its significance is checked by looking in a table of critical values of K_D, where $K_D = ND$, N is no more than 40, and when $n_1 = n_2 = N$. This table will give significance values for both two-tailed (different from) or one-tailed, (greater than *or* less than specified) hypotheses.

If n_1 and n_2 are both over 40 it is not necessary that $n_1 = n_2$, and in this case the significance of D (not K_D) can be checked in a table of critical values of D in the Kolmogorov-Smirnov two-sample test; this table will give significance levels for a two-tailed test. For a one-tailed test (where the researcher is interested in greater than relationships rather than different from) when both n_1 and n_2 are over 40, the significance of D is tested by looking at a table of chi-square values for d.f. $= 2$; this method approximates the desired result when n_1 and n_2 are large. When they are small it may be used, but the test is apt to be "conservative"—tending to find results not significant when they are.

Wald-Wolfowitz Runs Test

Like the K_D test, this test is appropriate at the ordinal level for two independent samples drawn from the same or identical populations, and assumes the variable studied has a continuous underlying distribution. The two samples result in a series of A-scores and B-scores—for example, A may be a 1970 sample, and the A-scores are city riot severity scores; B may be a 1969 sample, with B-scores the riot severity scores for that year. The A- and B-scores are combined into one ordered list, from the lowest-scoring to the highest-scoring units. By ordering the scores from both samples in this manner,[7] the researcher can look at the "group" row in Table 8.11 and, by direct inspection, count the number of runs. In the example illustrated there are 10 runs for 16 units.

Table 8.11   Runs Table for the Wald-Wolfowitz Test

Score	1	1	2	3	4	5	5	6	7	8	9	9	10	11	12	14
Group	A	B	B	A	B	A	A	A	B	A	A	B	A	B	B	B

The Wald-Wolfowitz method tests the difference between two samples; it tests differences of central tendency, variability, and other distribution differences. Differences in distribution will tend to reduce the number of runs; for example, samples with different medians will tend to generate runs with a bunching of A-scores around the sample A median and B-scores around the sample B median. If neither sample A nor sample B is over 20 in size, the researcher can look in the table of critical values for r in the runs test. For two samples of size 8 the table tells us that the number of runs must be 4 or less, or 14 or more, for us to conclude that the samples are significantly different; since our $r = 10$ falls between these, we fail to reject the null hypothesis that the scores of 1970 and 1969 are the same.

---

[7] Identical scores are ordered by a random method; the decision to put the A-score of 1 first rather than the B-score of 1 was determined by random tables.

If either or both samples are over 20 in size, the table cannot be used; instead, the normal table may be used as an approximation, using exactly the same formula for normal z values given for the one-sample runs test in the discussion of samples over 20. Finally, a special word must be said about *ties*—units of the A-sample having the same score as units of the B-sample. Random ordering is only one possible way of dealing with ties; instead, for instance, the A-units could always be placed before the B-units or vice versa. Siegel recommends ordering the data several ways and seeing if every ordering gives the same result, where either all orderings result in acceptance of the null hypothesis, or all result in its rejection. The Wald-Wolfowitz test is not applicable when the number of ties is large.

Mann-Whitney *U* Test

Finally, the Mann-Whitney U test is also used for ordinal-level, two-sample significance tests. In this technique the two samples are combined exactly as in the Wald-Wolfowitz runs test. U^a equals the number of A-scores preceding the first B, plus the number preceding the second B, etc., where A is the smaller sample and B is the larger sample. Using the example given in Table 8.11 for the Wald-Wolfowitz runs test,

$$U = 1 + 1 + 2 + 5 + 7 + 8 + 8 + 8 = 40$$

This is a way of measuring the likelihood that one sample gets consistently higher scores than the other; if so, then we conclude that the two populations are significantly different. A companion statistic, U^b, equals the product of the samples sizes minus U^a:

$$U^b = n_A n_B - U^a = 8 \times 8 - 40 = 24$$

U is either U^a or U^b, whichever is smaller.

To check the significance of two samples by the U test, different methods are used according to the sample size:

1. If both samples are 8 or less, a table of probabilities for U may be consulted. In the example, for $n_1 = 8$, $n_2 = 8$, and $U = 24$, the corresponding value is .221. This means that the difference measured by the U statistics would occur by chance alone 22.1% of the time; since this is far above the 5% level, we do *not* conclude that the two samples are different.

2. If the larger sample is between 9 and 20, a table of critical values of U is consulted in an analogous manner, for one- or two-tailed tests.

3. For larger samples, a normal table approximates the desired result, where

$$z = \frac{U - \frac{n_1 n_2}{2}}{\sqrt{\frac{(n_1 n_2)\,(n_1 + n_2 + 1)}{12}}}$$

Again, this is a formula that transforms U into a normal z value by subtracting a specified mean and dividing by a specified standard deviation.

For the ordinal-level, two-sample case where the two samples are related—samples composed of matched pairs, or the same individuals at two time periods—the **sign test** and the **Wilcoxon matched-pairs signed-ranks test** are used; for the k-sample case, **Friedman two-way analysis of variance** is used.[8]

Kruskal-Wallis *H* Test

For the ordinal-level, k-sample case where the samples are independent, the Kruskal-Wallis H test (one-way analysis of variance by ranks) is used to test significance of differences among samples, when variables are assumed to have continuous underlying distributions. It tests significance of differences of averages only, as opposed to differences in variations, skewness, etc., and is related to the chi-square distribution:

$$H = \frac{12}{N(N+1)} \sum \frac{R}{n} - 3(N+1)$$
$$\text{d.f.} = k - 1$$

The H statistic is computed by the above formula, where N is the number of observations in all samples together, n is the number of observations in any particular sample, R is the number of ranks in

---

[8] These topics are covered in detail by Siegel and many other texts, but are not usually emphasized in introductory political science applications.

any particular sample, and k is the number of samples. First, data from all samples are ordered as in the Wald-Wolfowitz or Mann-Whitney tests. Second, the data scores are renumbered from 1 to N, with 1 corresponding to the lowest score, 2 to the next-lowest, and on up to N, the highest score—1 to N are the "ranks." Third, using these rank scores, data for each sample are listed by rank. Fourth, these rank scores are added up for each sample; these sums are the R scores. Fifth, the H value is determined by the formula above. If there are many ties, H is divided by the quantity

$$1 - \frac{\Sigma t^3 - t}{N^3 - N}$$

where t is the number of ties in any sample (the numerator is a sum for all samples), and N is, as before, the total number of observations in all samples together. Finally, if *all* samples are of size 5 or less, a table of probabilities associated with H may be consulted. If the samples are larger, a standard chi-square table may be consulted, using H as the chi-square value and degrees of freedom as the number of samples minus one; if the corresponding chi-square value is equal to or less than the H value, then the difference is significant at the level indicated by the table.

SUMMARY: WHICH TEST OF SIGNIFICANCE?

If the data are not a sample but an enumeration, or if the sample is not random, then a test of significance is not appropriate at all. If the data are assumed to be normally distributed and interval in nature, then the standard z tests, t tests for small samples, or F tests for differences between means are appropriate; if not, chi-square or the Fisher exact test for small samples are used.

In addition there are many special tests of significance that make no assumption about distribution of data. If data are nominal, the binomial case is appropriate for 2-by-2 tables when sample size is so small that chi-square is inappropriate; the Fisher exact test is a binomial test for the two-sample case. Neither these nor the McNemar test for the significance of changes in before-after studies assume a continuous underlying distribution. The Cochran Q test is another nominal-level significance test, extending the McNemar technique to more than two samples.

For ordinal-level data, the Kolmogorov-Smirnov test is used when the underlying variable is continuous; for discontinuous variables, the test is conservative, tending to find some significant relationships insignificant. It is definitely preferred over the chi-square test when small cell frequencies force combining of rows or columns in the chi-square test. The Kolmogorov-Smirnov one-tailed test and the Mann-Whitney U test are appropriate for two independent samples in testing differences of central tendency. For testing differences in general, the Kolmogorov-Smirnov two-tailed test and the chi-square tests are appropriate, as is the Wald-Wolfowitz runs test. The one-sample runs test is used with dichotomous data to test whether a sample was taken at random. The Kruskal-Wallis test is most appropriate for more than 2 samples and is considered one of the most sensitive nonparametric tests, although the chi-square k-sample test must be used when the data are in the form of frequencies rather than ordinal scores.

9

Association and Validity

In addition to the texts cited in the previous chapter,
see Leo Goodman and William Kruskal, "Measures of Association
for Cross Classifications" (Bobbs-Merrill reprints, Nos. S405-406).
See also Sidney Siegel, *Nonparametric Statistics for the
Behavioral Sciences* (McGraw-Hill, 1965).

So far we have discussed *tests of significance,* statistics used in answering the question, "Does *any* relationship between variables exist, or are the results possibly by chance alone?" **Measures of association** answer the question, "How strong is the relationship?" Many significant relationships are not strong, and some that are strong are not significant. For example, a strong relationship based on only a few cases might well be insignificant.

Like tests of significance, there are many measures of association. In the next chapter we will discuss *correlation,* which is a common type of measure of association. In this section we will discuss measures of association used with tabular data—data presented in cross-table form rather than in lists.

WHICH MEASURE OF ASSOCIATION?

There is no substitute for working with a particular statistic on known sets of data to see how it is affected by changes in the data.

Every statistic has peculiar attributes, and decisions of appropriateness must be made in each research problem. Sometimes several measures will be used; at a general level, however, the researcher may make four decisions in selecting an appropriate measure of association:

1. He must decide the *level* of his data—is it nominal, ordinal, or better? If he is comparing a nominal variable with an ordinal variable he must choose a statistic approporiate to the lower level, the nominal.
2. Are the *sizes of the tables* being studied 2-by-2 or are they larger, r-by-c?
3. Is the research hypothesis directional (asymmetric; *x* causes *y*) or nondirectional (symmetric; no causation specified)?
4. Is a measure based on chi-square desired, or a probabilistic measure?

With regard to this last question, social scientists have tended to prefer probabilistic measures because they (a) have an intrinsic meaning, unlike chi-square measures, which have no reference of meaning outside themselves; (b) tend to result in lower relationships

Table 9.1   Measures of Association

Nominal-Nominal

	2-by-2		r-by-c	
	χ^2	Prob.	χ^2	Prob.
Asymmetric		Lambda		Lambda
Symmetric	Phi-square	Yule's Q	Cramer's V (or tau c)	Lambda

Ordinal-Ordinal

	2-by-2		r-by-c	
	Nonprob.	Prob.	Nonprob.	Prob.
Asymmetric		Somer's d		Somer's d
Symmetric	Kendall's tau b	Gamma or Yule's Q	Kendall's tau c	Gamma

than chi-square measures; and (c) are specifically designed to measure association, not significance. Finally, if the variables are normally distributed along underlying continua and are at the ordinal or interval level, some measure of correlation (discussed in the next chapter) would be appropriate.

CHI-SQUARE-BASED MEASURES OF ASSOCIATION

Phi-square or **phi** (ϕ^2 or ϕ) is a possible measure when the variables are both true dichotomies. That is, the variables in a 2-by-2 table must be true dichotomies, such as male-female or white-nonwhite, not "compressed" continuous variables, such as high versus low income. Phi-square or phi *may* be used with compressed continuous data, but then interpretation of the measure becomes difficult. Only when both variables in the 2-by-2 table have the same marginals ($r_1 = c_1$ and $r_2 = c_2$) does phi vary between zero and 1.

Phi-square is equal to chi-square divided by N, the number of observations represented in the table, and is sometimes called "mean-square contingency." Phi equals the difference between diagonal products divided by the square root of the marginal products:

Table 9.2

	Male	Female	
Voted	$a = 140$	$b = 10$	$r_1 = 150$
Didn't Vote	$c = 10$	$d = 40$	$r_2 = 50$
	$c_1 = 150$	$c_2 = 50$	$N = 200$

$$\phi = \frac{ad - bc}{\sqrt{r_1 r_2 c_1 c_2}}$$

$$= \frac{5600 - 100}{\sqrt{56,250,000}}$$

$$= .73$$

It thus measures the strength of the relationship—number of cases on the main diagonal minus number not on main diagonal—adjusting for the given marginal distribution of the variables. In Table 9.2 both variables have the same marginals, but if they were different we should also have to calculate the maximum value of phi (phi_{max}):

$$\phi_{\text{max}} = \sqrt{\frac{s_i}{l_i} \times \frac{l_j}{s_j}}$$

Where s_i is the smallest row or column marginal

s_j is the smallest row marginal if s_i is a column marginal, or the smallest column marginal if s_i is a row marginal

l_i and l_j are the same for the largest row or column marginals

Tables with differing marginals will have differing maximum phi values, and hence comparability among a series of phi values for these tables would be very difficult. Even when phi values are comparable, they, like all chi-square measures, (a) are comparable only among themselves, (b) tend to understate one-way relationships, and (c) are very sensitive to shifts in marginal distributions.

Pearson's C

Several statistics have been developed to extend a chi-square measure of association to tables larger than 2-by-2. These include Pearson's C, Tschuprow's T, and Cramer's V. **Pearson's C,** also called the *contingency coefficient* and the coefficient of mean square contingency, is a traditional measure equal to the square root of chi-square divided by chi-square plus N:

$$C = \sqrt{\frac{\chi^2}{\chi^2 + N}}$$

Its upper limit is .71 in the 2-by-2 case and approaches 1 as the number of rows and columns increases. Moreover, C tends to underestimate the level of association, often resulting in an association of less than 1.0, even though all the observations are on the main diagonal (or, alternatively, on the off diagonal) of a table.[1] Some social scientists recommend computing C only for tables of at least 5-by-5 size, since only in these tables does maximum C approach 1.0. For normally-distributed, linearly-related variables, Pearson believed C was an approximation of product-moment correlation, r, used with interval data and discussed in the next chapter.

Tschuprow's T

This is a similar statistic equal to the square root of the quantity chi-square divided by N (the number of observations in the table) times the square root of the number of degrees of freedom (rows minus one times columns minus one):

---

[1] In square tables, $C_{max} = \sqrt{r-1/r}$, where $r =$ number of rows.

$$T = \sqrt{\frac{\chi^2}{N\sqrt{(r-1)(c-1)}}}$$

T has a limit of 1.0 in square tables, even those below the 5-by-5 size, when row marginals are identical to column marginals.

Cramer's V

Cramer's V is a chi-square measure of association for r-by-c tables and gives better norming—variation between zero and one—than does C or T, although until recently it has not been as widely used:

$$V = \sqrt{\frac{\chi^2}{mN}} \quad \text{where } m = (r-1) \text{ or } (c-1), \text{ whichever is smaller.}$$

Social scientists now generally prefer V over C or T, since it varies between 0 and 1 even in the case of tables which are not square—although, like C and T, its maximum value is less than 1.0 when row marginals are not identical to column marginals. Like T, V is the same as phi in the 2-by-2 case.

Table 9.3

Table A

	Male	Female	r_i
Republican	15	10	25
Democrat	5	20	25
c_i	20	30	$N=50$

chi-square = 8.33
$V = \sqrt{8.33/50} = .408$

Table C

	Male	Female	r_i
Republican	25	5	30
Democrat	5	15	20
c_i	30	20	$N=50$

chi-square = 17.02
$V = \sqrt{17.02/50} = .583$

Table B

	Male	Female	r_i
Republican	20	5	25
Democrat	0	25	25
c_i	20	30	$N=50$

chi-square = 33.33
$V = \sqrt{33.33/50} = .817$

Table D

	Male	Female	r_i
Republican	30	0	30
Democrat	0	20	20
c_i	30	20	$N=50$

chi-square = 50.00
$V = \sqrt{50/50} = 1.00$

The effect of marginal distributions in these statistics is illustrated in Table 9.3. Table A is a hypothetical distribution for a particular group, showing that in this group there is a certain tendency for males to be Republican and females to be Democrat. The strength of this relationship is $V = .408$; since this is a 2-by-2 table, this same figure holds for phi and T. This figure, .408, has no intrinsic meaning; .408 V is simply .408 V, and the strength of this can only be assessed by comparing it to Vs computed for other tables. Moreover, given the marginals which are unequal, the strongest possible relationship is illustrated in Table B, for which $V = .817$. Thus Table A is strong at the .408 V-level, where V has a maximum of .817.

Similarly, Table C illustrates the case where row marginals (30, 20) are identical to column marginals (30, 20), and where the relationship is strong at the $V = .583$ level. The marginals in Table C are such that it would be possible to have all the observations on one diagonal, as is illustrated in Table B. In that case the maximum V would be 1.0. Thus Table C is associated at the $V = .583$ level, where $V_{max} = 1.0$. Note that the maximum will be 1.0 when row marginals equal column marginals, and this happens when all of the observations are on just *one* of the diagonals.

OTHER MEASURES LACKING INDEPENDENT OPERATIONAL MEANING

For ordinal-level relationships, **Kendall's tau** is sometimes used. While it is not a chi-square-base measure, it is classed with them in Table 9.1 because it also lacks an operational meaning outside its own frame of reference. Variations of this, however, including Goodman and Kruskal's gamma and Somer's *d*, do have an operational meaning.

Before these measures of ordinal association can be discussed, it is necessary to introduce the concept of **paired observations** in a table. There are four basic kinds of pairs:

1. **Concordant pairs,** which fall on the main (right-sloping) diagonal.
2. **Discordant pairs,** which fall on the off diagonal (slopes down to the left).
3. **Pairs tied on x,** the independent variable.
4. **Pairs tied on y,** the dependent variable.

Example A

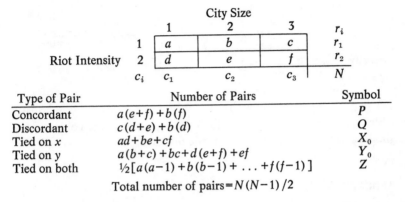

Type of Pair	Number of Pairs	Symbol
Concordant	$a(e+f)+b(f)$	P
Discordant	$c(d+e)+b(d)$	Q
Tied on x	$ad+be+cf$	X_0
Tied on y	$a(b+c)+bc+d(e+f)+ef$	Y_0
Tied on both	$\frac{1}{2}[a(a-1)+b(b-1)+ \ldots +f(f-1)]$	Z

Total number of pairs $= N(N-1)/2$

As the example shows, a pair is concordant, consistent with a relation on the main diagonal, if it is on one of the main diagonals (a–e, a–ef, or b–f). A pair is discordant if it is associated with one of the off diagonals (c–e, c–ed, or b–d), making it inconsistent with a main diagonal relationship. In addition a pair could be merely tied on x if it is in a column (a–d, b–e, or c–f), while in a row it is tied on y (a–b, a–c, b–c, d–e, d–f, or e–f). Finally, the entries within any cell may constitute pairs tied on both x and y.

Kendall's tau-*b*

Most often used for 2-by-2 tables, **Kendall's tau-b** may also be used for other size arrays as well. It is equal to the excess of concordant over discordant pairs $(P-Q)$,[2] divided by a term representing the geometric mean between the number of pairs not tied on x and the number of pairs not tied on y:

$$\text{tau-}b = \frac{P-Q}{\sqrt{(P+Q+Y_0)(P+Q+X_0)}}$$

As will be seen in the discussion on Somer's *d*, it is this averaging of pairs tied to the dependent variable with pairs tied to the independent variable that makes tau a nondirectional (symmetric) statistic.

---

[2] If the main relationship is on the off diagonal, this will be negative.

Example B

		City Size		
		1	2	r_i
Riot	1	1	0	1
Intensity	2	3	4	7
	c_i	4	4	8

$$\text{tau-}b = \frac{4-0}{\sqrt{(4+0+12)(4+0+3)}}$$

$$= 4/\sqrt{112} = .37$$

Tau-*b* reaches a maximum of 1.0 only when $r = c$—only in square tables—*and* when the row marginals are the same as the column marginals, and when all entries are on one diagonal.

Kendall's tau-c

This is a variant of tau-*b* for larger tables. It equals the excess of concordant over discordant pairs times another term representing an adjustment for the size of the table:

$$\text{tau-}c = (P-Q)(2m/N^2[m-1])$$

where m = the number of rows *or* the number of columns, whichever is smaller.[3]

Example C

		City Size			
		1	2	3	r_i
	1	4	2	0	6
Riot Intensity	2	2	3	4	9
	c_i	6	5	4	15

$$\text{tau-}c = (36-4)(4/15^2[1])$$
$$= 32(4/225)$$
$$= 128/225 = .57$$

Kendall's tau is used in preference to Cramer's *V* or other nominal-level statistics when dealing with ordinal-level data because it measures strength of deviation from statistical independence toward monotonic correlation, whereas the nominal-level statistics measure any deviation from statistical independence—that is, from the "expected" value, given the marginal distribution. Tau-*c* has the advantage of reaching a maximum of 1.0 even for rectangular tables,

[3] Note that this differs from the *m* used in Cramer's *V*.

whereas tau-*b* reaches 1.0 only for square tables. The main problem with these measures is that they lack an operational meaning, tau-*b*s being comparable only with other tau-*b*s, for instance, with no clear meanings attached to values between 0 (statistical independence) and 1 (perfect monotonic correlation).

MEASURES HAVING OPERATIONAL MEANING (PROBABILITY MEASURES)

There are three measures that are related to Kendall's tau but which have an intrinsic meaning enabling comparison outside their own internal framework. These are Goodman and Kruskal's gamma, Yule's Q (previously discussed in connection with scaling), and Somer's *d*.

Goodman and Kruskal's Gamma

This is a symmetric measure based on the difference between concordant and discordant pairs. It equals this difference $(P-Q)$ as a percentage of both consistent and discordant pairs $(P+Q)$:

$$\gamma = P - Q/P + Q$$

In Example B, for instance, gamma $= 4 - 0/4 + 0 = 1.0$, since *all* larger communities had more severe riots. In Example C, gamma $= (36-4)/(36+4)$, or .80; this reflects the fact that in this example there were very few discordant pairs (the off-diagonal products totaled $Q=4$) and many consistent (concordant) pairs $(P=36)$. Yules Q is simply gamma for 2-by-2 tables:

$$Q = ad - bc/ad + bc = \gamma$$

Somer's *d*

Somer's *d* is gamma modified to penalize for pairs tied on x only, in directional (asymmetric) hypotheses in which x causes or predicts y; and to penalize for pairs tied on y only, in hypotheses in which y causes or predicts x:

$$d_{yx} = P - Q/P + Q + Y_0 \qquad \text{for the hypothesis that}$$
$$x \text{ causes or predicts } y$$

$$d_{xy} = P - Q/P + Q + X_0 \qquad \text{for the hypothesis that}$$
$$y \text{ causes or predicts } x$$

It is thus an *asymmetric statistic,* its value depending on the direction of the researcher's hypothesis.

Somer's d reaches a maximum of 1.0 when all entries are on the main diagonal in a square table, or if all values take on a monotonic relationship in a rectangular table. By monotonic is meant that, for hypotheses in which x causes or predicts y (d_{yx}, "y on x"), every value of y is associated with just one x value. For hypotheses in which y causes or predicts x, a monotonic relationship involves each x value having entries on just one y value.

Example D

	City Size (x)			
	1	2	3	r_i
Riot Intensity (y) 1	6	0	0	6
2	0	5	4	9
c_i	6	5	4	15

$d_{yx} = 54 - 0/54 + 0 + 20 = .73$

$d_{xy} = 54 - 0/54 + 0 + 0 = 1.0$

tau-$c = 54(4/15^2) = .96$

Example D, for instance, is monotonic for d_{xy} but not for d_{yx}. This example also illustrates how Somer's d takes on different values according to the direction of the hypothesis—in Example D, only d_{yx} is relevant, since one would not predict that city size is caused by riot intensity; similarly, the symmetric statistic tau-c also overstates the strength of the relationship since it is not restricted to relationships in just one direction.[4]

Percent Difference

Percent difference is a simple traditional measure for 2-by-2 tables equal to d_{yx}. It is computed by subtracting the difference, measured as percentages, between the first and second columns in either row.

[4] For square tables, tau-b is the geometric mean between d_{xy} and d_{yx}.

Example B Again

	City Size			
		1	2	r_i
Riot	1	1 (25%)	0 (0%)	1
Intensity	2	3 (75%)	4 (100%)	7
	c_i	4 (100%)	4 (100%)	8

$$\%d = .25 - 0 = .25$$
$$= 1.0 - .75 = .25$$
$$d_{yx} = 4/4 + 0 + 12 = .25$$
$$d_{xy} = 4/4 + 0 + 3 = .57$$
$$\text{tau-}b = .38 \quad \text{gamma} = 1.0$$

Lambda

Gamma and Somer's d are considered as pairs of observations consistent with the relationship (symmetric relationships for gamma, asymmetric for d) as a percentage of all relevant pairs. **Lambda,** the last measure of association to be discussed, has an operational meaning in terms of *probable reduction of error.* A gamma of .60 means that 60% of the relevant pairs are consistent with the relationship, where "consistent" is defined as $P - Q$, and "relevant" as the denominator. A lambda of .60 means that knowing the independent variable will reduce by 60% the number of errors made in predicting the dependent variable. For example, knowing city size might reduce by 60% the number of errors in predicting riot severity.

Lambda asymmetric equals the number of errors of prediction made when only the marginals of the dependent variable are known minus the number when the marginals of the independent variable are known, as a proportion of the number of errors when only the dependent is known. **Lambda$_{se}$** is the standard statistic,

$$\text{lambda}_{se} = \frac{(\Sigma f_i) - F_d}{N - F_d}$$

where f_i = the largest frequency for each class of the independent (x) variable

F_d = the largest marginal value of the dependent variable

but it has three companions. **Lambda$_{sp}$** is based on probable improvement of prediction, not reduction of error:

$$\text{lambda}_{sp} = \frac{(\Sigma f_i) - F_d}{F_d}$$

Lambda$_{pe}$ and **lambda**$_{pp}$ are statistics for reduction of error and improvement of prediction measures respectively, where the table is expressed in terms of percentages (p), not scores (s).

Lambda cannot be computed if all the entries lie in just one row (column) of the independent variable, but otherwise it varies between 0 and 1. It is 0 when knowing the independent variable is of no help in prediction; it may be 0 even though there is not complete statistical independence. It is 1 only if a unit's x (independent variable) classification completely determines its y (dependent) classification. Lambda is unaffected by the ordering of columns or rows, and hence may be used with nominal-level data.

Example E

		City Size (x)				
		1	2	3	r_i	
Riot	1	80 (67%)	9 (90%)	1 (10%)	90	(167)
Severity (y)	2	40 (33%)	1 (10%)	9 (90%)	50	(133)
	c_i	120 (100%)	10 (100%)	10 (100%)	140	(300)

$$\text{lambda}_{se} = \frac{(80+9+9)-90}{140-90} = .160$$

$$\text{lambda}_{pe} = \frac{(67+90+90)-167}{300-167} = .600$$

$$\text{lambda}_{sp} = \frac{(80+9+9)-90}{90} = .089$$

$$\text{lambda}_{pp} = \frac{(67+90+90)-167}{167} = .479$$

Example E illustrates the great difference in results obtained for the same table, depending on which version of lambda is applied. Lambda$_{se}$, suggested by Guttman and developed by Goodman and Kruskal, equals .160 for this table. Knowing the independent variable, city size, reduces by 16% the number of errors in predicting riot severity. On the other hand, lambda$_{sp}$ tells us that the number of correct predictions is improved only 8.9%. Others have argued that when the independent (x) marginals are highly unequal, as they are in this example, it is better to express the table in percentages and then act *as if* the percentages were scores. This has the effect of giving the reduction of error or improvement of prediction for the case which *would* (but actually does not) exist if each class of the independent variable had the same number of cases—for example, if city sizes 2 and 3 had as many cases as does city size 1, which actually has 120 in comparison with 10 each for 2 and 3. *If* independent variable classes were equal, then errors of prediction would be reduced 60% and correct predictions increased 47.9%.

Which lambda should be used in a particular case? The researcher must first decide if he is interested in reduction of error or improvement of prediction; often both kinds of statistics will be desired. If only one is used and the researcher is indifferent, lambda$_{se}$ has been far more widely used than its companions. Second, if the independent (x) variable margins are highly unequal, the researcher should seriously consider computing lambda$_{pe}$ or lambda$_{pp}$—otherwise strong relationships in independent variable classes with small numbers of cases (as with city sizes 2 and 3 in the example) may be obscured. Third, if the largest dependent marginal is a very large proportion of N, then the researcher should consider computing lambda$_{sp}$ or lambda$_{pp}$, since otherwise the small denominator that would occur in the lambda$_{se}$ and lambda$_{pe}$ formulas would lead to misleadingly large measures of association. Since each of the four statistics provides a distinct bit of information, it may often be useful to present all four lambda measures in each case. Note, however, that lambda is an asymmetric measure whose value would usually be different if the dependent and independent variables were switched; by switching, computing lambda both ways, and averaging, **lambda symmetric** may be derived.

VALIDITY

After asking whether a relationship exists at all (significance) and how strong it is (association), the researcher must be careful to ask if the relationship has **validity.** Social scientists have distinguished four types of validity: predictive, concurrent, content, and construct validity.

Predictive Validity

Here the researcher is concerned with whether the relationship found for one set of data will hold for a future set of data. If it worked once, will it work again? Two dimensions must be considered here: time and group. How much or how little may we validly say? Is the relationship the same for all time periods, or just recent times, or perhaps only for a particular month? Is the relationship the same for all groups everywhere in the world, only for American groups, or perhaps only true for a particular group in a particular city? In assessing this type of validity, the political scientist correlates results for his research group with similar studies for other groups and other time periods.

The correlation[5] coefficient between the observed results and the results in a second set of data is sometimes called the "validity coefficient." When the second set is a restudy, the coefficient is sometimes called a "coefficient of stability." When the second set is a parallel study conducted concurrently, the coefficient is called a "coefficient of equivalence." If the second set is really a subset of the original study, as when every other observation is considered part of a "second" study, the coefficient of correlation between the two is called the "coefficient of internal consistency."

Concurrent Validity

This brings us to concurrent validity, the question of whether the relation will hold for a control set of data. The coefficient of internal consistency (also called the split-halves test) is of this type. **Reliability** by the Spearman-Brown measure[6] for split halves equals twice the coefficient of internal consistency divided by 1 plus that coefficient:

$$r_t = 2r_{ic}/1 + r_{ic}$$

These coefficients require an interval level of data, and are used primarily in assessing the validity of *measures* (scales, tests) rather than *relationships*. Such scales and tests are ordinarily expected to have a reliability of .90 or higher to be accepted.

In testing the concurrent validity of a relationship, the more common problem in political science, the control set of data may consist of paired individuals with characteristics matched by age, sex, education, social class or other control variables. Or the control set may consist of a group of random individuals (or groups, cities, etc.) not

---

[5] Correlation is a type of measure of association, discussed in the next chapter.

[6] The study is arbitrarily divided into two by random process.

"exposed" in a before-after study—for example, not exposed to a political campaign technique in a study of the relation between a candidate's issue stand and his popularity. Or the members of the control group may be selected by a random split-halves method.

Predictive and concurrent validity are categories of the more general type, **criterion validity.** The question of control data also raises the question of whether all the relevant variables have been controlled for, as by multivariate analysis, partial correlation, or some other technique. One may find a strong relationship between religion and political identification, for example, but find that this relationship "disappears" when social class is introduced as a control variable. This question of possible control variables is called the question of **spuriousness,** and can be met only by creativity on the part of the researcher in anticipating the relevance of possible control variables not present in the initial relationship.

Another area of concern relating to criterion validity is that of **logical fallacy,** raising again the question, "For which group or groups the relationship is valid?" Religion may be related to party preference

Figure 9.1   Types of Fallacies

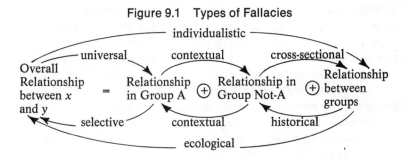

in some groups but not in others. Moreover, it may be related between groups but not within any particular group. For example, it could happen that predominantly Catholic states vote Democratic and predominantly Protestant states vote Republican, yet within any particular state Protestants and Catholics vote the same; this would occur if Protestants voted Democratic in predominantly Catholic states, and Catholics voted Republican in Protestant states.

Thus there are three types of relationships: relationship within a particular group, relationship between groups, and the overall relationship that combines these two. Logical fallacies occur by confusing these three types. What is true overall is not necessarily true within any particular group (universal fallacy) or between groups (individualistic fallacy). What is true in a particular group is not necessarily true overall (selective fallacy), or in another group (contextual fallacy), or between groups (cross-sectional fallacy). What is true between groups need not be true within any particular group (historical fallacy) or true overall (ecological fallacy). Some writers refer to all of these logical fallacies as *ecological fallacies.*

The problem of fallacy is a serious one, since the political scientist very often has only group data[7] such as number of Catholics by state and number of Democrats by state. One cannot logically reason from group data to individual relationships. The fact that Catholic states have many Democrats suggests but *does not* logically prove that individual Catholics tend to be Democrats.

Content Validity

This is also called *face validity,* and refers more to the validity of measures than of relationships. Social scientists usually insist that measures seem, on the face, to measure what they claim to. First, questions should seem to relate to the subject and cover the full range that is relevant. A test of tolerance levels composed of items dealing only with racial issues would not have *content validity,* since the content of the test fails to deal with non-racial aspects of tolerance. Second, the method of gathering data must, on the face, seem to be proper. Generally, random sampling or full enumeration are considered necessary in a valid study, although less rigorous standards are applied to exploratory studies.

Construct Validity

This also relates to validity of measures, asking if the researcher is truly measuring what he thinks he is. If the researcher is using a measure of racial tolerance, even though its content *seems* valid, is he really measuring racial tolerance or is he measuring something

---

[7] Group data is sometimes referred to as "ecological data," in contrast to "individual data."

else? This question cannot be answered unless the measure of racial tolerance can be assessed against some other standard considered accepted and non-debatable. The researcher can only see if the measure works in the expected direction for groups that, for whatever reasons, he *assumes* to be tolerant. Or the measure can be tested to see if it works in the expected direction with regard to other standardized tests; for example, the index of intolerance should correlate, one might *assume*, with the widely-used measure of "authoritarian personality."

Factor Validity

Finally, factor validity is a special topic, with a statistical meaning for validity. Validity is sometimes arbitrarily defined as "factor communality," or the percent of variance in the dependent (y) variable explained by all the factors in factor analysis. This communality is called h^2, and equals the sum of the squares of the factor loadings. Factor validity thus measures validity solely in terms of predictability: do the independent variables or factors predict the variance of the dependent variable? Because of this special, limited meaning of validity, other approaches to validity should normally be employed.

10

Correlation

Brief basic introductions to correlation are found in virtually all of the introductory texts mentioned in earlier chapters, including Weiss, Chapter 11; Yeomans, Chapter 5.5; and Allen Bernstein's concise *Handbook of Statistics Solutions for the Behavioral Sciences,* Chapter 6 (Holt, Rinehart & Winston paperback, 1964).

One of the best treatments, far more comprehensive, is N. M. Downie and R. W. Heath, *Basic Statistical Methods,* Second Edition (Harper & Row paperback, 1965), Chapters 7 and 16. For treatment of nonparametric correlation see Sidney Siegel, *Nonparametric Statistics for the Behavioral Sciences,* Chapter 9 (McGraw-Hill, 1956). The more advanced student will find a convenient review in Andrew Baggaley, *Intermediate Correlation Methods* (Wiley, 1964), Chapters 3–5.

Correlation is a category of measures of association, usually dealing with data presented in lists rather than tables. The most common kinds of correlation require interval (metric) data. Some of the measures of association discussed in the previous section are also termed "correlation statistics," used in correlation of data below the interval level. This chapter will discuss correlation at the interval level first, and then other forms of correlation.

PEARSONIAN, PARTIAL, AND NON-LINEAR CORRELATION

Pearsonian Product-moment Correlation, *r*

Pearsonian correlation, *r*, varies from 0 to 1, or 0 to −1 for negative relationships, as the points representing *x* and *y* on a scatter diagram move from a random arrangement to a straight line. Thus

Figure 10.1

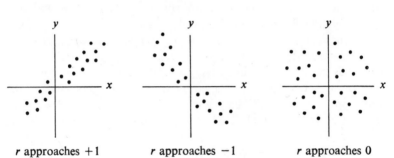

r approaches +1   *r* approaches −1   *r* approaches 0

Pearsonian correlation assumes that the relationship between *x* and *y* is *linear*. If the relationship is on a curve (*curvilinear*), then *r* will be misleadingly low. Furthermore, these techniques assume *homoscedas-*

Figure 10.2

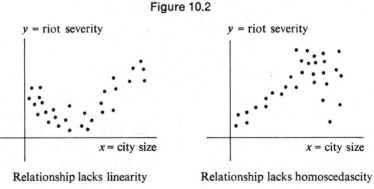

Relationship lacks linearity   Relationship lacks homoscedascity

(a)   (b)

city of the variables. The *x* variable must not have a low variance for some values of *y* and a high variance for other values of *y*. That is, not only must a straight line rather than a curved line be drawn through the paired (*x,y*) points (linearity), but the spread of points around the line should be about the same all along the line (homoscedascity).

For example, the relationship shown in Figure 10.2(a) is curvilinear; there is a clear pattern of covariation, but it cannot be summarized by one straight line. Figure 10.2(b) lacks homoscedascity even though a straight line could be drawn through the points because the relationship is much stronger for smaller cities (*x*) than larger. If the relationship is nonlinear, lacks homoscedascity, or is below the interval level of measurement, the assumptions involved in Pearsonian correlation are not met. Linearity and homoscedascity are most easily checked by visual inspection of a scatter diagram. Finally, Pearsonian *r* will vary between 0 and ±1 only if both variables being correlated have the same underlying (usually normal) distribution.

Pearsonian correlation is called *product-moment* correlation, the term "product-moment" being a mathematical term referring to the mean of a product, which is what *r* is based on. Pearsonian *r* equals the sum of the product of *x* and *y* deviations from their respective means divided by the value that sum would have if the observations fell perfectly on a straight line.

Definitional formula for *r*:

$$r = \frac{\Sigma (x - \bar{x})(y - \bar{y})}{\sqrt{\Sigma (x - \bar{x})^2 \Sigma (y - \bar{y})^2}}$$

Computational formula for *r*:

$$r = \frac{N\Sigma (xy) - (\Sigma x)(\Sigma y)}{\sqrt{[N\Sigma x^2 - (\Sigma x)^2][N\Sigma y^2 - \Sigma (y)^2]}}$$

In the **definitional formula** for *r*, the numerator measures the deviation of the *x* and *y* scores from mean *x* and mean *y* (see Figure 10.3). When the data form a straight line, points with high *x* deviations (high $x - \bar{x}$) will also have high *y* deviations; those with low *x* deviations will have low *y* deviations. In Table 10.1, a list of *x* values is paired in a perfect linear relationship with a list of *y* values. As a result, low *x* deviations are matched by low *y* deviations, medium by medium, high by high. When each *x* deviation is multiplied by its respective *y* deviation, a list of deviation products is derived that adds up to 20. The student may experiment by rearranging the *y*

Figure 10.3

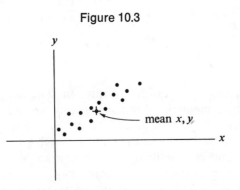

mean *x, y*

column to see that no other arrangement would result in a sum as high as 20; any deviation from perfect linearity reduces the sum of deviation products.

Table 10.1   A Table of Deviation Products

x	y	$x-\bar{x}$	$y-\bar{y}$	$(x-\bar{x})(y-\bar{y})$
1	2	−2	−4	8
2	4	−1	−2	2
3	6	0	0	0
4	8	1	2	2
5	10	2	4	8
$\bar{x}=3$	$\bar{y}=6$			20

Also in the definitional formula of *r*, the denominator states the maximum value that the numerator can take. Since in the example the relationship is perfect, the denominator equals 20 also. The student may again experiment by rearranging the original *y* column to show that while any rearrangement of the column from its illustrated perfect linear relationship diminishes the numerator, it does not affect the denominator.

Pearson's *r* thus uses the product-moment method of measuring degree of linearity as a criterion for correlation. Perfect correlation is perfect linearity, and the correlation coefficient itself is a ratio of

Table 10.2   Computing the Maximum Deviation Product

$x-\bar{x}$	$y-\bar{y}$	$(x-\bar{x})^2$	$(y-\bar{y})^2$
-2	-4	4	16
-1	-2	1	4
0	0	0	0
1	2	1	4
2	4	4	16
		10	40

$$\Sigma(x-\bar{x})^2\,\Sigma(y-\bar{y})^2 = 10(40) = 400$$
$$\text{m.d.p.} = \sqrt{\Sigma(x-\bar{x})^2\,\Sigma(y-\bar{y})^2} = \sqrt{400} = 20$$

observed linearity to perfect linearity. In computing r in practice, however, the **computational formula** is used, which is the mathematical equivalent of the definitional formula, but which avoids the need to compute deviations from the mean for each pair of observations. Also as a means of simplifying computation, certain *data transformation rules* are available: x or y scores may be added to, subtracted from, divided or multiplied by any constant without affecting the correlation coefficient, since none of these operations affect the linearity of the relationship between x and y; roots or power func-

Table 10.3

Town	Goldwater votes (x)	Nixon votes (y)	x'	y'	x'^2	y'^2	$x'y'$
1	100	130	0	3	0	9	0
2	102	120	2	2	4	4	4
3	105	110	5	1	25	1	5
4	103	150	3	5	9	25	15
5	100	140	0	4	0	16	0
			10	15	38	55	24

$$
\begin{aligned}
r &= \frac{N\Sigma(xy) - (\Sigma x)(\Sigma y)}{\sqrt{[N\Sigma x^2 - (\Sigma x)^2][N\Sigma y^2 - (\Sigma y)^2]}} \\[2mm]
&= \frac{5(24) - 10(15)}{\sqrt{[5(38) - 100][5(55) - 225]}} \\[2mm]
&= \frac{120 - 150}{\sqrt{(190 - 100)(275 - 225)}} = \frac{-30}{\sqrt{90(50)}} \\[2mm]
&= \frac{-30}{\sqrt{4500}} = \frac{-30}{10\sqrt{45}} = \frac{-3}{\sqrt{45}} = \frac{-3}{6.71} \\[2mm]
&= -.45
\end{aligned}
$$

tions would affect *r*, however. Moreover, transformations applied to *x* need not be applied to *y*.

Taking a simple example shown in Table 10.3, suppose we sampled five small communities whose voting population had not changed and found the number voting for Goldwater in 1964 and for Nixon in 1968, labelling these votes *x* and *y*. These may be simplified, first by subtracting 100 from *x* to get *x'*, then transforming *y* by subtracting 100 and dividing by 10 to get *y'*. These transformations enable us to work with small numbers in the computational formula, eventually arriving at $r = -.45$. This shows there is a medium negative correlation between groups on voting for Goldwater and voting for Nixon, at least for these five towns. It would be a historical fallacy, discussed in the last chapter, to conclude that this necessarily means that individuals who voted for Goldwater tended not to vote for Nixon; what is true between groups is not necessarily true within groups at the individual level.

One way of transforming the data would be to take both *x* and *y*, subtract from each their respective means, and divide each by their respective standard deviations. Note that this is the way to transform *raw scores* into *normal scores*: subtract the mean and divide by the standard deviation. If the scores are in normal form, then *r* equals the sum of the products of the normal (standard) scores divided by *N*:

$$r = \Sigma z_x z_y / N$$

This formula is mathematically equivalent to both the definitional and computational formulas.

Coefficient of Determination, r^2

The square of the correlation coefficient, r^2, is considered to be the proportion of the variance in the dependent variable "explained" by the independent variable. If the correlation between income and an index of "sense of political efficacy" is .60, then the square of this, .36, is the fraction of the variance in political efficacy explained by income. This implies that a correlation of .60 is not twice as strong as one of .30, since .36 is more than twice .09.

Partial Correlation

Partial correlation is correlation between two variables controlling for one or more other variables, as between income and sense of political efficacy, controlling for educational level. When education is held constant, does the correlation of .60 between income and efficacy diminish or disappear? This question is answered by using the partial correlation coefficient with education as a control:

First-order partial (one control):

$$r_{ij.k} = \frac{r_{ij} - (r_{ik})(r_{jk})}{\sqrt{1 - (r_{ik})^2} \times \sqrt{1 - (r_{jk})^2}}$$

As many control variables may be used at the same time as desired, although ordinarily measurement error and intercorrelation of control variables makes controlling for more than three variables at the same time unlikely to be meaningful. Note that each higher-order partial correlation equation requires computation of all lower orders of partial correlation:

Second-order partial (two controls):

$$r_{ij.kl} = \frac{r_{ij} - (r_{jl.k})(r_{il.k})}{\sqrt{1 - (r_{il.k})^2} \times \sqrt{1 - (r_{jl.k})^2}}$$

Third-order partial (three controls):

$$r_{ij.klm} = \frac{r_{ij} - (r_{im.kl})(r_{jm.kl})}{\sqrt{1 - (r_{im.kl})^2} \times \sqrt{1 - (r_{jm.kl})^2}}$$

As will be seen in a later chapter, partial correlation coefficients are important in "causal modeling," building and testing mathematical models of political reality. Significance of partial correlation is tested by the F test, where:

$$F = (r_{ij.k}^2 / 1 - r_{ij.k}^2)(N - k - 1)$$

In this formula, k equals the number of independent and control variables. After computing the F value by this formula, the student may determine whether the partial correlation coefficient is significant by consulting the *F* distribution table in the Appendix, for 1 and $(N - k - 1)$ degrees of freedom.

Significance of the Correlation Coefficient

Like any measure of association, a strong correlation does not assure significance.[1] The smaller the sample size the higher *r* must be to be significant. The significance of *r* may be read directly from a table of coefficients of correlation and *t* ratios, where degrees of freedom equals sample size minus 2. If our sample included only 5 observations, then sample size 5 minus 2 = 3 would be the number of degrees of freedom. For 3 degrees of freedom, the table tells us that *r* must be .878 or higher to be significant at the .05 level, and .959 or higher to be significant at the .01 level. At the .05 level, for a sample size of 25, *r* must be .396; for 100, .195; for 1000, .062.

If such a table is unavailable, critical values of *r* may be determined from a *t* table by the formula:

$$r_{\mathrm{crit}} = \sqrt{t^2/t^2 + (N - 2)}$$

For a certain number of degrees of freedom (the researcher's sample size minus 2) and the desired level of significance (.05, .01, or whatever), a value of *t* may be read and placed in the formula. For sample size 25 and significance level .05, $t = 2.069$; the student may use this in the r_{crit} formula to see for himself if the minimum significant value of *r* is .396 as stated above. Note that the *t* (and *z* and *F*) test *assumes* both variables are normally distributed and have the same variance.

Correlation Coefficient and Range of the Data

In testing the significance of *r*, however, the researcher must keep in mind that the magnitude of *r* is "artificially" low when the range of the data is narrow. For example, the correlation between unemployment and labor rioting is .77 for the years 1927–1963, but only .34 for the years 1930–1939. This is not primarily because there was some strong correlation after the 1930s, but rather because low unem-

---

[1] Significance is relevant only for random samples, not enumerations.

ployment and low rates of labor rioting after 1939 served to increase the range of both variables. When the variables being correlated do not vary greatly, the correlation coefficient is unlikely to be large. Because this is so, social scientists increasingly report the variance along with the correlation coefficients.[2]

Eta Coefficient for Non-linear Relationships

Whenever a relation is curvilinear, r understates the amount of correlation. Even a perfect curvilinear correlation might conceivably have an r of zero. When the relationship is linear, r equals eta; in non-linear relationships, the degree to which r is less than eta measures the extent to which the relation is nonlinear. If visual inspection of a scatter diagram such as illustrated in Figure 10.1 suggests curvilinearity, eta should be computed:

1. *If* the data are interval;
2. *If* the frequencies in each column are large enough to give stability to the column means (note this is *not* the case in Table 10.4, which uses low frequencies for simplicity); and
3. *If* there are enough columns to give the grand mean of the column means stability.

Note also that having y-columns and x-rows instead of the customary reverse will ordinarily result in a different value for eta, appropriate when the hypothesis is that y causes or predicts x.

As indicated by Table 10.4, eta (η_{yx}) equals the square root of the sum of squares for y between columns (Σy_b^2 in turn equal to the sum of the mean squared y values associated with each x column, minus the squared sum of y values associated with all columns divided by N) divided by the total sum of squares for y ($\Sigma y_t^2 =$ the sum of the weighted squared frequencies of y minus the average weighted squared frequency of y). The numerator and denominator in this complicated formula serve very much like their counterparts in the correlation equation; to the extent x and y are related—linearly, parabolically,

---

[2] Some authors have developed "corrections" for range of data; see J. P. Guilford, *Psychometric Methods* (New York: McGraw-Hill, 1954).

Table 10.4   Computation Schedule for Eta Data in Scatterplot Form

Data

x	y
1	1
2	2
3	3
4	4
5	3
6	2
7	1

$y \backslash x$	1	2	3	4	5	6	7
4				1			
3			1		1		
2		1				1	
1	1						1
f	1	1	1	1	1	1	1

A f	B y	C $f(y)$	D $f(y)^2$	E x-class (column)	F f	G $\Sigma y'$	H $(\Sigma y')^2$	I $(\Sigma y')^2/f$
1	4	4	16	1	1	1	1	1
2	3	6	18	2	1	2	4	4
2	2	4	8	3	1	3	9	9
2	1	2	2	4	1	4	16	16
				5	1	3	9	9
				6	1	2	4	4
				7	1	1	1	1
$N=7$		$\Sigma f(y)=16$	$\Sigma f(y)^2=44$		$N=7$	$\Sigma(\Sigma y')=16$		$(\Sigma y')^2/f=44$

$$\text{Eta}^2 = \Sigma y_b^2 / \Sigma y_t^2 \quad \text{where} \quad \Sigma y_t^2 = \Sigma f(y)^2 - \frac{[\Sigma f(y)]^2}{N} = 44 - \frac{16^2}{7} = 7.4$$

$$\text{and} \quad y_b^2 = \Sigma \left[\frac{(\Sigma y')^2}{f} \right] - \frac{[\Sigma(\Sigma y')]^2}{N} = 44 - \frac{16^2}{7} = 7.4$$

Therefore $\text{Eta} = \sqrt{7.4/7.4} = 1.0$

or in any manner—the numerator will be as large as the denominator and eta will approach 1. Eta varies from 0 to 1.0, and has no sign since it measures only relationship, not direction of relationship.

In the example given in the computation schedule, simple data are given for x and y; when these are put into the form of a scatterplot, showing y frequencies for each x value, that is, for each column, the perfect curvilinear relationship is evident. The needed derivations from the data are computed in columns A through I of Table 10.4. Column A gives the frequencies for each y value (each row). The y values are listed in column B, while column C is the product of columns A and B. The value $f(y)^2$ is derived in column D by multiplying columns B and C.

Column E lists the values x may take. Although column E does not enter into the computations, it is listed to aid in understanding columns F through I. Column F shows the frequencies of each x value, while G is the $f(y)$ associated with each x value (with each column). For example, there is one entry in column 2, and this entry corresponds to a y value of 2. Therefore a 2 is entered opposite x-value 2 in column G. Column H gives the values in column G, squared, and I gives the values in column H divided by the x frequencies in column F.

This laborious process results in the availability of all the statistical components needed in computing eta. The denominator, Σy_t^2, is the sum of column D minus the sum of column C, squared and divided by N, equalling 11.4 in the example. The numerator, Σy_b^2, equals the sum of column I minus the sum of column G, squared and divided by N. Eta, sometimes called the **correlation ratio,** is the square root of this ratio, 1.0 in this case, showing a perfect relationship. The student may experiment for himself by rearranging the original y data values to show that any other arrangement will result in a lower value of eta.

As for r, there is way of *testing the significance of eta*—the F test. Using the formula

$$F = \frac{\Sigma y_b^2/c-1}{\Sigma y_t - \Sigma y_b^2/N-c}$$

where Σy_b^2 is the numerator of eta,
Σy_t^2 is the denominator of eta,
c is the number of columns, and
N the number of entries in the table

the F ratio is computed. The researcher uses a table of the distribution of F, seeing whether the computed value of F is as large as that in the table, for the level of significance he desires (usually .05 or .01) and for degrees of freedom equal to $c-1$ *and* to $N-c$.[3] If the computed F value is as large as that in the table, eta is considered significant. In Table 10.4, and in any perfect relationship, the denominator of the F ratio is 0 and therefore significance is indeterminate (not computable) as it is when $N \leq c$.

CORRELATION STATISTICS FOR ORDINAL-LEVEL DATA

Kendall's Rank Correlation

Tau is a correlation measure used in association of two sets of rank-ordered data. For example, we might want to correlate students ordered by their class rank (x, the independent variable) with students ranked by their scores on an index of level of political information (y, the dependent variable). First, the x scores, the ordinal data for the independent variable, are listed by their rank order from lowest to highest. Second, the y scores, the ordinal data for the dependent

Table 10.5

x	1	2	3.5	3.5	5	6	7	8	9	10	11	12	
y	4	2	2	5	6	7.5	2	7.5	9	11.5	10	11.5	$N = 12$

variable, are listed as pairs of the x scores. In Table 10.5, the student with the highest class rank, 1, has a political information level that ranks 4th; that is this student had the fourth highest score—the score itself was not necessarily 4. The 2nd, 3.5th, and 7th students by class rank were in a three-way tie for first place by information level.

Third, S, a measure of the consistency of the y ranks with the x ranks, is computed. If when the data have been arranged as in steps 1 and 2 there is a perfect rank correlation, then all values in the y row to the right of any given y value will be as large or larger (smaller if correlation is negative) than that value. S is thus the sum of the number of higher minus lower y values to the right of each y value. For example, the first y value in Table 10.5 is 4, which has 8 higher and 3 lower values to the right. The next y value is 2, which has 8

[3] The F table requires use of two degrees-of-freedom measures.

higher and none lower, ignoring values that are equal to it. The third y value is also 2, which is paired with an x value (3.5) that is itself tied with another equal x value. In the case of these x ties, the y values paired with each of the tied x values are ignored. Thus, ignoring the y value of 5, the third y value has 7 higher and no lower y values to the right. S is the sum of all these differences:

$$S = (8-3) + (8-0) + (7-0) + (7-1) + (6-1)$$
$$+ (5-1) + (5-0) + (4-0) + (3-0) +$$
$$(1-1) + (1-0) = 48$$

$$\text{tau} = 2S/N(N-1) \qquad = S/\tfrac{1}{2}N(N-1)$$
$$= 2(48)/12(12-1) = 96/132$$
$$= .727$$

Although tau is not directly comparable to Pearson's r in magnitude —.727 tau is not equivalent to .727 r—it does tend to be significant at the same level for the same data. When the data are derived from a random sample, *significance of tau* is tested by use of the normal (z) tables, where $z_{\text{tau}} = T/s_T$:[4]

Computational formula for the significance of tau:

$$z = T/s_T = \text{T}/\sqrt{2(2N+5)/9N(N-1)}$$
$$= .727/\sqrt{2(24+5)/9(12)\,11} = .727/\sqrt{58/1188}$$
$$= 3.39$$

When applied to the data in Table 10.4, z has a value of 3.39; the proportion of the normal curve read directly from the normal table corresponding to 3.39 is .0003. Thus, when N is 12, a tau of .727 is significant at the .0003 level.[5]

Spearman's rho

Rho (ρ) is an older measure than tau, simple to compute—it is sometimes used as a quick but rough approximation to r, and often

----

[4] $T = \text{tau}$; $s_T = $ standard deviation of tau.

[5] Kendall has also developed a *partial rank correlation coefficient* for use in controlling for third variables in ordinal relationships. This coefficient is discussed in Siegel, pp. 223–229. See Siegel also for a table of significance of tau when $N \leq 10$.

used when data are rank-order in form but assumed to be based on an underlying interval level of measurement. For example, states ranked 1 to 50 in terms of unemployment rates (x) might be correlated with states ranked 1 to 50 by number of riots experienced during the year. Rho is sometimes called *rank difference correlation* and is a product-moment correlation coefficient for ranked data, interpreted like *r*:

1. The *x* and *y* data are arranged by rank orders as in steps 1 and 2 of the tau procedure, from lowest to highest unemployment rates, and the paired values for number of riots.
2. Each *y* value is subtracted from its corresponding *x* value.
3. This difference is squared.
4. The squared difference (D^2) is used in the *computational formula for rho:*

$$\rho = 1 - [6\Sigma D^2 / N(N^2 - 1)]$$

Table 10.6

x	1	2	3.5	3.5	5	6	7	8	9	10	11	12
y	4	2	2	5	6	7.5	2	17.5	9	11.5	10	11.5
D	−3	0	1.5	−1.5	−1	−1.5	5	.5	0	−1.5	1	.5
D²	9	0	2.25	2.25	1	2.25	25	.25	0	2.25	1	.25

$\Sigma D^2 = 45.5$ $N = 12$

$$\text{rho} = \rho = 1 - [6(45.5)/12(144-1)]$$
$$= 1 - (273/1716) = 1 - .159$$
$$= .841$$

The definitional formula for rho is the same as that for *r*; the derivation for the computational formula when *x* and *y* are ranks is given in Siegel, page 203.

The *significance of rho* is computed by the use of *t* tables when *N* is over 10. Using Table 10.6,

$$t = (\rho/\sqrt{1 - \rho^2})(\sqrt{N-2})$$
$$= (.841/\sqrt{1 - .841^2})(\sqrt{12-2})$$
$$= (.841/.540)(3.16) = 4.93$$
$$\text{d.f.} = N - 2 = 12 - 2 = 10$$

t equals 4.93 and degrees of freedom equals 10. For 10 d.f. at the .01 level, the t table shows that the computed t must be at least 3.17. Since 4.93 is more than this, we may conclude rho is significant at the .01 level. When N is 10 or less, critical levels of significance may be read directly from a table of critical values of r_s.

OTHER CORRELATION STATISTICS

The **contingency coefficient**, C, discussed in the last chapter ($C = \chi^2/\chi^2 + N$), is often used as a correlation statistic for nominal data. C has the advantage of being applicable to any level of data, any underlying distributions, whether there is underlying continuity or not. It has the disadvantage that it reaches a maximum which is variable and less than 1; it is not operationally meaningful; and the data must meet chi-square requirements—no more than 20% of cells may have an expected frequency under 5 and no cells under 1.

Phi, also discussed in the previous chapter, is used when both independent and dependent variables are true dichotomies, not condensations of continuous variables (phi $= ad - bc / \sqrt{r_1 r_2 c_1 c_2}$). Both C and phi are significant for a table if chi-square is significant. Phi reaches a maximum of 1, but otherwise has the same advantages and disadvantages as C, and may be used with forced dichotomies.

Tetrachoric correlation, r_t, is used when both variables are assumed to be forced dichotomies—continuous variables condensed into dichotomies—and when the marginals are 70:30 or less extremely split. The computation of r_t is extremely complicated and tables have been developed as an aid. Tetrachoric correlation is a function of the dividend of the marginal products in a 2-by-2 table, and is read from a tables of estimates of r_t for various values of ad/bc after the dividend

Table 10.7

		Class Rank (x)		r_i
		Top Half	Bottom Half	
Information Level (y)	High	140	10	150
	Low	10	40	50
	c_i	150	50	200

$r_t = f\ (ad/bc)$ if ad is larger (correlation is positive)
  or $f(bc/ad)$ if ad is less (correlation is negative)

$= f(56)$

has been computed. In Table 10.7, the dividend is 56; looking this up in a table of r_t, we find it corresponds to $r_t = .93$.[6]

Two further coefficients have been developed for the case when one of the variables is continuous and the other dichotomous. If the dichotomous variable is a true dichotomy, point-biserial correlation is used; if forced, biserial is used.

Point-biserial Correlation

Point-biserial correlation, r_{pb}, requires that the continuous variable be the independent variable and be of interval level. It is a product-moment coefficient and is interpreted like the Pearsonian r. When x is the independent variable (e.g., political information level) and y is the dichotomous dependent variable (e.g., voting or not voting), r_{pb} equals the x mean for one dichotomous class minus the x mean for the total, divided by the standard deviation of x and multiplied by the root of the dividend of the proportions of cases in each class of the dichotomous y variable, as shown in Table 10.8.

Point-biserial correlation is most often used in **item analysis**, testing to see if test or index items discriminate well between individuals who score high by some criterion and those who score low. For example, the criterion, the continuous x variable, might be scores on a standardized scale of authoritarianism, and the item, the dichotomous y variable, might be endorsing or not endorsing the statement "Communists should be allowed to teach at the state university." Items with a high point-biserial correlation with the authoritarianism scale discriminate well between persons with high and low measured authoritarianism, and would presumably be used in a survey or test on this subject.

In Table 10.4, point-biserial correlation is computed easily:

1. Units of data are listed in the first column (units may be persons, cities, years, etc.); the corresponding x score (information level in the example) listed in a second column; and the y score (vote, in the example, where 1 = voted and 0 = didn't vote) in a third.
2. The mean of the x column and its standard deviation are computed, along with the x mean for those units whose y value was 1. Also computed are p and q, the proportions voting and not voting.
3. These values are placed in the formula for r_{pb}, generating a coefficient of .49.

[6] Also for this table, phi equals .73.

Table 10.8

Person	Information Level (x)	Vote (y)
1	84	1
2	73	1
3	69	0
4	65	1
5	60	0
6	51	1
7	42	1
8	38	0
9	33	0
10	20	0
	$\overline{535}$	$\overline{5}$

$$\bar{x} = 535/10 = 53.5$$
$$\bar{x}_y = (84 + 73 + 65 + 51 + 42)/5 = 63$$
$$s_x = \sqrt{\Sigma(x-\bar{x})^2/N}$$
$$\text{or for a sample,}$$
$$= \sqrt{\Sigma(x-\bar{x})^2/N-1}$$
$$= 19.1$$

$$r_{pb} = [(\bar{x}_y - \bar{x})/s](\sqrt{p/q}), \text{ where}$$

$\bar{x}$ is the mean of the independent variable

$\bar{x}_y$ is the mean of the x values for the cases where the y value is 1

s_x the standard deviation of x; for samples, the sample standard deviation of x

p the proportion of cases in y having a value of 1

$q = 1 - p$

$$r_{pb} = [(63 - 53.5)/19.1](\sqrt{\frac{1}{2}/\frac{1}{2}})$$
$$= .49$$
$$\text{d.f.} = N - 2 = 8$$

Significance of r_{pb} is computed by use of a t table, as with rho, for degrees of freedom equal to $N - 2$:

$$t = r_{pb}\sqrt{N-2}/\sqrt{1-r_{pb}^2}$$
$$= .49\sqrt{8}/\sqrt{1-.49^2}$$
$$= 1.60$$

In the example the computed t value is 1.60. Looking in a table of t values for d.f. $= 8$, we find that at the .05 level a t of 2.306 is required. Since the computed t is smaller than this value, the point-biserial correlation is *not* significant even at the .05 level.

Biserial Correlation

This is a similar coefficient, designed for cases where the dichotomous variable is actually a forced condensation of an underlying continuous variable. Its formula

$$r_b = (\bar{x}_y - \bar{x}/s_x)\,(p/y)$$

is identical to that for point-biserial correlation, except that p/y is substituted for $\sqrt{p/q}$. The term y represents the ordinate on a normal

Figure 10.4

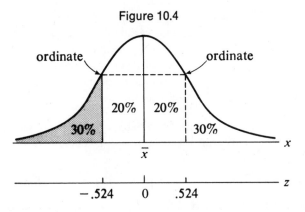

curve where the pth unit of x would fall. This ordinate is read from the normal tables. Suppose p equalled .30. Then by definition the proportion between this and the mean would be .20. Looking in the normal tables, we find 20% of the area lies between $z = .524$ and the mean, and when this is so the ordinate is .873, as illustrated in Figure 10.4. Otherwise, the computation is the same as for point-biserial correlation. Both are parametric statistics used in item analysis, and the **significance of biserial correlation** is also tested by the t table, where $t = r_b/(\sqrt{pq}/y\sqrt{N})$, with notation as before.

Triserial Correlation

Finally, **triserial correlation** was developed by Jaspen for the case when an ordinal trichotomy (such as low, medium, and high riot severity) is to be correlated with a continuous interval-level, normally-distributed variable (such as unemployment rates):

$$r_{tri} = \frac{y_h(\bar{x}_h) + (y_m - y_h)\bar{x}_m - y_m\bar{x}_l}{s_t y_h^2/p_h + (y_m - y_h)^2/p_m + y_m^2/p_l}$$

where y_h, y_m, y_l are normal curve ordinates, as in biserial correlation, related to

$p_h, p_m, p_l,$ which are the proportions of observations in the three classes of the trichotomous variable.

$\bar{x}_h, \bar{x}_m, \bar{x}_l$ are the x means (the means of the continuous variable) for those observations falling into the three classes of the trichotomous (y) variable, and

s_t is the standard deviation of all the x values combined.

Triserial correlation appears formidable, but it is in fact a logical extension of the biserial coefficient and is computed in a similar manner.

CONCLUSION: WHICH COEFFICIENT OF CORRELATION?

Before the student becomes overwhelmed with the various types of correlation, the confusion may be placed in perspective by noting that in practice only a few types are widely used in political science. *Most common* is the use of Pearsonian r as a measure of correlation between two normally-distributed, interval-level variables, such as rates of increase of income with proportion of votes cast for the incumbent party—r may be used if data are similarly distributed, but then significance cannot be tested. Often r is controlled for a third variable (e.g., proportion of population urban, or level of education) or even a fourth and fifth variable, by means of partial correlation $(r_{ij.k})$. The next chapter will show how, with "multiple correlation" (R), one can also correlate a variable with several other variables at once. Eta, used for curvilinear correlation, is not much used, perhaps reflecting the newness of recent quantitative methods of a sophisticated nature in the discipline, and also reflecting the difficulty of discerning *any* clear, quantifiable relationships with socal data.

If the data are not normally distributed, the contingency coefficient C is appropriate at the nominal level, and Spearman's rho or Kendall's tau at the ordinal or higher levels. Chi-square goodness-of-fit test may be applied to test the normality of the data. Dichotomous data may be handled by the phi coefficient.

If the data contain one continuous variable and a true dichotomy, point-biserial correlation is used; if a forced dichotomy, biserial; and if an ordered trichotomy, triserial. Tetrachoric correlation is used when two dichotomous variables are being studied, both of which are assumed to represent underlying continuities.

The correlation statistics are simply more measures of association, used in giving a number to the strength of a relationship. Studying a relationship in detail is better than summarizing it with a number, but political scientists must often deal with many relationships for many cases, making it desirable to have a summary statistic to help in quick comparisons. Where possible, multivariate analysis using tables and control subtables, and other forms of detailed analysis should be undertaken to get beyond the summary statistic, which, because it summarizes, loses information.

In an early chapter it was stated that the purpose of statistics is to simplify by losing information. Chapter 11 will discuss other techniques related to the product-moment correlation that are used to simplify relationships even further. Sometimes these techniques, like factor analysis, are called more "sophisticated." They further simplify the data, but their computation is more complex. Like all statistics, they are "sophisticated" only if appropriate to the data and research needs of the political scientist.

11

Regression and Factor Analysis

Sound introductions to regression are contained in several texts already mentioned—Downie and Heath, Chapter 8; Yeomans, Chapter 5—as well as most statistics texts, including P. Games and G. Klare, *Elementary Statistics: Data Analysis for the Behavioral Sciences* (McGraw-Hill, 1967), Chapter 14. An elementary introduction to the terminology of factor analysis is contained in Phillips, Chapter 11, while the more advanced student might refer to Baggaley, pp. 91–167.

More advanced applications in measurement are contained in George Bohrnstedt's article, "Observations on the Measurement of Change," in E. F. Borgatta, ed., *Sociological Methodology 1969* (Jossey-Bass, 1969), Chapter 4. Chapters 10–14 of Edward J. Kane, *Economic Statistics and Econometrics* (Harper & Row, 1968) discuss the use of regression in economic modeling.

The *American Political Science Review* regularly carries articles applying regression and factor analysis, as, for example, S. J. Cimbala, "Foreign Policy As an Issue Area" (*APSR:* March, 1969).

Correlation makes no assumptions about causality. If x and y are correlated, we still have no reason to conclude that one causes the other: x may cause y, y may cause x, there may be mutual causation, both may be caused by a third variable, or there may be an intervening variable. **Regression** is used instead of correlation when our hypothesis is such that we wish to assert causation, to investigate whether x causes y. Like correlation, regression requires interval data and linear, homoscedasic relationships, and similarly distributed variables, usually normally distributed. When significance tests are used, both variables must be normally distributed. Because it is not affected by the range (variance) of the data as is the correlation coefficient, the unstandardized regression coefficient may be preferred in the measurement of association in explaining change.

Factor analysis builds on the correlation statistic in a different way. It is a method of attempting to identify the common factors that underlie a large number of variables, or to explore underlying factors uniting groups of people. For example, for a set of senators, which votes belong together? (We may identify foreign policy, presidential support, domestic welfare dimensions, or underlying factors as criteria to group votes.) Or for a set of votes, which senators belong together? (We may identify Southern, city, liberal coalition, or other underlying criteria for grouping senators.) When the researcher is dealing with a large number of variables, many of them may be overlapping and redundant; factor analysis can serve as an exploratory means of collapsing a large number of variables into a smaller number of factors, manageable in formulating political models. It starts with a correlation matrix—Pearsonian for normally-distributed data—of each variable with every other variable, and ends up with a table showing the "loading" of each variable on a small number of underlying factors, where some variables will be heavily loaded on one factor and some on another.

REGRESSION AND MULTIPLE CORRELATION

The student should already be familiar with some of the concepts used in regression, such as the **scatter diagram** of x and y values on a **rectangular coordinate system,** where x is the *independent* and y the *dependent variable,* as illustrated in Figure 11.1. In addition, sometimes a third (or more) variable is held *constant* as a **control.** In a political science experiment, for example, decision-makers could be

Figure 11.1

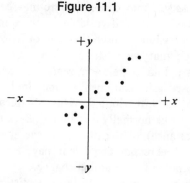

asked to choose between competitive and cooperative strategies (the dependent variable) under different patterns of payoffs (the independent variable) when both are selected as pairs matched by age, education, income and other characteristics (the control variables).

Figure 11.2

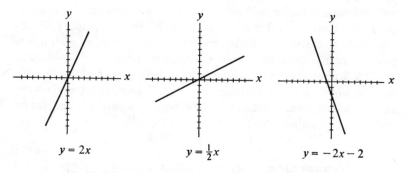

$$y = 2x \qquad y = \frac{1}{2}x \qquad y = -2x - 2$$

Regression is a way of drawing a line through a scatter diagram that best summarizes the scatter. The formula for such a line takes the form

$$y = bx + c$$

where b is the regression coefficient and c is some constant equal to the y intercept of the regression line, the point on the y axis where the line intersects. The regression coefficient is the slope of the regression line.

Least-squares Regression

What criterion should be used to draw the "best" summary line through points on a scatter diagram? In simple cases, one might well approximate the best solution by simply inspecting the diagram visually and drawing a line through it by intuition—the freehand or "black thread" method—although the subjectivity of this procedure makes it impossible to test "goodness." The best line is considered to be one where squared vertical deviations of the points from the line are minimized.[1]

In least-squares regression, the first two statistics to be computed are the regression coefficient, b, and the constant, c. This is relatively simple, since the constant is a function of x and b, while b itself, the regression coefficient, is intimately related to the correlation coefficient. The correlation coefficient is a standardized regression coefficient, adjusted for the ratio of the standard deviations. The formulas given below are for the hypothesis that x causes or predicts y; if the reverse were hypothesized, the xs and ys in the formulas could be reversed and a different regression coefficient computed. Thus, every set of data has two usually different regression coefficients, b_{yx} and b_{xy}:

$$b_{yx} = \frac{\Sigma yx - N\bar{x}\bar{y}}{\Sigma (x-\bar{x})^2} = r\frac{s_x}{s_y}$$

$$= \frac{\Sigma xy - N\bar{x}\bar{y}}{\Sigma x^2 - [(\Sigma x)^2/N]} = \text{computational formula for } b$$

$$c_{yx} = \bar{y} - b_{yx}x$$

To take an example with actual data shown in Table 11.1, we might hypothesize that unemployment (x) causes labor rioting (y), at least for the 1930s. Computation of the regression equation involves simply

---

[1] Deviations must be squared because there is always a horizontal line such that the sum of the raw deviations is zero.

Table 11.1

Year	Unemploy- ment (x)	Riots (y)	xy	x^2	y^2
1930	8.7%	3	26.1	75.69	9
1931	15.9	28	445.2	252.81	784
1932	23.6	21	495.6	556.96	441
1933	24.9	17	423.3	620.01	289
1934	21.7	37	802.9	470.89	1369
1935	20.1	30	603.0	404.01	900
1936	16.9	31	523.9	285.61	961
1937	14.3	22	314.6	204.49	484
1938	19.0	2	38.0	361.00	4
1939	17.2	9	154.8	295.84	81

$$\Sigma x = 182.3 \quad \Sigma y = 200 \quad \Sigma xy = 3827.4 \quad \Sigma x^2 = 3527.31 \quad y^2 = 5322$$
$$\bar{x} = 18.23 \quad \bar{y} = 20$$

$$b_{yx} = \frac{\Sigma xy - N\bar{x}\bar{y}}{\Sigma x^2 - [(\Sigma x)^2/N]}$$

$$= \frac{3,827.40 - 3,646.00}{3,527.31 - (33,233.29/10)} = \frac{181.4}{203.98} = .889$$

$$c = \bar{y} - b_{yx}\bar{x} = 20.0 - .889(18.23) = 3.79$$

$$y = .889x + 3.79$$

listing x and y, their products, and x^2, and finding the sum of these lists. From there it is a short step to substituting the observed values into the regression coefficient equation; when the coefficient is computed it may be used in the second equation to derive the constant. The result is an equation that may be used to predict number of labor riots (y) from unemployment rate (x). For example, in a year in which unemployment was 10% we would expect $.889(10) + 3.79$, or approximately 13 labor riots.

Standard Error of Estimate, s_{yx}

Computing the regression equation is not enough. We must still decide how *confident* we should be about our predictions using the equation. The standard error of estimate, s_{yx}, may be used on normally-distributed interval data to answer this question. This statistic equals the root of the sum of the squared differences between observed minus expected y values, divided by $N - 2$:

$$s_{yx} = \sqrt{\frac{\Sigma (y_o - y_e)^2}{N-2}} \text{ (definitional formula)}$$

The observed and expected y values are listed, their differences squared, summed, divided by $N-2$ and the square root taken, in the definitional formula.

However, this is equivalent to another procedure that seems more complex but is actually easier, based on data already computed in arriving at the linear regression coefficient:

$$s_{xy} = \sqrt{\frac{\Sigma y^2 - [(\Sigma xy)^2 / \Sigma x^2]}{N-2}} \quad \text{(computational formula)}$$

$$= \sqrt{\frac{5322 - (14,648,991 / 3,527.31)}{10 - 2}}$$

$$= \sqrt{\frac{5322 - 4153}{8}} = \sqrt{\frac{1169}{8}}$$

$$= 12.1$$

All that is necessary is to determine the sum of y^2, substitute the other values, and work the equation through. In this case the standard error of estimate is 12.1 This means that any y value (predicted number of riots) estimated by the regression equation will be within ± 12.1 of the real value 68% of the time, within ± 24.2 about 95% of the time. Because N is small in this case, standard error of estimate is large, and we cannot be very confident about our predictions. At the 95% level our estimate of 13 riots on the basis of 10% unemployment would have to be rephrased to 13 riots, ± 24! Clearly these wide confidence limits undermine the validity of our predictions. Because this is always a possibility, standard error of estimate must be given along with regression predictions, a procedure that is also applicable to multiple regression.

Multiple Regression and Multiple Correlation

Multiple regression is a way of predicting the dependent variable from two or more independent variables. Multiple correlation is a closely-related statistic used in determining the proportion of variance of the dependent variable explained by two or more independent variables. Since computation of these statistics is so laborious that it is always done by computer, only the three-variable (one dependent, two independent) case will be discussed.

If x_1 is the dependent variable (e.g., number of labor riots) and x_2 and x_3 are the independent variables (e.g., unemployment and real wages), then the formula for the multiple regression line looks like this:

$$x_1 = b_{12.3}(x_2) + b_{13.2}(x_3) + c_{1.23}$$

The dependent variable equals the partial regression coefficient of the dependent with the first independent variable, controlling for the second, times the first independent variable, plus a similar quantity for the second independent variable, plus a constant. Computation of the partial regression coefficients involves computation of the simple regression coefficients first, after which the formulas below may be used to arrive at a prediction equation for the dependent variable:

$$b_{12.3} = b_{12} - (b_{13})(b_{32})/1 - (b_{23})(b_{32})$$

$$b_{13.2} = b_{13} - (b_{12})(b_{23})/1 - (b_{32})(b_{23})$$

$$c_{1.23} = x_1 - b_{12.3}(x_2) - b_{13.2}(x_3)$$

The partial b coefficients in such a prediction equation are called **unstandardized regression coefficients.** Because these are not affected by the range of the data, as are correlation coefficients, some have argued for their use as measures of assocation in explaining change. Their disadvantage, however, is that they cannot be compared to tell the relative importance of each independent variable in predicting the dependent variable. Therefore, **standardized regression coefficients,** also called **beta weights,** are obtained by multiplying the partial b coefficients by the ratio of the standard deviation of the independent variable to the standard deviation of the dependent variable.[2] The formula for the standardized multiple regression line, where the data (x_1, x_2, x_3) are standardized, looks like this:

$$x_1 = b_{12.3}(s_2/s_1)(x_2) + b_{13.2}(s_3/s_1)(x_3) + c_{1.23}$$

[2] Note: $r^2_{IJ.K} = (\text{beta}_{IJ.K})(\text{beta}_{JI.K})$.

The standardized formula will result in the following sort of equation:

$$\text{number of riots } (x_1) = .50 \times \text{unemployment rate } (x_2)$$
$$+ .10 \times \text{real wages} + 3.9$$

Multiple correlation, R, is the square root of the proportion of the variance in the dependent variable "explained" by the independent variables. Thus it is very closely related to standardized multiple regression. In the three-variable case, R may be computed directly from the formula:

$$R_{12.3} = \sqrt{r_{12}^2 + r_{13.2}^2 (1 - r_{12}^2)}$$
$$= \sqrt{r_{12}^2 + r_{13}^2 - 2r_{12}r_{13}r_{23}/1 - r_{23}^2}$$

By using this formula with the data in Table 11.2, it may be shown, that unemployment and real wages "explain" about 63.5% of the variance in labor rioting between 1927 and 1963. The **significance of multiple correlation,** R, is tested by the F test, where F is the ratio of

Table 11.2

	x_1	x_2	x_3
Riots (x_1)	—	.768	−.662
Unemployment (x_2)	.768	—	−.651
Wages (x_3)	−.662	−.651	—

$$R_{1.23}^2 = \frac{r_{12}^2 + r_{13}^2 - 2r_{12}r_{13}r_{23}}{1 - r_{23}^2}$$

$$= \frac{(.768)^2 + (-.662)^2 - 2(.768)(-.651)(-.662)}{1 - (-.651)^2}$$

$$= .635$$

proportion explained (R^2) to proportion not explained $(1 - R^2)$. For Table 11.2, for degrees of freedom equal to k (the number of independent variables; 2 in this case) and $n - k - 1$ (where n is the number of units; 36 in this case, one for each year), computation of F is as follows:

$$F = R^2 (N - k - 1) / (1 - R^2) k$$

$$= (.635) (36 - 2 - 1) / (.365) (2)$$

$$= 28.71$$

Looking in an F table for k (2) and $n - k - 1$ (33) degrees of freedom, a value of 3.29 is required for significance at the .05 level, and 5.31 for the .01 level. Since our computed F (28.71) is much larger, we may conclude that R is significant at the .01 level.

Finally, a few words of caution in the use of multiple correlation must be mentioned. First, it is inadvisable to use more than four or five predictor (independent) variables, since in social science there is usually too much intercorrelation of such variables, and because of the danger of compounding sampling bias. Second, there is the problem of "multicollinearity." The more highly related the predictor variables are, the lower the contribution of each to R will be. Thus the contribution of three socio-economic variables (education, income, occupational status) may be less than one political variable's contribution to R, simply because there are three socio-economic variables and one political variable; in such a case it would be wrong to conclude that the political variable was the most important.

This problem is illustrated when **stepwise regression** is used. Stepwise regression is a method, usually used with computers, whereby a regression equation is computed with one independent variable, a second equation is computed with two variables, then a third variable may be added, etc. First a correlation matrix is computed. The computer selects as the first independent variable that variable with the strongest correlation with the dependent variable and computes the first step regression equation. It then computes a partial correlation matrix, using the first independent variable as a control. The second independent variable chosen is that with the strongest partial correlation with the dependent variable, and the second step regression equation is computed, and so on. If income is chosen as the first independent variable, then it is unlikely that occupational prestige, which is highly related, will be chosen second because its partial correlation (controlling for income) with the dependent variable will be low—even though it too may be causally important.

Kendall's Coefficient of Concordance, *W*

W is a kind of multiple correlation for *ordinal* data, extending the function of rho and tau (Chapter 10) to more than two variables. The first step in computing W is to present a table of the ranked data such

Table 11.3

N	1	2	3	4	5	6
Riot rank	1	2	3	4	5	6
k Unemployment rank	1	4	3	5	2	6
Wage rank	3	2	1	4	5	6
R_i	5	8	7	13	12	18

$$\Sigma R_i = 63 \qquad \overline{R} = 10.5$$

$$|R_i - \overline{R}| = 5.5 \quad 3.5 \quad 1.5$$
$$2.5 \quad 2.5 \quad 7.5$$

$$(R_i - \overline{R})^2 = 30.25 \quad 12.25 \quad 2.25$$
$$6.25 \quad 6.25 \quad 56.25$$

$$\Sigma (R_i - \overline{R})^2 = 113.5$$

$$W = \frac{\Sigma (R_i - \overline{R})^2}{k^2 (N^3 - N)/12}$$

$$= \frac{113.5}{(3)^2 (6^3 - 6)/12}$$

$$= 113.5/157.5$$
$$= .721$$

as shown in Table 11.3 listing a number of variables (k; 3 in the example) down the side and a number of units (N; 6 in the example) across the top.

If there were perfect association among the variables, then the column sums (R_i) should be $1k$, $2k$, $3k$, . . . , Nk, when the dependent variable (riot rank, listed first) is ranked in order. Note that negatively correlated variables, like wages and rioting (rioting goes up as wages goes down) must be reverse ranked in this procedure. That is, if perfect association held, the first column would have all 1s, the second all 2s, etc., adding in this case to 3, 6, 9, etc. Kendall's W is a measure of the extent to which this happens.

In computing W, the second step is to add up the columns, find the mean column total (equal to $\Sigma R_i/N$), subtract from each column total the mean column total, square these differences and add them up. This gives the numerator.

Third, the denominator is computed by placing the numbers for k (number of variables; note change in meaning) and N (number of units) in the formula and working it through. W is the second step divided by the third step, equal to .721 in this case.

Note that in the case of *ties* average ranks may be used; since ties tend to lower W when they are numerous, an adjustment should be made. The adjustment for a large number of tied ranks is to subtract from the denominator in the formula for W an amount equal to

$$\Sigma \, (t^3 - t) \, / 12$$

In this adjustment, t equals the number of ties at any given value for each row. In the first row, there may be three ties for first place, two ties for fourth place; in the second row, there may be two ties for second place and four ties for fourth place, etc.— $(t^3 - t)/12$ is calculated for 3, 2, 2, 4, . . . ties and summed.

The **significance of** W may be tested by chi-square when N is 8 or higher. In this test, chi-square equals:

$$\chi^2_w = \frac{\Sigma \, (R_i - \overline{R})^2}{kN \, (N - 1) \, / 12} \quad \text{where} \quad \text{d.f.} = N - 1$$

The notation is the same as for the formula for W. If the chi-square value computed by this formula is as large as that in the chi-square table, W is considered significant. When N is 7 or less, a table of critical values of s in the Kendall coefficient of concordance may be consulted, where s is the numerator in the formula for W. If the computed s (113.5 in Table 11.3) is as large as the critical value in the reference table (as it is in the example), then W is considered significant. Also available when N is small is a table of values of the coefficient of concordance significant at various levels, listing how high W must be to be significant at the .05 or .01 levels, for various N and k.

FACTOR ANALYSIS

Given a table of correlations showing the correlation of each variable with every other variable, what is the minimum number of common factors needed to account for all the relationships? Or, more simply, what variables share a common underlying factor with what other variables? These are questions raised in **factor analysis.** The solution to a factor analysis problem yields a table like Table 11.4,

Table 11.4

Variable	Factor 1	Factor 2	Factor 3	Communality (h^2)
1	.1346	.4256	.6879*	.6726
2	.0327	−.7807*	.0717	.6158
3	−.4888	−.2762	.6780*	.7750
4	−.3770	−.2403	.7433*	.7526
5	.0968	.8170*	.0036	.6770
6	−.9416*	−.1128	.2431	.9586
7	−.8993*	−.1514	.2833	.9120
8	−.8202*	.0905	.0447	.6831
9	−.6050*	.5256	−.0486	.6448

* Indicates those variables most heavily loaded on a given factor.

showing for each variable how much it is loaded on each factor (e.g., variable 2 is loaded −.7807 on factor 2), and the proportion of variance in the variable explained by all the factors together (the communalities; e.g., all three factors explain 61.58% of the variance in variable 2). Thus nine variables can be simplified into three underlying factors, a process of simplification that necessarily loses information. Factor 1 is associated with variables 6 to 9, factor 2 is most associated with variables 2 and 5, and factor 3 with variables 1, 3, and 4.

Especially in exploratory studies, the researcher may find it useful to form his hypotheses in terms of these three underlying factors, more simple than using the nine variables directly. The question is, of course, what do the factors represent? This is a crucial problem in factor analysis, since this technique can never tell the researcher what to call the factors. He must infer what they represent from knowledge of which variables are loaded on them. For example, if variables 6 to

9 are education, income, occupational status, and level of political information, he might guess that factor 1 may represent an underlying socio-economic factor. If variables 2 and 5 are support of larger federal role and Americans for Democratic Action ratings, factor 2 might be called a "liberalness" factor. Clearly, this is all very arbitrary, especially since variables may be loaded (like variable 9) on more than one factor. For this reason many social scientists believe factor analysis is best used in an exploratory way.

Factor analysis may be used to reduce the number of variables into a smaller number of underlying factors. The communality, h^2 (similar in meaning to r^2 and R^2), of the dependent variable is sometimes called "factor validity" coefficient and is taken as a measure of validity; it represents the proportion of the variance in the dependent variable explained by all the factors underlying all the variables in the analysis. Factor analysis is sometimes used in causal modelling (discussed in the next chapter) on the assumption that variables grouped together in a model should tend to be loaded on the same underlying factors.

Programming Options in Factor Analysis

Factor analysis is so complex in computation that it is virtually always done by computer, and for this reason the introductory mathematics of factor analysis are not given.[3] Here only a further discussion of the terms used in factor analysis will be presented, with special reference to decisions the researcher must make in selecting which factor analysis computer program to use for his data.

Nature of Analysis

The first decision involves the nature of the analysis being undertaken. Typically the researcher is interested in uncovering a few (2 to 10) factors that underlie several (10 to 50) variables, with data based on many (100 to 1000) people. For example, what are the factors

---

[3] Refer to the readings cited for this chapter, or to the more complete treatment in Harry Harmon's *Modern Factor Analysis* (Chicago: University of Chicago Press, 1960).

that underlie a set of 50 votes by 100 senators? This is known as the **R-technique.** Alternatively, the researcher might be interested in uncovering a few (2 to 10) factors that unite several persons (usually 10 to 50), with data based on many variables. For example, what are the factors uniting factions of Senate Democrats, based on data for at least 100 votes? This is called the **Q-technique,** and will enable identification of subgroups of like senators as measured by the 100 votes.

Thus the *R*-technique is based on the correlation of measures or variables for a population of persons on one occasion. The *Q*-technique is based on the correlation of persons, for a population of measures on one occasion. Two less-used techniques remain: the *P*-technique and the *O*-technique. The **P-technique** is based on the correlation of measures for a population (a number) of occasions for one person. The *P*-technique might be used, for example, to study the changing composition of political indicators as measures over time. The **O-technique** is less common, involving the correlation of occasions for a population of measures for one person. The *O*-technique could be used to group occasions according to the ways they affect performance on a series of political measures or indicators as applied to one senator, for example.

Finally, the *S*-technique and the *T*-technique round out the logical possibilities. The **S-technique** is based on the correlation of persons for a number (population) of occasions on one measure. It addresses itself to a question of the sort, "Which groups of senators are homogeneous over time with regard to a particular measure, as a measure of support for larger federal role?" The **T-technique** involves the correlation of occasions for a population of persons for one measure. It is relevant to a question of the sort, "How may occasions be grouped according to how they, for a particular measure such as support for larger federal role, are associated with different cluster patterns of senators?"

The *R*-technique is by far the most common; *O, P, S,* and *T*-techniques are rarely used in political science, although this disuse is not due to methodological shortcomings. Which technique is used is solely a matter of what the researcher's question is. Whichever is chosen, the first step in factor analysis is to generate a correlation matrix of each variable with every other variable (*R*-technique), each person with every other person (*Q*-technique), or whatever correlation is appropriate. Table 11.5 summarizes the various factor analysis techniques and their uses.

Table 11.5

Technique	Correlation of	For a Population of	Holding Constant
O	occasions	measures	one person
P	measures	occasions	one person
Q	persons	measures	one occasion
R*	measures	persons	one occasion
S	persons	occasions	one measure
T	occasions	persons	one measure

* The *R*-technique is the one most commonly used in political science.

Method of Extracting the Factors

Once the correlation matrix has been constructed, there remains the central question, "By what criteria are the factors to be extracted?" The **cluster method** is the simplest approach, akin to the "freehand method" in regression analysis, in that it does not result in a unique factor solution.

Assuming the *R*-technique[4] with a correlation of variables, the researcher begins with the two variables most correlated with each other and computes their *B* coefficient. *B* equals the ratio of the average of the correlations of each variable within the cluster with every other variable in the cluster $(\overline{G})$, to the average correlation of variables not in the cluster $(\overline{T})$, or $B = \overline{G}/\overline{T}$. The first two variables are assumed to belong to the same factor. A third variable is selected, the one for which the sum of its correlations with each of the two variables already in the cluster is highest. The *B* coefficient is again computed, and if the addition of the third variable does not significantly lower the *B* coefficient, it too is considered to belong to the factor. This process is continued until addition of a variable significantly lowers the *B* coefficient. Then the process is repeated to extract a second factor, using the remaining variables not clustered in the first factor. The process is repeated for a third, fourth, or however many factors may be extracted.

The **centroid method** is more advanced, although it too fails to yield a unique solution for the minimum number of factors that can explain the correlation matrix. It is considered a fair approximation to the more accurate principal-components method discussed below,

---

[4] The *R*-technique is assumed throughout the remainder of the discussion.

and is computationally far easier. One starts with the correlation matrix **(step 1)**, using whatever kind of correlation is appropriate to the nature of the analysis. Here, the R-technique is assumed. **Step 2** is simply to add up the correlations in each column. **Step 3** notes the highest correlation in each column, and in **step 4** this is added to the column sum of correlations. In **step 5,** m is computed, where m is the reciprocal of the square root of the total of the sums computed in step 4. The value m is multiplied by each of the step 4 sums to give the values in **step 6.** These are the loadings of each variable on the first factor. Variable 1, for instance, has an unrotated loading of .37 on the first factor (rotation is discussed below).

In **step 7** the first residual correlation matrix is computed. Computing residuals is based on the fact that a correlation between variable A and variable B equals the factor loading of A on factor 1 times the loading of B on factor 1, plus the loading of A on factor 2 times B's

Table 11.6   Centroid Method

Correlation Matrix

Step	Variable	1	2	3	4	5	
	1	—	.00	.20	.00	.40	
	2	.00	—	.30	.40	.60	
1	3	.20	.30	—	.00	.80	
	4	.00	.40	.00	—	.00	
	5	.40	.60	.80	.00	—	
2	$\Sigma r=$	.60	1.3	1.3	.40	1.8	
3	$r_{\max}=$	.40	.6	.8	.40	.8	
4	$\Sigma r_t=$	1.0	1.9	2.1	.80	1.6	$\Sigma(\Sigma r_t)=7.4$
5				$m=1/\sqrt{\Sigma(\Sigma r_t)}=1/\sqrt{7.4}=.368$				
6	$m\Sigma r_t=$	.37	.70	.77	.29	.59	

		1	2	3	4	5	
	1 (.37)	—	−.26	−.08	−.11	.18	
	2 (.70)	−.26	—	−.24	−.20	−.19	First
7	3 (.77)	−.08	−.24	—	−.22	.35	Unreflected
	4 (.29)	−.11	.20	−.22	—	−.17	Residual
	5 (.59)	.18	.19	.35	−.17	—	Matrix

First Unreflected Residual Matrix

	Variable	1	2*	3	4*	5	
	1	—	−.26	−.08	−.11	.18	
	2*	−.26	—	−.24	.20	.19	
8	3	−.08	−.24	—	−.22	.35	

Table 11.6   *(Continued)*

	4*	$-.11$	.20	$-.22$	—	$-.17$
	5	.18	.19	.35	$-.17$	—
9	$\Sigma r=-.27$	$-.11$	$-.19$	$-.30$	.55	$\Sigma(\Sigma r)=-.32$
10	col. 4 reflected $= -.05$	$-.51$	.25	.30*	.89	
11	col. 2 reflected $= .47$	.51*	.73	.70	.51	

First Reflected Residual Matrix

	Variable	1	2	3	4	5
	1	—	.26	$-.08$	.11	.18
12	2	.26	—	.24	.20	$-.19$
	3	$-.08$	.24	—	.22	.35
	4	.11	.20	.22	—	.17
	5	.18	$-.19$	.35	.17	—
13	$\Sigma r=$	.47	.51	.73	.70	.51
14	$r_{max}=$	.26	.26	.35	.22	.35
15	$r_t=$	.73	.77	1.08	.99	.86 $\Sigma(\Sigma r_t)=4.43$
16	$m=1/\sqrt{\Sigma(\Sigma r_t)}=1/\sqrt{4.43}=.475$					
17	$m\Sigma r_t=$	.35	$-.37$	.51	$-.47$	.41

loading on factor 2, . . . plus the factor loading of A on factor n, times the loading of B on factor n. In step 7, the entries in the first unreflected residual correlation matrix are obtained by multiplying the respective row and column factor loadings and subtracting that result from the original cell entry. For example, the entry in column 1, row 2 is obtained by multiplying the column loading (.37) times the row variable loading (.70), and subtracting the result (.26) from the original entry (.00), giving a residual loading of $-.26$.

Step 8 is simply to recopy these unreflected residual entries onto a new table. **Step 9** (as in step 2) is to add up the column residual correlations. If any of the sums in step 9 are negative, which is usually the case, it is necessary to *reflect* the residual matrix. If all are positive, the researcher can skip to step 14. *Reflection* is begun in **step 10** by taking the largest negative sum in step 9 ($-.30$, in column 4) and entering it as a positive value under the line for step 10. An asterisk is placed beside that column and row number to indicate its reflection. The other entries in step 10 are derived by doubling that row's entry for each column, changing its sign and adding it to the column sum computed in step 9. For example, the reflected value for the first column equals the unreflected residual entry ($-.11$), doubled

$(-.22)$, with its sign changed $(.22)$, and added to the sum computed in step 9 $[.22 + (-.27) = -.05]$.

If any of the final entries in step 10 are negative, the process is repeated. **Step 11** is such a repetition, done for the highest negative value in step 10, namely the $-.51$ entry in column 2. Performed exactly as in step 10, this step results in sums that are all positive. Sometimes many repetitions are necessary, even requiring reflection of a column more than one time. Note that the one exception in repetitions of step 10 is that signs are *not* reversed before adding the doubled value for entries in columns that have previously been reflected once (or three or any odd number of times). In step 11, for example, the .20 entry in the second row, fourth column is left positive after it is doubled; it is then added to the .30 sum in step 10, to give a step 11 entry of .70.

Step 12 is to copy the first reflected residual correlation matrix. In absolute terms, the reflected matrix has exactly the same entries as the unreflected matrix. The difference is that it has different signs. The signs in the unreflected matrix (step 8) are reversed *if* they

1. Are in rows that have been reflected (and have an asterisk) but in columns that have *not* been reflected (and therefore do not have an asterisk),
2. Or, vice versa, are in reflected columns but not in reflected rows.

Steps 13 through **16** repeat steps 2 through 5, this time using the reflected residual matrix instead of the original correlation matrix. **Step 17** repeats step 6, giving the absolute values of the factor loadings of each variable on the *second* factor. The sign given each of these loadings depends on the number of times the variable column has been reflected:

1. If it was reflected once or an odd number of times, its sign is the reverse of its sign in the previous factor.
2. If it was not reflected or was reflected an even number of times, its sign remains the same as in the previous factor.

Further steps may be undertaken in a similar fashion to compute the second unreflected residual matrix, reflect it, and get the factor loadings for the third factor, and so on. The **communality,** h^2, for each variable equals the sum of the squared loadings of that variable on all the factors.

The **principle-components** or **principle-factor method** is more complicated than the centroid method, but is used in most computer programs for factor analysis because it gives a unique least-squares solution. That is, the principle-components (also called principle-axes) method first extracts the factor that accounts for the greatest variance, then extracts the factor accounting for the second greatest variance, and so on. The centroid method may well give more factors than are necessary to account for a given percentage of the variance. Several other methods of extracting factors are available, but these are rarely used in political science.

Number of Factors to Extract

In the discussion of the centroid method it was mentioned that further steps (actually repetitions of previous steps) might be taken to compute a third, fourth, or indefinite number of sets of factor loadings. The decision of how many factors to extract is arbitrary, depending on the researcher's particular needs, but several criteria might be mentioned.

A rule of thumb for most social science data is that factors extracted after the third are unlikely to account for much additional variance. **Tucker's phi** criterion is based on the significance of the decrease in the cell entries of reflected residual matrices.[5] Using the notation given in the centroid method example, phi is $\Sigma(\Sigma r_i)$ for the $(n+1)$th reflected residual matrix divided by the corresponding statistic for the nth residual matrix; if this phi coefficient is larger than $(N-1)/(N+1)$, where N is the number of variables, then there are at least n significant factors.

Coomb's Criterion is applicable only where the original correlation matrix contains no negative entries significantly different from zero. When the number of negative entries remaining in a residual table after reflection is not significantly different from the corresponding value in a table of critical values of Coomb's criterion, then enough factors have been extracted.

Humphrey's Rule is based on the significance of correlation. The factor is considered not significant unless the product of the two highest factor loadings exceeds two standard errors of a zero correla-

[5] Note that entries on the third matrix tend to be smaller than those on the second, those on the fourth smaller than those on the third, etc.

tion coefficient. Finally, most computer programs allow the reseacher to have computation stopped after the xth factor has been extracted, or when the last factor contributes less than x^2 to h^2, where the researcher specifies x according to his particular research needs.

Method of Rotation

If the research is dealing with n (say 5) variables, then one could conceive of data represented as points in n-dimensional (e.g., 5-dimensional) space. The factors may be thought of as vectors through these points, similar to the way a regression line is drawn through a scatter diagram. Factor loadings describe the location of these vectors with respect to reference axes, axes of an n-dimensional space. These axes are arbitrarily located according to which method is used to extract the factors. The meaning of all this is simply that the factor loadings will not be understandable to the researcher *until* the original axes are rotated about the origin to a new position. This new position depends on research needs.

The mathematics of factor rotation is beyond the scope of an introductory work, but a few terms may be set forth. First, the researcher may decide whether he wants orthogonal or oblique rotation. *Orthogonal rotation* has the advantage that it leaves each of the reference axes perpendicular (orthogonal) to one another, making each of the factors independent of one another. Thus the researcher can be sure that each factor underlying a set of variables is a completely different factor. *Oblique rotation* does not necessarily leave the axes perpendicular, and hence the factors are unlikely to be mutually independent. It has the advantage, however, that the factors can account for more of the variance.

If orthogonal rotation is selected, the **varimax method** is usually used. This method rotates the reference axes so as to maximize the variance of each factor, so that each factor is identified with certain variables and not with others; in other words, each variable will *tend* to load heavily on only one factor. The varimax method has the advantage that the factors will be more easily labelled than with other methods, since it will be more clear what variables are associated with which factors. The **quartimax method** maximizes the variance of the squared factor loadings, so that factors tend to be general for the same variables, the advantage being that larger factor loadings are maximized and small loadings minimized. Some computer programs exist to give a **biquartimax solution,** which gives equal weight to the varimax and quartimax criteria. Or the researcher may use **orthomax-c,** where *c* varies from zero to one and the researcher may specify the exact proportion of weighting to be given to either criterion (e.g., $c = .34$ would indicate a 34:66 weighting of quartimax to varimax criteria).

If the rotation chosen is oblique, analogous methods exist. The **oblimax method** maximizes the kurtosis[6] of a function of the frequency distribution of rotated factor loadings, with the result that each variable will tend to be heavily loaded on one factor and have low loadings on other factors. The **quartimax-oblique method** minimizes the sum of the cross-products of the squared factor loadings and has the advantages of the quartimax method for orthogonal rotations.

CONCLUSION

To repeat a point made before: a technique is sophisticated only if it is appropriate to the researcher's needs and data resources. Factor analysis in particular is subject to misuse, requiring as it does metric (interval) data. Consistency of factor analytic results is improved if the data are normalized, although this is not necessary. The assumptions behind the correlation matrix on which factor analysis is built should be met, notably linearity and homoscedascity of relationship. Pearsonian product-moment correlation is typically used on normally distributed metric data gathered by enumeration of random sample, although other product-moment correlation statistics may be used instead. Biserial or rank-difference correlations may be used as estimates of product-moment coefficients, if necessary. The phi coefficient should not be used, nor should different types of coefficients be mixed in a single correlation matrix. Because of this last restriction, dichotomous variables should not be mixed with continuous variables, and there is thus a limitation on the types of variables that can be placed together in factor analysis. On the other hand, it is unclear just how much conclusions are likely to be in error if these

[6] Kurtosis is a measure of the peakedness of a distribution. Technically, it is the ratio of half the distance between the .25 and .75 marks in a distribution, to the distance between the .10 and .90 marks. Thus, $K = .5 (Q_3 - Q_1) / P_{90} - P_{10}$.

and other restrictions mentioned earlier are not met. Many political scientists prefer to restrict factor analysis to the exploratory stages of investigation. Here again, the beginning political researcher may well find it advantageous to approach the same subject from several differing approaches and techniques.

12

Causal Modelling

The basic concept of making causal inferences from correlation and partial correlation statistics is presented in Chapters 2 and 3 of Hubert M. Blalock, Jr., *Causal Inferences in Nonexperimental Research* (University of North Carolina paperback, 1967). This may be followed by consulting "Theory Building and Causal Inferences," also by Blalock, in H. M. and A. B. Blalock, eds., *Methodology in Social Research* (McGraw-Hill, 1968), Chapter 5. The best presentation of path analysis, the one followed closely here, is "Principles of Path Analysis" by Kenneth C. Land, Chapter 1 in Borgatta, *Sociological Methodology 1969* mentioned in Chapter 11.

In the same volume David Heise discusses "Problems of Path Analysis and Causal Inference" and Otis Dudley Duncan treats specific examples in "Contingencies in Constructing Causal Models." The Blalock method of causal modelling is illustrated by Arthur Goldberg's article, "Discerning a Causal Pattern Among Data on Voting Behavior" in the December, 1966 issue of the *American Political Science Review.* Path analysis is illustrated in Hayward Alker's treatment of the Lerner and other theories of modernization in "Causal Inference and Political Analysis" (Arnold Foundation reprints, 1966; originally in *Mathematical Applications in Political Science, II).*

In *Methodology in Social Research* listed in the readings, Hubert Blalock has an opening chapter titled "The Measurement Problem: The Gap Between the Languages of Theory and Research." The heart of the problem of using statistical techniques in political science is precisely that unfortunate discontinuity which exists between data and theories that are built on the data.

The general problem is, "How can we tell when the data we have gathered are consistent with our hypothesized image of the manner in which what we are investigating is caused?" We have already discussed use of tables, measures of association, and other quantitative ways of attacking this question; this chapter presents the most recent methods now being developed to answer the question. Often, however, the student will find his data do not warrant the use of these "sophisticated" techniques.

When the term "cause" is used, the student should be aware that the political scientist does not, when he is using statistics, necessarily use the term in its day-to-day sense. The phrase "*X* causes *Y*" is often a shorthand substitute for the phrase "The variation in *X* can be used to explain the variation in *Y*, even when other factors are taken into account." Usually such statements are expressed in probabilistic terms, and the difference between explaining the variation and understanding the causation is great.

In the case of interpreting rioting, for example, the "real" causes no doubt involve factors going back even to man's biological makeup. While it may be true that an "instinct toward aggression" may be one of the underlying causes of rioting, obviously such a relatively constant variable cannot be used to predict (explain) the variation in frequency of rioting. In explaining the variation in any phenomenon, statistical techniques—including partial correlation and path analysis —look to those causes or factors that vary with what is being studied, even though many other less variable causes may be involved in very important ways.

CAUSAL ANALYSIS USING CORRELATION COEFFICIENTS

Both correlation and partial correlation statistics are commonly used to check the validity of hypothesized models of reality. This sort of causal modelling is appropriate when:

1. The causal arrows in the model are unidirectional, and
2. The model is recursive (i.e., when none of the endogenous variables can be both a cause and an effect of another endogenous variable).

For example, in the model below, causation is unidirectional and recursive:

Figure 12.1

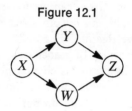

All the arrows go only one way and each of the variables can be expressed in terms of themselves as follows:

$$X = e_x \qquad (e_x = \text{error factor associated with } x)$$

$$Y = b_{yx}Y + e_y$$

$$W = b_{wx.y}W + 0Y + e_w$$

$$Z = 0X + b_{zy.xw} + b_{zw.xy} + e_z$$

This is a set of recursive regression equations for the model in Figure 12.1, where the es represent error factors and the bs represent ordinary regression coefficients or partial regression coefficients.

Furthermore, by use of partial correlation coefficients, it is possible to check the data against this model. For example, since the model (1) assumes that the whole effect of X on Z operates through Y and W, and since we assume (2) that the error factors (and other exogenous factors) associated with W, X, Y, and Z are statistically independent, then if Y and W are held constant, the correlation of X with Z should drop to zero. That is,

$$r_{xz.yw} = 0$$

In the Arthur Goldberg article in the readings, a more complex model involving additional partial correlation tests is developed to explain the variation in presidential vote choice. The six variables involved, partial correlation predictions, and actual partial correlations are given in Table 12.1.

Table 12.1

Variables

1—*FSC*—Father's Sociological Traits
2—*FPI*—Father's Party Identification
3—*RSC*—Respondent's Sociological Traits
4—*RPI*—Respondent's Party Identification
5—*RPA*—Respondent's Partisan Attitudes
6—*RV*—Respondent's Presidential Vote

Predicted Results	Actual Results
$r_{41.23} = 0$	.017
$r_{32.1} = 0$	.101
$r_{43.12} = 0$	.130
$r_{64.1235} = 0$	.365
$r_{62.1345} = 0$	−.022

Model

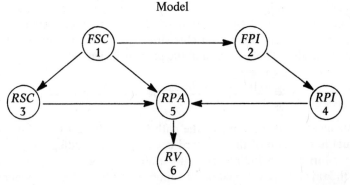

Source: Arthur S. Goldberg, "Discerning a Causal Pattern Among Data on Voting Behavior," *American Political Science Review* (December 1966), Fig. 1, by permission of the publisher.

Note that the problem mentioned earlier, that of attempting to control for more than two variables through partial correlation, is a problem that appears here. For that reason, the tests which are most interesting, those involving the dependent variable (presidential vote choice), are the least reliable.

Beyond this, however, how much of a residual—actual results deviating from the predicted zero level—is permissible in a "good" model? There is no real answer to this question, although with political science data residuals at the .100 level or less are ordinarily considered acceptable. As with so many other statistics, however, a more fruitful way of evaluating the residuals to a particular model is by comparing them with the residuals resulting from another model of the same variables and same data. That is, the researcher should attempt to compute residuals to several different recursive causal arrangements of his variables and then look to see which arrangement results in the lowest residuals; that model is ordinarily the one most supported by the data.[1]

CAUSAL ANALYSIS USING PATH COEFFICIENTS

Path analysis uses coefficients that measure the amount of variation in a particular dependent variable *directly* attributable to another variable. With correlation coefficients, indirect effect of one variable with another is included, whereas with path coefficients the indirect effects of all other variables are controlled for. That is, the path coefficient measures the fraction of the standard deviation of the endogenous (dependent) variable directly attributable to the designated variable. The definition of the path coefficient is

$$p_{ij} = \frac{\sigma_{i.12 \ldots (j-1)(j+1) \ldots na}}{\sigma_i} \times \frac{\sigma_j}{\sigma_{j.12 \ldots (i-1)(i+1) \ldots}}$$

This means that the value of the path from variable j to variable i is equal to the ratio of the standard deviation in i, holding constant all other variables including residual variable a and excepting variable j, to the raw standard deviation of i times the ratio of the raw standard deviation in j to the standard deviation in j, holding constant all variables except i.

Another term used in path analysis is the "path regression coefficient," which is the unstandardized form of the path coefficient:

[1] Refer to the Goldberg article to see how he uses some of the high residuals to his first model as criteria for formulating other superior models to explain presidential vote choice.

$$c_{ij} = p_{ij}\left(\frac{\sigma_i}{\sigma_j}\right)$$

The general procedure in path analysis is to

1. Draw a recursive model of the phenomenon using variables for which appropriate data are available.
2. Specify the equations that describe the causal system in the model.
3. Derive values for the path coefficients by solution of these multiple equations.

Finally, of course, the path coefficients are used to aid the testing of models and the construction of theories.

Drawing a Recursive Model

Let us start with a simple 3-variable model, the hypothesis that two independent variables, economic reversal (X_1) and intensity of social movement activity (X_2), cause the variation in the dependent variable, frequency of rioting (X_3). Assume that we have already gotten beyond the problems, formidable in themselves, of defining these terms and gathering valid measurements. Then our model would look like this, where X_a is a residual factor that includes the error factor:

Figure 12.2

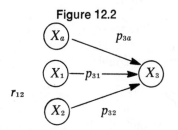

Note that we assume the residual factor is uncorrelated with the independent variables. Given this sort of model, we can now express each of the relationships in equation form.

Specifying Path Estimation Equations

First we can write the equation which says that the dependent variable is a function of the paths from the independent variables and the residual variable:[2]

$$Z_3 = p_{3a}Z_a + p_{31}Z_1 + p_{32}Z_2$$

Then we can write the equations which show that the correlations of the independent variables with the dependent variable are a function of the paths between a given independent variable and the dependent variable, plus the path between one independent variable and another:

$$r_{31} = p_{31} + p_{32}r_{12}$$

$$r_{32} = p_{32} + p_{31}r_{12}$$

Of course, all correlations can be computed quantitatively from the observed data, so we know these values from the start. The last equations to be written involve the dependent variable and the residual variable:

$$r_{33} = 1 = p_{31}r_{31} + p_{32}r_{32} + p_{3a}^2$$

$$p_{3a} = 1 - (p_{31}r_{31} + p_{32}r_{32}) = 1 - R^2$$

$$p_{3a} = 1 - R^2$$

R^2, of course, is the coefficient of multiple correlation, discussed in an earlier chapter. That is, it is the coefficient of the combined correlation of the independent variables (X_1 and X_2) with the dependent variable (X_3).

Before continuing to the third step, it should be pointed out that a parallel set of equations involving regression coefficients and path regression coefficients could also be written for the same model:

$$b_{31} = c_{31} + c_{32}b_{21}$$

$$b_{32} = c_{32} + c_{31}b_{12}$$

[2] The X variables are expressed in their standardized Z form.

Deriving Values of the Path Coefficients

We are now in a position to solve the path estimation equations for p_{ij} by any of the standard algebraic means. This solution, clearly outlined in the Kenneth Land reading, is as follows for the case of p_{31}.

Start with the equation:

$$r_{31} = p_{31} + p_{32}r_{12}$$

Transform to place p_{31} to the left of the equal sign:

$$p_{31} = r_{31} - p_{32}r_{12}$$

and by the same process,

$$p_{32} = r_{32} - p_{31}r_{12}$$

By substituting for p_{32} in the equation for p_{31} we get:

$$p_{31} = r_{31} - (r_{32} - p_{31}r_{12})\, r_{12}$$

$$= r_{31} - r_{32}r_{12} + p_{31}r_{12}r_{12}$$

Subtract $p_{31}r_{12}^2$ from both sides of the equation:

$$p_{31}(1 - r_{12}^2) = r_{31} - r_{32}r_{12}$$

Then solve for p_{31} by dividing each side by $(1 - r_{12}^2)$:

$$p_{31} = \frac{r_{31} - r_{32}r_{12}}{1 - r_{12}^2}$$

By the same process the path regression coefficient, c_{ij}, can be computed in terms of standard regression coefficient, b_{ji}.

Determining Direct and Indirect Effects

Path coefficients are extremely useful in interpreting the meaning of correlation coefficients. In our hypothetical example, recall that X_1 was economic reversal (ER), X_2 was intensity of social movement action *(SM)*, and the dependent variable X_3 was frequency of rioting *(FR)*.

Also recall from the path estimation equations that

$$r_{31} = p_{31} + r_{12}p_{32}$$

That is, the correlation between rioting *(FR)* and economic reversal *(ER)* can be quantitatively divided into two parts, the first (p_{31}) representing *direct* effect of *ER* on *FR*, and the second $(r_{12}p_{32})$ representing the *indirect* effects of *ER* on *FR* due to *ER*'s relation to other independent variables—in this case, to *SM*.

Or to put it another way, the total indirect effect (TIE) of *ER* on *FR* is equal to

$$r_{12}p_{32} = TIE \text{ of } 1 \text{ on } 3 = r_{31} - p_{31}^{\cdot}$$

Note also that p_{3a} represents the proportion of the standard deviation in the dependent variable and p_{3a}^2 represents the proportion of the variance in the dependent variable attributable to all causes including error other than the independent variables:

$$p_{3a}^2 = \text{unexplained variance} = 1 - R^2$$

In fact, since there is unexplained variance (including error variance) in the independent variables as well as the dependent variables, our model should have looked like this:

Figure 12.3

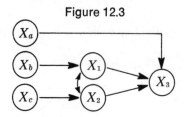

The paths from X_b to X_1 and from X_c *to* X_2 are computed the same as for that from X_a to X_3:

$$p_{3a} = \sqrt{1 - R^2} \qquad \text{where } R \text{ is } X_1 + X_2 \text{ on } X_3$$

$$p_{1b} = \sqrt{1 - R^2} \qquad \text{where } R \text{ is } X_2 + X_3 \text{ on } X_1$$

$$p_{2c} = \sqrt{1 - R^2} \qquad \text{where } R \text{ is } X_1 + X_3 \text{ on } X_2$$

In a complete path analysis diagram, every endogenous factor will have a residual term (p with a letter subscript).

Assumptions Involved in Path Analysis

The researcher, of course, starts with his data in standardized score (Z) form. He must assume that his data are interval data. For example, if his analysis deals with a score representing negative attitudes created by riots, where one person scored 80 and another 40, that is assumed to mean that the first person is twice as negative as the second—in just the same way that 80 riots is twice as many as 40 riots. Dichotomies can be used (male-female, white-nonwhite), but they are assumed to be real dichotomies, not arbitrary divisions of underlying continua. Land, Labovitz, and other social scientists have argued, however, that the treating of near-interval social science data as if they were interval does not ordinarily lead to significant errors.

The second assumption is that relationships among variables are homoscedascic, linear, and additive. The researcher should draw scatter diagrams of his variables to visually assess the linearity of his data. Sometimes nonlinear data can be transformed to linear form, as by applying logarithms to both sides of the equation.

Third, results will vary according to the causal assumptions. The model assumes that causation flows in the direction implied by the arrows. It also assumes that the causation occurs at one point in time, or at several points if a multistage model, as discussed by Land, is specified. That is, the path coefficients cannot be used to prove whether the causal priorities hypothesized are "true" or not; they can only be used to aid further research, as by determining the path implications of two alternative causal arrangements of the variables.

Fourth, and implied in the third, is that all system inputs must be clearly presented and differentiated from the dependent variable. In addition, the causal priorities of the independent variables must be specified. No reciprocal relations or feedback loops between variables are allowed.

Fifth, perhaps most important, the residual terms (in the example, those with letter subscripts) are assumed in each case to be uncorrelated with any of the other determining variables in the equation. Moreover, the residuals must be uncorrelated with one another, have mean values of zero, and be normally distributed.

Testing the Significance of Path Coefficients

As with testing the significance of correlation coefficients, the F and t tests are used. Recall also that if a large sample is involved, a statistic may be significant but nevertheless be so low that it is not strong or particularly important. The fact that the F and t tests are "parametric" (i.e., involve assumptions about the distribution of the variables) is the reason why the residuals must be assumed to be normally distributed.[3]

The formula for testing the path coefficient p_{ij} would be:

$$F = \frac{p_{ij}^2 \, (n-2)}{1 - p_{ij}^2}$$

In this formula p_{ji} represents the standard correlation coefficient between j and i, while n represents the number of observations made on i and j. One then takes this value of F, computes the two associated degrees of freedom

$$d.f._{.1} = 1 \qquad\qquad d.f._{.2} = n-2,$$

and consults a table of critical deviations of F for the .05 level and .01 level, or whatever level the researcher deems adequate. In consulting such a table he will see, for example, that at the .05 level for $n = 62$, F must be 4.00 or higher to consider the path coefficient significant ($p_{ij} = .25$ or higher would be significant in this case). For small samples, a t test would be used instead of an F test.

Using Tests of Significance in Model-building

Paths that are not statistically significant may, after an examination of the implications, be dropped from the model. That is, the F test can serve as a criterion for improving causal models if used in conjunction with path analysis. Since path coefficients measure only the *direct* contribution of one variable to another, this is preferable to

---

[3] These tests, along with F and t tables, are presented in any standard statistics text, such as Theodore Anderson and Morris Zelditch, *A Basic Course in Statistics with Sociological Applications,* Second Edition (New York: Holt, Rinehart and Winston, 1968).

the earlier method of deleting causal arrows in a model when the correlation between the variables was statistically insignificant.

Example: Unemployment, Real Wages, and Rioting

The data in this example are taken from a study of American labor disturbances between 1927 and 1963. For simplicity, only three variables will be considered: annual frequency of rioting (*RIOT*), the unemployment rate (*UEMP*), and adjusted weekly wages in 1947–49 dollars (*AWWG*). By methods discussed in the previous section on correlation, the following product-moment correlation matrix was generated:

Table 12.2

Variable	1 *UEMP*	2 *AWWG*	3 *RIOT*
UEMP	1.000	−.651	.768
AWWG		1.000	−.662
RIOT			1.000

The multiple correlation R of *UEMP* and *AWWG* with *RIOT* was .797

These correlation coefficients are all significant above the .01 level.

As a first step, a hypothetical causal diagram is drawn with the correlation coefficients written in:

Figure 12.4

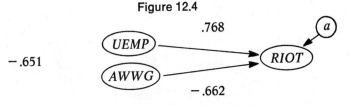

If any of the correlation coefficients between variables linked in this causal diagram were not statistically significant, of course, the researcher would ordinarily rethink his model to adjust for this.

Step 2 is to specify the path estimation equations. These equations are the same as those worked earlier in this chapter, where it was shown that

$$p_{31} = \frac{r_{31} - r_{32}r_{12}}{1 - r_{12}^2}$$

By substituting the values of r derived from the data, we get:

$$p_{31} = \frac{.768 - (-.662)(-.651)}{1 - (-.651)^2} = \frac{.337}{.576} = .585$$

One of the path estimation equations derived previously was:

$$r_{32} = p_{32} + p_{31}r_{12}$$

By subtracting $p_{31}r_{12}$ from each side we obtain the formula for p_{32}:

$$p_{32} = r_{32} - p_{31}r_{12}$$

Since we already know the value of p_{31} we can substitute the values:

$$p_{32} = -.662 - (.585)(-.651) = -.281$$

The last path, p_{3a}, is the root of 1 minus the multiple correlation, discussed on page 000.

$$p_{3a} = \sqrt{1 - R^2} = \sqrt{1 - (.796)^2} = .604$$

At this point the casual model may be redrawn, writing in the path coefficients, after checking their significance on an F table:

Figure 12.5

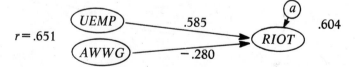

The last step involves *using path coefficients to partition the variance of the dependent variable:* this is possible because the correlation of the dependent variable with itself can be expressed as a function of path coefficients:

$$r_{33} = 1 = p_{31}r_{31} + p_{32}r_{32} + p_{3a}^2$$

By substituting the values derived above, we get:

$$r_{33} = (.585)\,(.768) + (-.280)\,(-.662) + (.604)^2$$

$$= .449 + .185 + .365$$

$$\cong 1.00$$

Thus we can conclude that the path from unemployment to riot frequency accounted for .449 of the variance in rioting, changes in real wages accounted for another .185, and other factors not specified in the causal model, including error, accounted for the remaining .365 of the variation, assuming causality actually flowed in the direction indicated by the arrows.

In the end, the quantitative techniques, from crosstables through path analysis, can only serve to reject causal hypotheses, not accept them. Path analysis, or any other technique, can only tell the researcher if the data are consistent with his hypothesis. The data in this example, for instance, are consistent with the hypothesis that economic factors such as employment and real wage rates are main causes of labor rioting. But we have not proved that they are causes, only that the data does not disprove the hypothesis. Unfortunately, that is all that may ever be done—and it is an important reason why the same subject must be approached from a number of different techniques and approaches before a final explanation is attempted. How to accomplish this synthesis with elegance is the task of more advanced texts in political science methodology.

Appendix A

Examples of Computer Routines for Political Science Applications

Every computer is different, and most university computer centers will have their own "prepackaged" programs for social science data. In using these programs, the researcher needs to understand only a minimum of programming. In fact, these are sometimes called "cookbook" programs, since it is only necessary to follow the directions! To give an idea of how these easy-to-use prepackaged programs work, three are presented here, each designed for IBM's smallest computer, the 1130. Larger computers can do more, of course, but the principles involved are the same.

1. A Program for Crosstabulation and Chi-square

This program[1] is designed to construct up to 200 *r*-by-*c* tables, using up to 400 variables and an unlimited number of respondents, where the variables range from 0 to 9 in integers. Thus, if there are three levels of incomes and 5 levels of political attitudes, the program would print a 3-by-5 table, giving also the chi-square significance for the table.

Step 1. Starting in column 1 of an IBM card, type up a "job card":

---

[1] The program for crosstabulation was written by Karl Deirup.

// JOB T

This card tells the computer your job is starting; if desired, or if your computer center requires it, you can also place your identification number (usually starting in column 51) and name (usually starting in column 63) on this card. The computer will then print these at the top of each page of the print-out.

Step 2. After the job card comes a stack of program cards. This is the "prepackaged" part. As an illustration, these program cards are listed here, with a brief description of how the program works.

```
// FOR
*IOCS(CARD,1132PRINTER,DISK)
* ONE WORD INTEGERS
      DEFINE FILE 1 (20000, 1, U, NEXT)
      DIMENSION ISCOR(400),ANAME(400,2)KRT1(200),KRT2(200),
     1NROW(200),NCOL(200),INTRY(10,10),MARGR(10),MARGC(10),
     2CLMPC(10),RWMPC(10),PERCN(10,10)
```

(This part of the program sets aside space for 200 10-by-10 tables, 400 variables, and other space needed.)

```
    1 DO 10 I = 1, 400
   10 ISCOR (I) = 0
      DO 11 I = 1, 2000, 400
   11 WRITE (1'I) (ISCOR(J), J = 1, 400)
```

(These cards set the spaces set aside for tables and variables equal to zero to begin with.)

```
      READ (2, 101) NV, NCT, NDATA, ((ANAME(I,J), J= 1,2),
     I = 1, NV)
  101 FORMAT (I3,11X,I3,11X,I5/ (26A3,2X))
```

(These direct the computer to read the first control card, discussed in step 3, plus name cards discussed in step 4.)

```
      WRITE (3,102) ((ANAME(I,J),J=1,2), I = 1,NV)
  102 FORMAT (1H1,2A3,14(1X,2A3)/15X,15(1X,2A3)
```

(Computer is instructed to write variable names, for automatic listing of the first ten data cards.)

```
      READ (2, 103) (KRT1(I), KRT2(I) NROW(I), NCOL(I), I = 1, NCT)
  103 FORMAT (5(I3, 2X, I3, 1X, I2, 2X, I2, 1X))
```

(Computer reads the crosstab control cards discussed in step 5.)

```
      DO 12 J = 1, NDATA
      READ (2,104) (ISCOR(I), I = 1, NV)
  104 FORMAT (70I1,10X)
```

```
      WRITE (3,105)(ISCOR(I), I = 1, NV)
105 FORMAT (/(15I7),15X)
      DO 12 I = 1, NCT
      IJK1 = KRT1(I)
      IJK2 = KRT2(I)
      M1 = 100*(I−1) & 10*(ISCOR(IJK1)) & ISCOR(IJK2) & 1
      READ (1'M1) M2
      M2 = M2 & 1
  12 WRITE (1'M1) M2
```

(These cards are a "DO loop" repeated once for each respondent and resulting in calculation of the entries in each cell. The first two cards after the initial DO 12 card enable the computer to read the data cards discussed in step 6. The next two cards provide for printing out data cards, and the remaining cards are a secondary DO loop within the main DO loop and are repeated once per table.)

```
      JPGCH = 0
      DO 24 I = 1, NCT
      IJK1 = KRT1(I)
      IJK2 = KRT2(I)
      JPGCH = JPGCH − (17&3*NROW(I))
      IF (JPGCH) 14,13,13
  13 WRITE (3,106)(ANAME(IJK1,K),K=1,2),IJK1,(ANAME(IJK2,K),K=1,2),
      1IJK2
106 FORMAT (//////1X,2A3,' IS ROWS (',I3,1H),3X,2A3,' IS COLUMNS
      1(',I3,',')')
      GO TO 15
  14 JPGCH = 57 − (11&3*NROW(I))
      WRITE (3,107)(ANAME(IJK1,K),K=1,2),IJK1,(ANAME(IJK2,K),K=1,2),
      1IJK2
107 FORMAT (1H1,2A3,' IS ROWS (',I3,')',3X,2A3,' IS COLUMNS
      1(',I3,')')
```

(This part of the program provides for centering tables on print-out pages and for writing the heading of each table.)

```
  15 IR = NROW(I)
      IC = NCOL(I)
      DO 16 KR = 1,IR
      DO 16 KC = 1,IC
      M3 = 100*(I−1) & 10*(KR−1) & KC
  16 READ (1'M3) INTRY(KR,KC)
      ISUMC = 0
      DO 20 KC = 1,IC
      MARGC(KC)= 0
      DO 19 KR = 1,IR
  19 MARGC(KC) = MARGC(KC) & INTRY(KR,KC)
  20 ISUMC = ISUMC & MARGC(KC)
      DO 27 KC = 1, IC
```

```
 27 CLMPC(KC) = MARGC(KC)*100.0/ISUMC
    ISUMR = 0
    DO 18 KR = 1,IR
    MARGR(KR) = 0
    DO 17 KC = 1,IC
    PERCN(KR,KC) = INTRY(KR,KC)*100.0/MARGC(KC)
 17 MARGR(KR) = MARGR(KR) & INTRY(KR,KC)
    RWMPC(KR) = MARGR(KR)*100.0/ISUMR
 18 ISUMR = ISUMR & MARGR(KR)
```

(These DO loops read out all the cell entries for a table, calculate the column and row marginals, cell entries as a percent of column totals, and marginal totals as a percent of *N*.)

```
    SUMR = ISUMR
    CHISQ = 0
    DO 21 KR = 1,IR
    DO 21 KC = 1,IC
    EXPF = MARGR(KR) * MARGC(KC) / SUMR
 21 CHISQ = CHISQ & (INTRY(KR,KC)-EXPF)**2/EXPF
```

(This section of the program calculates the chi-square value for each table.)

```
     ICL = IC - 1
     WRITE (3,108)(KC, KC = 1, ICL)
 108 FORMAT (/12X,'0',9I10)
     DO 22 KR = 1,IR
     KRL = KR - 1
     WRITE (3,109) KRL, (INTRY(KR,KC,)KC = 1,IC),MARGR(KR)
 109 FORMAT (/1X,I3,11I10)
  22 WRITE (3,112) (PERCN(KR,KC),KC=1,IC), RWMPC(KR)
 112 FORMAT (9X,11(F6.1'PCT'))
     WRITE (3,110) (MARGC(KC), KC = 1,IC),ISUMR
 110 FORMAT (//4X,11I10)
     WRITE (3,113) (CLMPC(KC),KC=1,IC)
 113 FORMAT (9X,10(F6.1,'PCT'))
     IDF = (NROW(I)-1) * (NCOL(I)-1)
     WRITE (3,114) IDF
 114 FORMAT ('0',I3,' DEGREES OF FREEDOM')
     IF (ISMR-ISUMC) 23,24,23
  23 WRITE (3,111) ISUMR,ISUMC
 111 FORMAT ('ERROR ** SUM OF ROW MARGINALS =',I5,', SUM OF
    1COLUMN MARGINALS =',I5)
  24 WRITE (3,115) CHISQ
 115 FORMAT ('0CHI SQUARE =',F9.3)
     CALL EXIT
     END
// XEQ
```

(These cards provide for all the information to be printed out in table form, along with variable names, percentages, marginals, chi-square value and number of degrees of freedom.)

Step 3. Now comes the "cookbook" part, telling the computer just what is wanted through "control cards." The first control card, immediately after the // XEQ card, tells the computer how many variables are on the data cards (cols. 1–3), how many tables are to be computed (cols. 15–17), and the number of respondents or units of data (cols. 29–33). For example:

015 VARIABLES 007 CROSSTABS 00125 UNITS OF DATA

Step 4. Next the variable names are listed, using six letters per variable name and a maximum of thirteen names per card, and using as many cards as are needed up to a maximum of 400 variable names. If no names are needed, just put in the appropriate number of blank IBM cards, the same number as if names were used. For example:

VAR001VAR002VAR003VAR004VAR005VAR006VAR007VAR008VAR009VAR010

Step 5. The next control cards tell the computer which two variables are to be tabled in each table. The computer is told the number of the variable that is to be the row variable in the table (cols. 1–3), the number of the column variable (cols. 6–8), the number of rows to be in the table (cols. 10–11) and the number of columns (cols. 14–15). This sequence may be repeated to give instructions for 5 tables per card, using as many cards as are necessary for up to 200 tables. For example, to crosstabulate variable 1 by variable 2 in a 3-by-6 table, and to tabulate variable 6 by variable 5 in a 10-by-2 table:

001BY002(03BY06)006BY005(10BY02)

Step 6. After these control cards, the researcher then enters his data cards, where the variables range from 0 to 9 and are listed from column 1 to column 70, using as many data cards per respondent as are necessary. Columns 71–80 are reserved for a card identification number, if desired. (If the data are differently arranged, FORMAT 104 in the program may be changed.) Finally, some machines require a blank card at the end of the data. Providing the data cards, filling out a few control cards and a job card, and adding on the prepackaged program is all there is to it.

2.   A Program for Stepwise Linear Regression

IBM supplies "prepackaged" statistical programs, relatively easy to use even by those unfamiliar with programming. The IBM regression program for the 1130 can handle up to 30 variables, far more than used in most political science applications.

Step 1.   The job card, the same as in crosstabulation.

Step 2.   The prepackaged program, stored on a computer disk. This program is "called out" by copying the next two cards:

```
// XEQ REGR        01
*LOCALREGR,FMTRD,PRNTB,DATRD,MXRAD,TRAN
```

(This call-out routine comes in different versions, so the user must check with his computer center for the prepackaged programs in use there.)

Step 3.   An input-output units card, telling the computer what machines to use for reading-in the data (cols. 1–2, usually '02' for the card reader as an input device) ; for output of computed matrices if desired (cols. 3–4, usually also '02') and the main output switch (cols. 5–6, usually '00' for printer output) :

```
                       020200
```

Step 4.   A job title card; whatever the researcher puts here will be printed at the top of each page of the output. A job number, which is arbitrary, goes in columns 1–4, and any title desired in columns 9–80:

```
       0001        LABOR RIOTING REGRESSION
```

Step 5.   An option card, where entries in columns 1–44 indicate choices the researcher may make about computation and output of the regression analysis. Columns 1–2 list the number of variables, columns 3–4 list the input type, etc. The user will find all this information in an "1130 Statistical System User's Manual." Among the options available is one to print out the correlation matrix of each variable with every other variable (cols. 21–22). Also columns 25–26 can be marked to instruct the computer to stop after computing the correlation matrix, not doing regression analysis at all. Thus, this is also a program for Pearsonian correlation. There is also an option for printing out the regression results after each step (cols. 25–26). In the first step the computer will compute a regression equation with the strongest correlated variable as an independent variable, in the second step two independent variables will be used, in the third step three, etc., until criteria are reached specified in the last three options. An option card would look like this:

070100000000000000001020100010.010.010.0001

Step 6. Next come one or more variable name cards, the same as in step 4 of the crosstabulation program, except that only four letters are allowed per name:

RIOTWAGEUEMPSTRKVOTEPRTYHOME

Step 7. The next card is a variable format card, describing how the data are positioned on data cards. For example:

(I4,I1,F2.0,1X,4F4.2,F4.0,1X,F2.1)

The format card above reads as follows: the data are arranged with a 4-digit identification number, a 1-digit identification number, a unit of data 2 digits long with 0 digits to the right of the decimal, one space (1X), 4 units of data each 4 digits long and each with 2 of these digits to the right of the decimal, a unit 4 digits long with no digits to the right of the decimal, a space, and a last unit of data 2 digits long with one of these digits to the right of the decimal.

Step 8. Then the deck of data cards is inserted. For the format in the above example, they would look like this:

00010128 12342345345645671111 22
00020249 02938475674839292222 33
etc.

Step 9. A card with a −1 entry in the first two columns is placed after the last data card, followed by a blank card, and the program is ready to run.

3. A Program for Factor Analysis

IBM also supplies a very similar program for factor analysis, based on Pearsonian correlation and providing options for orthogonal or oblique rotations, which uses the principle-components method of extracting factors.

Step 1. Job card, same as before.

Step 2. The prepackaged factor analysis program is called from the disk containing the statistical package by copying these cards:

```
// XEQ FCTR       05
*LOCALFCTR,FMTRD,DATRD,PRNTB,MXRAD,TRAN
*LOCALFCTR1,TRIDI,QR,INVRS
*LOCALFCTR2,VECTR,PRNT
*LOCALFCTR3,VARMX,PROMX,SCORE,BFOUT
*LOCALCOREL,PRNT
```

Again, these cards may vary according to the version in use; most computer centers will have an analogous prepackaged factor analysis program, however.

Steps 3 and 4. The input-output units and the job title cards, same as before.

Step 5. The factor analysis option card, similar to the regression option card, but providing for output of the correlation matrix, varimax orthogonal rotation, oblique rotation, and outputs of various matrices involved in computation of factor analysis. These options are also described in the same manual. An option card might look like this:

```
900100000000000000000100020301020000000100010100000000000010101
```

Steps 6 to 9. The remainder of the steps are the same as in regression analysis, involving variable name card(s), then a variable format card, a data deck, a negative identification card, and a blank card. With these, the program would be ready to run.

Appendix B

Tables

TABLE I.   Squares and Square Roots

Number	Square	Square root	Number	Square	Square root
1	1	1.0000	31	9 61	5.5678
2	4	1.4142	32	10 24	5.6569
3	9	1.7321	33	10 89	5.7446
4	16	2.0000	34	11 56	5.8310
5	25	2.2361	35	12 25	5.9161
6	36	2.4495	36	12 96	6.0000
7	49	2.6458	37	13 69	6.0828
8	64	2.8284	38	14 44	6.1644
9	81	3.0000	39	15 21	6.2450
10	1 00	3.1623	40	16 00	6.3246
11	1 21	3.3166	41	16 81	6.4031
12	1 44	3.4641	42	17 64	6.4807
13	1 69	3.6056	43	18 49	6.5574
14	1 96	3.7417	44	19 36	6.6332
15	2 25	3.8730	45	20 25	6.7082
16	2 56	4.0000	46	21 16	6.7823
17	2 89	4.1231	47	22 09	6.8557
18	3 24	4.2426	48	23 04	6.9282
19	3 61	4.3589	49	24 01	7.0000
20	4 00	4.4721	50	25 00	7.0711
21	4 41	4.5826	51	26 01	7.1414
22	4 84	4.6904	52	27 04	7.2111
23	5 29	4.7958	53	28 09	7.2801
24	5 76	4.8990	54	29 16	7.3485
25	6 25	5.0000	55	30 25	7.4162
26	6 76	5.0990	56	31 36	7.4833
27	7 29	5.1962	57	32 49	7.5498
28	7 84	5.2915	58	33 64	7.6158
29	8 41	5.3852	59	34 81	7.6811
30	9 00	5.4772	60	36 00	7.7460

Source: H. Sorenson, *Statistics for Students of Psychology and Education* (New York: McGraw-Hill Book Company, Inc., 1936), Table 72, pp. 347–359, © Copyright McGraw-Hill Book Company, Inc., with the kind permission of the publisher.

Table I. Squares and Square Roots *(Continued)*

Number	Square	Square root	Number	Square	Square root
61	37 21	7.8102	101	1 02 01	10.0499
62	38 44	7.8740	102	1 04 04	10.0995
63	39 69	7.9373	103	1 06 09	10.1489
64	40 96	8.0000	104	1 08 16	10.1980
65	42 25	8.0623	105	1 10 25	10.2470
66	43 56	8.1240	106	1 12 36	10.2956
67	44 89	8.1854	107	1 14 49	10.3441
68	46 24	8.2462	108	1 16 64	10.3923
69	47 61	8.3066	109	1 18 81	10.4403
70	49 00	8.3666	110	1 21 00	10.4881
71	50 41	8.4261	111	1 23 21	10.5357
72	51 84	8.4853	112	1 25 44	10.5830
73	53 29	8.5440	113	1 27 69	10.6301
74	54 76	8.6023	114	1 29 96	10.6771
75	56 25	8.6603	115	1 32 25	10.7238
76	57 76	8.7178	116	1 34 56	10.7703
77	59 29	8.7750	117	1 36 89	10.8167
78	60 84	8.8318	118	1 39 24	10.8628
79	62 41	8.8882	119	1 41 61	10.9087
80	64 00	8.9443	120	1 44 00	10.9545
81	65 61	9.0000	121	1 46 41	11.0000
82	67 24	9.0554	122	1 48 84	11.0454
83	68 89	9.1104	123	1 51 29	11.0905
84	70 56	9.1652	124	1 53 76	11.1355
85	72 25	9.2195	125	1 56 25	11.1803
86	73 96	9.2736	126	1 58 76	11.2250
87	75 69	9.3274	127	1 61 29	11.2694
88	77 44	9.3808	128	1 63 84	11.3137
89	79 21	9.4340	129	1 66 41	11.3578
90	81 00	9.4868	130	1 69 00	11.4018
91	82 81	9.5394	131	1 71 61	11.4455
92	84 64	9.5917	132	1 74 24	11.4891
93	86 49	9.6437	133	1 76 89	11.5326
94	88 36	9.6954	134	1 79 56	11.5758
95	90 25	9.7468	135	1 82 25	11.6190
96	92 16	9.7980	136	1 84 96	11.6619
97	94 09	9.8489	137	1 87 69	11.7047
98	96 04	9.8995	138	1 90 44	11.7473
99	98 01	9.9499	139	1 93 21	11.7898
100	1 00 00	10.0000	140	1 96 00	11.8322

Table I.   Squares and Square Roots *(Continued)*

Number	Square	Square root	Number	Square	Square root
141	1 98 81	11.8743	181	3 27 61	13.4536
142	2 01 64	11.9164	182	3 31 24	13.4907
143	2 04 49	11.9583	183	3 34 89	13.5277
144	2 07 36	12.0000	184	3 38 56	13.5647
145	2 10 25	12.0416	185	3 42 25	13.6015
146	2 13 16	12.0830	186	3 45 96	13.6382
147	2 16 09	12.1244	187	3 49 69	13.6748
148	2 19 04	12.1655	188	3 53 44	13.7113
149	2 22 01	12.2066	189	3 57 21	13.7477
150	2 25 00	12.2474	190	3 61 00	13.7840
151	2 28 01	12.2882	191	3 64 81	13.8203
152	2 31 04	12.3288	192	3 68 64	13.8564
153	2 34 09	12.3693	193	3 72 49	13.8924
154	2 37 16	12.4097	194	3 76 36	13.9284
155	2 40 25	12.4499	195	3 80 25	13.9642
156	2 43 36	12.4900	196	3 84 16	14.0000
157	2 46 49	12.5300	197	3 88 09	14.0357
158	2 49 64	12.5698	198	3 92 04	14.0712
159	2 52 81	12.6095	199	3 96 01	14.1067
160	2 56 00	12.6491	200	4 00 00	14.1421
161	2 59 21	12.6886	201	4 04 01	14.1774
162	2 62 44	12.7279	202	4 08 04	14.2127
163	2 65 69	12.7671	203	4 12 09	14.2478
164	2 68 96	12.8062	204	4 16 16	14.2829
165	2 72 25	12.8452	205	4 20 25	14.3178
166	2 75 56	12.8841	206	4 24 36	14.3527
167	2 78 89	12.9228	207	4 28 49	14.3875
168	2 82 24	12.9615	208	4 32 64	14.4222
169	2 85 61	13.0000	209	4 36 81	14.4568
170	2 89 00	13.0384	210	4 41 00	14.4914
171	2 92 41	13.0767	211	4 45 21	14.5258
172	2 95 84	13.1149	212	4 49 44	14.5602
173	2 99 29	13.1529	213	4 53 69	14.5945
174	3 02 76	13.1909	214	4 57 96	14.6287
175	3 06 25	13.2288	215	4 62 25	14.6629
176	3 09 76	13.2665	216	4 66 56	14.6969
177	3 13 29	13.3041	217	4 70 89	14.7309
178	3 16 84	13.3417	218	4 75 24	14.7648
179	3 20 41	13.3791	219	4 79 61	14.7986
180	3 24 00	13.4164	220	4 84 00	14.8324

Table I.   Squares and Square Roots *(Continued)*

Number	Square	Square root	Number	Square	Square root
221	4 88 41	14.8661	261	6 81 21	16.1555
222	4 92 84	14.8997	262	6 86 44	16.1864
223	4 97 29	14.9332	263	6 91 69	16.2173
224	5 01 76	14.9666	264	6 96 96	16.2481
225	5 06 25	15.0000	265	7 02 25	16.2788
226	5 10 76	15.0333	266	7 07 56	16.3095
227	5 15 29	15.0665	267	7 12 89	16.3401
228	5 19 84	15.0997	268	7 18 24	16.3707
229	5 24 41	15.1327	269	7 23 61	16.4012
230	5 29 00	15.1658	270	7 29 00	16.4317
231	5 33 61	15.1987	271	7 34 41	16.4621
232	5 38 24	15.2315	272	7 39 84	16.4924
233	5 42 89	15.2643	273	7 45 29	16.5227
234	5 47 56	15.2971	274	7 50 76	16.5529
235	5 52 25	15.3297	275	7 56 25	16.5831
236	5 56 96	15.3623	276	7 61 76	16.6132
237	5 61 69	15.3948	277	7 67 29	16.6433
238	5 66 44	15.4272	278	7 72 84	16.6733
239	5 71 21	15.4596	279	7 78 41	16.7033
240	5 76 00	15.4919	280	7 84 00	16.7332
241	5 80 81	15.5242	281	7 89 61	16.7631
242	5 85 64	15.5563	282	7 95 24	16.7929
243	5 90 49	15.5885	283	8 00 89	16.8226
244	5 95 36	15.6205	284	8 06 56	16.8523
245	6 00 25	15.6525	285	8 12 25	16.8819
246	6 05 16	15.6844	286	8 17 96	16.9115
247	6 10 09	15.7162	287	8 23 69	16.9411
248	6 15 04	15.7480	288	8 29 44	16.9706
259	6 20 01	15.7797	289	8 35 21	17.0000
250	6 25 00	15.8114	290	8 41 00	17.0294
251	6 30 01	15.8430	291	8 46 81	17.0587
252	6 35 04	15.8745	292	8 52 64	17.0880
253	6 40 09	15.9060	293	8 58 49	17.1172
254	6 45 16	15.9374	294	8 64 36	17.1464
255	6 50 25	15.9687	295	8 70 25	17.1756
256	6 55 36	16.0000	296	8 76 16	17.2047
257	6 60 49	16.0312	297	8 82 09	17.2337
258	6 65 64	16.0624	298	8 88 04	17.2627
259	6 70 81	16.0935	299	8 94 01	17.2916
260	6 76 00	16.1245	300	9 00 00	17.3205

Table I.   Squares and Square Roots *(Continued)*

Number	Square	Square root	Number	Square	Square root
301	9 06 01	17.3494	341	11 62 81	18.4662
302	9 12 04	17.3781	342	11 69 64	18.4932
303	9 18 09	17.4069	343	11 76 49	18.5203
304	9 24 16	17.4356	344	11 83 36	18.5472
305	9 30 25	17.4642	345	11 90 25	18.5742
306	9 36 36	17.4929	346	11 97 16	18.6011
307	9 42 49	17.5214	347	12 04 09	18.6279
308	9 48 64	17.5499	348	12 11 04	18.6548
309	9 54 81	17.5784	349	12 18 01	18.6815
310	9 61 00	17.6068	350	12 25 00	18.7083
311	9 67 21	17.6352	351	12 32 01	18.7350
312	9 73 44	17.6635	352	12 39 04	18.7617
313	9 79 69	17.6918	353	12 46 09	18.7883
314	9 85 96	17.7200	354	12 53 16	18.8149
315	9 92 25	17.7482	355	12 60 25	18.8414
316	9 98 56	17.7764	356	12 67 36	18.8680
317	10 04 89	17.8045	357	12 74 49	18.8944
318	10 11 24	17.8326	358	12 81 64	18.9209
319	10 17 61	17.8606	359	12 88 81	18.9473
320	10 24 00	17.8885	360	12 96 00	18.9737
321	10 30 41	17.9165	361	13 03 21	19.0000
322	10 36 84	17.9444	362	13 10 44	19.0263
323	10 43 29	17.9722	363	13 17 69	19.0526
324	10 49 76	18.0000	364	13 24 96	19.0788
325	10 56 25	18.0278	365	13 32 25	19.1050
326	10 62 76	18.0555	366	13 39 56	19.1311
327	10 69 29	18.0831	367	13 46 89	19.1572
328	10 75 84	18.1108	368	13 54 24	19.1833
329	10 82 41	18.1384	369	13 61 61	19.2094
330	10 89 00	18.1659	370	13 69 00	19.2354
331	10 95 61	18.1934	371	13 76 41	19.2614
332	11 02 24	18.2209	372	13 83 84	19.2873
333	11 08 89	18.2483	373	13 91 29	19.3132
334	11 15 56	18.2757	374	13 98 76	19.3391
335	11 22 25	18.3030	375	14 06 25	19.3649
336	11 28 96	18.3303	376	14 13 76	19.3907
337	11 35 69	18.3576	377	14 21 29	19.4165
338	11 42 44	18.3848	378	14 28 84	19.4422
339	11 49 21	18.4120	379	14 36 41	19.4679
340	11 56 00	18.4391	380	14 44 00	19.4936

Table I.   Squares and Square Roots *(Continued)*

Number	Square	Square root	Number	Square	Square root
381	14 51 61	19.5192	421	17 72 41	20.5183
382	14 59 24	19.5448	422	17 80 84	20.5426
383	14 66 89	19.5704	423	17 89 29	20.5670
384	14 74 56	19.5959	424	17 97 76	20.5913
385	14 82 25	19.6214	425	18 06 25	20.6155
386	14 89 96	19.6469	426	18 14 76	20.6398
387	14 97 69	19.6723	427	18 23 29	20.6640
388	15 05 44	19.6977	428	18 31 84	20.6882
389	15 13 21	19.7231	429	18 40 41	20.7123
390	15 21 00	19.7484	430	18 49 00	20.7364
391	15 28 81	19.7737	431	18 57 61	20.7605
392	15 36 64	19.7990	432	18 66 24	20.7846
393	15 44 49	19.8242	433	18 74 89	20.8087
394	15 52 36	19.8494	434	18 83 56	20.8327
395	15 60 25	19.8746	435	18 92 25	20.8567
396	15 68 16	19.8997	436	19 00 96	20.8806
397	15 76 09	19.9249	437	19 09 69	20.9045
398	15 84 04	19.9499	438	19 18 44	20.9284
399	15 92 01	19.9750	439	19 27 21	20.9523
400	16 00 00	20.0000	440	19 36 00	20.9762
401	16 08 01	20.0250	441	19 44 81	21.0000
402	16 16 04	20.0499	442	19 53 64	21.0238
403	16 24 09	20.0749	443	19 62 49	21.0476
404	16 32 16	20.0998	444	19 71 36	21.0713
405	16 40 25	20.1246	445	19 80 25	21.0950
406	16 48 36	20.1494	446	19 89 16	21.1187
407	16 56 49	20.1742	447	19 98 09	21.1424
408	16 64 64	20.1990	448	20 07 04	21.1660
409	16 72 81	20.2237	449	20 16 01	21.1896
410	16 81 00	20.2485	450	20 25 00	21.2132
411	16 89 21	20.2731	451	20 34 01	21.2368
412	16 97 44	20.2978	452	20 43 04	21.2603
413	17 05 69	20.3224	453	20 52 09	21.2838
414	17 13 96	20.3470	454	20 61 16	21.3073
415	17 22 25	20.3715	455	20 70 25	21.3307
416	17 30 56	20.3961	456	20 79 36	21.3542
417	17 38 89	20.4206	457	20 88 49	21.3776
418	17 47 24	20.4450	458	20 97 64	21.4009
419	17 55 61	20.4695	459	21 06 81	21.4243
420	17 64 00	20.4939	460	21 16 00	21.4476

Appendix B

Table I.   Squares and Square Roots *(Continued)*

Number	Square	Square root	Number	Square	Square root
461	21 25 21	21.4709	501	25 10 01	22.3830
462	21 34 44	21.4942	502	25 20 04	22.4054
463	21 43 69	21.5174	503	25 30 09	22.4277
464	21 52 96	21.5407	504	25 40 16	22.4499
465	21 62 25	21.5639	505	25 50 25	22.4722
466	21 71 56	21.5870	506	25 60 36	22.4944
467	21 80 89	21.6102	507	25 70 49	22.5167
468	21 90 24	21.6333	508	25 80 64	22.5389
469	21 99 61	21.6564	509	25 90 81	22.5610
470	22 09 00	21.6795	510	26 01 00	22.5832
471	22 18 41	21.7025	511	26 11 21	22.6053
472	22 27 84	21.7256	512	25 21 44	22.6274
473	22 37 29	21.7486	513	26 31 69	22.6495
474	22 46 76	21.7715	514	26 41 96	22.6716
475	22 56 25	21.7945	515	26 52 25	22.6936
476	22 65 76	21.8174	516	22 62 56	22.7156
477	22 75 29	21.8403	517	26 72 89	22.7376
478	22 84 84	21.8632	518	26 83 24	22.7596
479	22 94 41	21.8861	519	26 93 61	22.7816
480	23 04 00	21.9089	520	27 04 00	22.8035
481	23 13 61	21.9317	521	27 14 41	22.8254
482	23 23 24	21.9545	522	27 24 84	22.8473
483	23 32 89	21.9773	523	27 35 29	22.8692
484	23 42 56	22.0000	524	27 45 76	22.8910
485	23 52 25	22.0227	525	27 56 25	22.9129
486	23 61 96	22.0454	526	27 66 76	22.9347
487	23 71 69	22.0681	527	27 77 29	22.9565
488	23 81 44	22.0907	528	27 87 84	22.9783
489	23 91 21	22.1133	529	27 98 41	23.0000
490	24 01 00	22.1359	530	28 09 00	23.0217
491	24 10 81	22.1585	531	28 19 61	23.0434
492	24 20 64	22.1811	532	28 30 24	23.0651
493	24 30 49	22.2036	533	28 40 89	23.0868
494	24 40 36	22.2261	534	28 51 56	23.1084
495	24 50 25	22.2486	535	28 62 25	23.1301
496	24 60 16	22.2711	536	28 72 96	23.1517
497	24 70 09	22.2935	537	28 83 69	23.1733
498	24 80 04	22.3159	538	28 94 44	23.1948
499	24 90 01	22.3383	539	29 05 21	23.2164
500	25 00 00	22.3607	540	29 16 00	23.2379

Table I.   Squares and Square Roots *(Continued)*

Number	Square	Square root	Number	Square	Square root
541	29 26 81	23.2594	581	33 75 61	24.1039
542	29 37 64	23.2809	582	33 87 24	24.1247
543	29 48 49	23.3024	583	33 98 89	24.1454
544	29 59 36	23.3238	584	34 10 56	24.1661
545	29 70 25	23.3452	585	34 22 25	24.1868
546	29 81 16	23.3666	586	34 33 96	24.2074
547	29 92 09	23.3880	587	34 45 69	24.2281
548	30 03 04	23.4094	588	34 57 44	24.2487
549	30 14 01	23.4307	589	34 69 21	24.2693
550	30 25 00	23.4521	590	34 81 00	24.2899
551	30 36 01	23.4734	591	34 92 81	24.3105
552	30 47 04	23.4947	592	35 04 64	24.3311
553	30 58 09	23.5160	593	35 16 49	24.3516
554	30 69 16	23.5372	594	35 28 36	24.3721
555	30 80 25	23.5584	595	35 40 25	24.3926
556	30 91 36	23.5797	596	35 52 16	24.4131
557	31 02 49	23.6008	597	35 64 09	24.4336
558	31 13 64	23.6220	598	35 76 04	24.4540
559	31 24 81	23.6432	599	35 88 01	24.4745
560	31 36 00	23.6643	600	36 00 00	24.4949
561	31 47 21	23.6854	601	36 12 01	24.5153
562	31 58 44	23.7065	602	36 24 04	24.5357
563	31 69 69	23.7276	603	36 36 09	24.5561
564	31 80 96	23.7487	604	36 48 16	24.5764
565	31 92 25	23.7697	605	36 60 25	24.5967
566	32 03 56	23.7908	606	36 72 36	24.6171
567	32 14 89	23.8118	607	36 84 49	24.6374
568	32 26 24	23.8328	608	36 96 64	24.6577
569	32 37 61	23.8537	609	37 08 81	24.6779
570	32 49 00	23.8747	610	37 21 00	24.6982
571	32 60 41	23.8956	611	37 33 21	24.7184
572	32 71 84	23.9165	612	37 45 44	24.7385
573	32 83 29	23.9374	613	37 57 69	24.7588
574	32 94 76	23.9583	614	37 69 96	24.7790
575	33 06 25	23.9792	615	37 82 25	24.7992
576	33 17 76	24.0000	616	37 94 56	24.8193
577	33 29 29	24.0208	617	38 06 89	24.8395
578	33 40 84	24.0416	618	38 19 24	24.8596
579	33 52 41	24.0624	619	38 31 61	24.8797
580	33 64 00	24.0832	620	38 44 00	24.8998

Appendix B

Table I. Squares and Square Roots *(Continued)*

Number	Square	Square root	Number	Square	Square root
621	38 56 41	24.9199	661	43 69 21	25.7099
622	38 68 84	24.9399	662	43 82 44	25.7294
623	38 81 29	24.9600	663	43 95 69	25.7488
624	38 93 76	24.9800	664	44 08 96	25.7682
625	39 06 25	25.0000	665	44 22 25	25.7876
626	39 18 76	25.0200	666	44 35 56	25.8070
627	39 31 29	25.0400	667	44 48 89	25.8263
628	39 43 84	25.0599	668	44 62 24	25.8457
629	39 56 41	25.0799	669	44 75 61	25.8650
630	39 69 00	25.0998	670	44 89 00	25.8844
631	39 81 61	25.1197	671	45 02 41	25.9037
632	39 94 24	25.1396	672	45 15 84	25.9230
633	40 06 89	25.1595	673	45 29 29	25.9422
634	40 19 56	25.1794	674	45 42 76	25.9615
635	40 32 25	25.1992	675	45 56 25	25.9808
636	40 44 96	25.2190	676	45 69 76	26.0000
637	40 57 69	25.2389	677	45 83 29	26.0192
638	40 70 44	25.2587	678	45 96 84	26.0384
639	40 83 21	25.2784	679	46 10 41	26.0576
640	40 96 00	25.2982	680	46 24 00	26.0768
641	41 08 81	25.3180	681	46 37 61	26.0960
642	41 21 64	25.3377	682	46 51 24	26.1151
643	41 34 49	25.3574	683	46 64 89	26.1343
644	41 47 36	25.3772	684	46 78 56	26.1534
645	41 60 25	25.3969	685	46 92 25	26.1725
646	41 73 16	25.4165	686	47 05 96	26.1916
647	41 86 09	25.4362	687	47 19 69	26.2107
648	41 99 04	25.4558	688	47 33 44	26.2298
649	42 12 01	25.4755	689	47 47 21	26.2488
650	42 25 00	25.4951	690	47 61 00	26.2679
651	42 38 01	25.5147	691	47 74 81	26.2869
652	42 51 04	25.5343	692	47 88 64	26.3059
653	42 64 09	25.5539	693	48 02 49	26.3249
654	42 77 16	25.5734	694	48 16 36	26.3439
655	42 90 25	25.5930	695	48 30 25	26.3629
656	43 03 36	25.6125	696	48 44 16	26.3818
657	43 16 49	25.6320	697	48 58 09	26.4008
658	43 29 64	25.6515	698	48 72 04	26.4197
659	43 42 81	25.6710	699	48 86 01	26.4386
660	43 56 00	25.6905	700	49 00 00	26.4575

Table I.   Squares and Square Roots *(Continued)*

Number	Square	Square root	Number	Square	Square root
701	49 14 01	26.4764	741	54 90 81	27.2213
702	49 28 04	26.4953	742	55 05 64	27.2397
703	49 42 09	26.5141	743	55 20 49	27.2580
704	49 56 16	26.5330	744	55 35 36	27.2764
705	49 70 25	26.5518	745	55 50 25	27.2947
706	49 84 36	26.5707	746	55 65 16	27.3130
707	49 98 49	26.5895	747	55 80 09	27.3313
708	50 12 64	26.6083	748	55 95 04	27.3496
709	50 26 81	26.6271	749	56 10 01	27.3679
710	50 41 00	26.6458	750	56 25 00	27.3861
711	50 55 21	26.6646	751	56 40 01	27.4044
712	50 69 44	26.6833	752	56 55 04	27.4226
713	50 83 69	26.7021	753	56 70 09	27.4408
714	50 97 96	26.7208	754	56 85 16	27.4591
715	51 12 25	26.7395	755	57 00 25	27.4773
716	51 26 56	26.7582	756	57 15 36	27.4955
717	51 40 89	26.7769	757	57 30 49	27.5136
718	51 55 24	26.7955	758	57 45 64	27.5318
719	51 69 61	26.8142	759	57 60 81	27.5500
720	51 84 00	26.8328	760	57 76 00	27.5681
721	51 98 41	26.8514	761	57 91 21	27.5862
722	52 12 84	26.8701	762	58 06 44	27.6043
723	52 27 29	26.8887	763	58 21 69	27.6225
724	52 41 76	26.9072	764	58 36 96	27.6405
725	52 56 25	26.9258	765	58 52 25	27.6586
726	52 70 76	26.9444	766	58 67 56	27.6767
727	52 85 29	26.9629	767	58 82 89	27.6948
728	52 99 84	26.9815	768	58 98 24	27.7128
729	53 14 41	27.0000	769	59 13 61	27.7308
730	53 29 00	27.0185	770	59 29 00	27.7489
731	53 43 61	27.0370	771	59 44 41	27.7669
732	53 58 24	27.0555	772	59 59 84	27.7849
733	53 72 89	27.0740	773	59 75 29	27.8029
734	53 87 56	27.0924	774	59 90 76	27.8209
735	54 02 25	27.1109	775	60 06 25	27.8388
736	54 16 96	27.1293	776	60 21 76	27.8568
737	54 31 69	27.1477	777	60 37 29	27.8747
738	54 46 44	27.1662	778	60 52 84	27.8927
739	54 61 27	27.1846	779	60 68 41	27.9106
740	54 76 00	27.2029	780	60 84 00	27.9285

Table I.   Squares and Square Roots *(Continued)*

Number	Square	Square root	Number	Square	Square root
781	60 99 61	27.9464	821	67 40 41	28.6531
782	61 15 24	27.9643	822	67 56 84	28.6705
783	61 30 89	27.9821	823	67 73 29	28.6880
784	61 46 56	28.0000	824	67 89 76	28.7054
785	61 62 25	28.0179	825	68 06 25	28.7228
786	61 77 96	28.0357	826	68 22 76	28.7402
787	61 93 69	28.0535	827	68 39 29	28.7576
788	62 09 44	28.0713	828	68 55 84	28.7750
789	62 25 21	28.0891	829	68 72 41	28.7924
790	62 41 00	28.1069	830	68 89 00	28.8097
791	62 56 81	28.1247	831	69 05 61	28.8271
792	62 72 64	28.1425	832	69 22 24	28.8444
793	62 88 49	28.1603	833	69 38 89	28.8617
794	63 04 36	28.1780	834	69 55 56	28.8791
795	63 20 25	28.1957	835	69 72 25	28.8964
796	63 36 16	28.2135	836	69 88 96	28.9137
797	63 52 09	28.2312	837	70 05 69	28.9310
798	63 68 04	28.2489	838	70 22 44	28.9482
799	63 84 01	28.2666	839	70 39 21	28.9655
800	64 00 00	28.2843	840	70 56 00	28.9828
801	64 16 01	28.3019	841	70 72 81	29.0000
802	64 32 04	28.3196	842	70 89 64	29.0172
803	64 48 09	28.3373	843	71 06 49	29.0345
804	64 64 16	28.3549	844	71 23 36	29.0517
805	64 80 25	28.3725	845	71 40 25	29.0689
806	64 96 36	28.3901	846	71 57 16	29.0861
807	65 12 49	28.4077	847	71 74 09	29.1033
808	65 28 64	28.4253	848	71 91 04	29.1204
809	65 44 81	28.4429	849	72 08 01	29.1376
810	65 61 00	28.4605	850	72 25 00	29.1548
811	65 77 21	28.4781	851	72 42 01	29.1719
812	65 93 44	28.4956	852	72 59 04	29.1890
813	66 09 69	28.5132	853	72 76 09	29.2062
814	66 25 96	28.5307	854	72 93 16	29.2233
815	66 42 25	28.5482	855	73 10 25	29.2404
816	66 58 56	28.5657	856	73 27 36	29.2575
817	66 74 89	28.5832	857	73 44 49	29.2746
818	66 91 24	28.6007	858	73 61 64	29.2916
819	67 07 61	28.6082	859	73 78 81	29.3087
820	67 24 00	28.6356	860	73 96 00	29.3258

Table I. Squares and Square Roots *(Continued)*

Number	Square	Square root	Number	Square	Square root
861	74 13 21	29.3428	901	81 18 01	30.0167
862	74 30 44	29.3598	902	81 36 04	30.0333
863	74 47 69	29.3769	903	81 54 09	30.0500
864	74 64 96	29.3939	904	81 72 16	30.0666
865	74 82 25	29.4109	905	81 90 25	30.0832
866	74 99 56	29.4279	906	82 08 36	30.0998
867	75 16 89	29.4449	907	82 26 49	30.1164
868	75 34 24	29.4618	908	82 44 64	30.1330
869	75 51 61	29.4788	909	82 62 81	30.1496
870	75 69 00	29.4958	910	82 81 00	30.1662
871	75 86 41	29.5127	911	82 99 21	30.1828
872	76 03 84	29.5296	912	83 17 44	30.1993
873	76 21 29	29.5466	913	83 35 69	30.2159
874	76 38 76	29.5635	914	83 53 96	30.2324
875	76 56 25	29.5804	915	83 72 25	30.2490
876	76 73 76	29.5973	916	83 90 56	30.2655
877	76 91 29	29.6142	917	84 08 89	30.2820
878	77 08 84	29.6311	918	84 27 24	30.2985
879	77 26 41	29.6479	919	84 45 61	30.3150
880	77 44 00	29.6648	920	84 64 00	30.3315
881	77 61 61	29.6816	921	84 82 41	30.3480
882	77 79 24	29.6985	922	85 00 84	30.3645
883	77 96 89	29.7153	923	85 19 29	30.3809
884	78 14 56	29.7321	924	85 37 76	30.3974
885	78 32 25	29.7489	925	85 56 25	30.4138
886	78 49 96	29.7658	926	85 74 76	30.4302
887	78 67 69	29.7825	927	85 93 29	30.4467
888	78 85 44	29.7993	928	86 11 84	30.4631
889	79 03 21	29.8161	929	86 30 41	30.4795
890	79 21 00	29.8329	930	86 49 00	30.4959
891	79 38 81	29.8496	931	86 67 61	30.5123
892	79 56 64	29.8664	932	86 86 24	30.5287
893	79 74 49	29.8831	933	87 04 89	30.5450
894	79 92 36	29.8998	934	87 23 56	30.5614
895	80 10 25	29.9166	935	87 42 25	30.5778
896	80 28 16	29.9333	936	87 60 96	30.5941
897	80 46 09	29.9500	937	87 79 69	30.6105
898	80 64 04	29.9666	938	87 98 44	30.6268
899	80 82 01	29.9833	939	88 17 21	30.6431
900	81 00 00	30.0000	940	88 36 00	30.6594

Appendix B

Table I. Squares and Square Roots *(Continued)*

Number	Square	Square root	Number	Square	Square root
941	88 54 81	30.6757	971	94 28 41	31.1609
942	88 73 64	30.6920	972	94 47 84	31.1769
943	88 92 49	30.7083	973	94 67 29	31.1929
944	89 11 36	30.7246	974	94 86 76	31.2090
945	89 30 25	30.7409	975	95 06 25	31.2250
946	89 49 16	30.7571	976	95 25 76	31.2410
947	89 68 09	30.7734	977	95 45 29	31.2570
948	89 87 04	30.7896	978	95 64 84	31.2730
949	90 06 01	30.8058	979	95 84 41	31.2890
950	90 25 00	30.8221	980	96 04 00	31.3050
951	90 44 01	30.8383	981	96 23 61	31.3209
952	90 63 04	30.8545	982	96 43 24	31.3369
953	90 82 09	30.8707	983	96 62 89	31.3528
954	91 01 16	30.8869	984	96 82 56	31.3688
955	91 20 25	30.9031	985	97 02 25	31.3847
956	91 39 36	30.9192	986	97 21 96	31.4006
957	91 58 49	30.9354	987	97 41 69	31.4166
958	91 77 64	30.9516	988	97 61 44	31.4325
959	91 96 81	30.9677	989	97 81 21	31.4484
960	92 16 00	30.9839	990	98 01 00	31.4643
961	92 35 21	31.0000	991	98 20 81	31.4802
962	92 54 44	31.0161	992	98 40 64	31.4960
963	92 73 69	31.0322	993	98 60 49	31.5119
964	92 92 96	31.0483	994	98 80 36	31.5278
965	93 12 25	31.0644	995	99 00 25	31.5436
966	93 31 56	31.0805	996	99 20 16	31.5595
967	93 50 89	31.0966	997	99 40 09	31.5753
968	93 70 24	31.1127	998	99 60 04	31.5911
969	93 89 61	31.1288	999	99 80 01	31.6070
970	94 09 00	31.1448	1000	100 00 00	31.6228

TABLE II.   Areas of the Normal Curve

$\frac{x}{\sigma}$	.00	.01	.02	.03	.04	.05	.06	.07	.08	.09
0.0	1.00000	.99995	.99980	.99955	.99920	.99875	.99820	.99755	.99685	.99596
0.1	.99501	.99396	.99283	.99158	.99025	.98881	.98728	.98565	.98393	.98211
0.2	.98020	.97819	.97609	.97390	.97161	.96923	.96676	.96420	.96156	.95882
0.3	.95600	.95309	.95010	.94702	.94387	.94055	.93723	.93382	.93024	.92677
0.4	.92312	.91399	.91558	.91169	.90774	.90371	.89961	.89543	.89119	.88688
0.5	.88250	.87805	.87353	.86896	.86432	.85962	.85488	.85006	.84519	.84060
0.6	.83527	.83023	.83514	.82010	.81481	.80957	.80429	.79896	.79459	.78817
0.7	.78270	.77721	.77167	.76610	.76048	.75484	.74916	.74342	.73769	.73193
0.8	.72615	.72033	.71448	.70861	.70272	.69681	.69087	.68493	.67896	.67298
0.9	.66689	.66097	.65494	.64891	.64287	.63683	.63077	.62472	.61865	.61259
1.0	.60653	.60047	.59440	.58834	.58228	.57623	.57017	.56414	.55810	.55209
1.1	.54607	.54007	.53409	.52812	.52214	.51620	.51027	.50437	.49848	.49260
1.2	.48675	.48092	.47511	.46933	.46357	.45793	.45212	.44644	.44078	.43516
1.3	.42956	.42399	.41845	.41294	.40747	.40202	.39661	.39123	.38569	.38058
1.4	.37531	.37007	.36487	.35971	.35459	.34950	.34445	.33944	.33447	.32954
1.5	.32465	.31980	.31500	.31023	.30550	.30082	.29618	.29158	.28702	.28251
1.6	.27804	.27361	.26923	.26489	.26059	.25634	.25213	.24797	.24385	.23978
1.7	.23575	.23176	.22782	.22392	.22008	.21627	.21251	.20879	.20511	.20148
1.8	.19790	.19436	.19086	.18741	.18400	.18064	.17732	.17904	.17081	.16762
1.9	.16448	.16137	.15831	.15530	.15232	.14939	.14650	.14364	.14083	.13806
2.0	.13534	.13265	.13000	.12740	.12483	.12230	.11981	.11737	.11496	.11259
2.1	.11025	.10795	.10570	.10347	.10129	.09914	.09702	.09495	.09290	.09090
2.2	.08892	.08698	.08507	.08320	.08136	.07956	.07778	.07604	.07433	.07265
2.3	.07100	.06939	.06780	.06624	.06471	.06321	.06174	.06029	.05888	.05750
2.4	.05614	.05481	.05350	.05222	.05096	.04973	.04852	.04737	.04618	.04505
2.5	.04394	.04285	.04179	.04074	.03972	.03873	.03775	.03680	.03586	.03494
2.6	.03405	.03317	.03232	.03148	.03066	.02986	.02908	.02831	.02757	.02684
2.7	.02612	.02542	.02474	.02408	.02343	.02280	.02218	.02157	.02098	.02040
2.8	.01984	.01929	.01876	.01823	.01772	.01723	.01674	.01627	.01581	.01536
2.9	.01492	.01449	.01408	.01367	.01328	.01288	.01252	.01215	.01179	.01145
3.0	.01111									
4.0	.00034									

Source: Herbert Arkin and Raymond R. Colton, *Tables for Statisticians* (New York: Barnes and Noble, Inc., 1950), Table 10, p. 114, with the kind permission of the publisher.

TABLE III. Ordinates of the Normal Curve

$\frac{x}{\sigma}$	.00	.01	.02	.03	.04	.05	.06	.07	.08	.09
0.0	.0000	.0040	.0080	.0120	.0159	.0199	.0239	.0279	.0319	.0359
0.1	.0398	.0438	.0478	.0517	.0557	.0596	.0636	.0675	.0714	.0753
0.2	.0793	.0832	.0871	.0910	.0948	.0987	.1026	.1064	.1103	.1141
0.3	.1179	.1217	.1255	.1293	.1331	.1368	.1406	.1443	.1480	.1517
0.4	.1554	.1591	.1628	.1664	.1700	.1736	.1772	.1808	.1844	.1879
0.5	.1915	.1950	.1985	.2019	.2054	.2088	.2123	.2157	.2190	.2224
0.6	.2257	.2291	.2324	.2357	.2389	.2422	.2454	.2486	.2518	.2549
0.7	.2580	.2612	.2642	.2673	.2704	.2734	.2764	.2794	.2823	.2852
0.8	.2881	.2910	.2939	.2967	.2995	.3023	.3051	.3078	.3106	.3133
0.9	.3159	.3186	.3212	.3238	.3264	.3289	.3315	.3340	.3365	.3389
1.0	.3413	.3438	.3461	.3485	.3508	.3531	.3554	.3577	.3599	.3621
1.1	.3643	.3665	.3686	.3718	.3729	.3749	.3770	.3790	.3810	.3830
1.2	.3849	.3869	.3888	.3907	.3925	.3944	.3962	.3980	.3997	.4015
1.3	.4032	.4049	.4066	.4083	.4099	.4115	.4131	.4147	.4162	.4177
1.4	.4192	.4207	.4222	.4236	.4251	.4265	.4279	.4292	.4306	.4319
1.5	.4332	.4345	.4357	.4370	.4382	.4394	.4406	.4418	.4430	.4441
1.6	.4452	.4463	.4474	.4485	.4495	.4505	.4515	.4525	.4535	.4545
1.7	.4554	.4564	.4573	.4582	.4591	.4599	.4608	.4616	.4625	.4633
1.8	.4641	.4649	.4656	.4664	.4671	.4678	.4686	.4693	.4699	.4706
1.9	.4713	.4719	.4726	.4732	.4738	.4744	.4750	.4758	.4762	.4767
2.0	.4772	.4778	.4783	.4788	.4793	.4798	.4803	.4808	.4812	.4817
2.1	.4821	.4826	.4830	.4834	.4838	.4842	.4846	.4850	.4854	.4857
2.2	.4861	.4865	.4868	.4871	.4875	.4878	.4881	.4884	.4887	.4890
2.3	.4893	.4896	.4898	.4901	.4904	.4906	.4909	.4911	.4913	.4916
2.4	.4918	.4920	.4922	.4925	.4927	.4929	.4931	.4932	.4934	.4936
2.5	.4938	.4940	.4941	.4943	.4945	.4946	.4948	.4949	.4951	.4952
2.6	.4953	.4955	.4956	.4957	.4959	.4960	.4961	.4962	.4963	.4964
2.7	.4965	.4966	.4967	.4968	.4969	.4970	.4971	.4972	.4973	.4974
2.8	.4974	.4975	.4976	.4977	.4977	.4978	.4979	.4980	.4980	.4981
2.9	.4981	.4982	.4983	.4984	.4984	.4984	.4985	.4985	.4986	.4986
3.0	.49865	.4987	.4987	.4988	.4988	.4988	.4989	.4989	.4989	.4990
3.1	.49903	.4991	.4991	.4991	.4992	.4992	.4992	.4992	.4993	.4993
4.0	.49997									

Source: Herbert Arkin and Raymond R. Colton, *Tables for Statisticians* (New York: Barnes and Noble, Inc., 1936), Table 11, p. 115, with the kind permission of the publisher.

TABLE IV.   Distribution of *t*

df	Level of significance for one-tailed test					
	.10	.05	.025	.01	.005	.0005
	Level of significance for two-tailed test					
	.20	.10	.05	.02	.01	.001
1	3.078	6.314	12.706	31.821	63.657	636.619
2	1.886	2.920	4.303	6.965	9.925	31.598
3	1.638	2.353	3.182	4.541	5.841	12.941
4	1.533	2.132	2.776	3.747	4.604	8.610
5	1.476	2.015	2.571	3.365	4.032	6.859
6	1.440	1.943	2.447	3.143	3.707	5.959
7	1.415	1.895	2.365	2.998	3.499	5.405
8	1.397	1.860	2.306	2.896	3.355	5.041
9	1.383	1.833	2.262	2.821	3.250	4.781
10	1.372	1.812	2.228	2.764	3.169	4.587
11	1.363	1.796	2.201	2.718	3.106	4.437
12	1.356	1.782	2.179	2.681	3.055	4.318
13	1.350	1.771	2.160	2.650	3.012	4.221
14	1.345	1.761	2.145	2.624	2.977	4.140
15	1.341	1.753	2.131	2.602	2.947	4.073
16	1.337	1.746	2.120	2.583	2.921	4.015
17	1.333	1.740	2.110	2.567	2.898	3.965
18	1.330	1.734	2.101	2.552	2.878	3.922
19	1.328	1.729	2.093	2.539	2.861	3.883
20	1.325	1.725	2.086	2.528	2.845	3.850
21	1.323	1.721	2.080	2.518	2.831	3.819
22	1.321	1.717	2.074	2.508	2.819	3.792
23	1.319	1.714	2.069	2.500	2.807	3.767
24	1.318	1.711	2.064	2.492	2.797	3.745
25	1.316	1.708	2.060	2.485	2.787	3.725
26	1.315	1.706	2.056	2.479	2.779	3.707
27	1.314	1.703	2.052	2.473	2.771	3.690
28	1.313	1.701	2.048	2.467	2.763	3.674
29	1.311	1.699	2.045	2.462	2.756	3.659
30	1.310	1.697	2.042	2.457	2.750	3.646
40	1.303	1.684	2.021	2.423	2.704	3.551
60	1.296	1.671	2.000	2.390	2.660	3.460
120	1.289	1.658	1.980	2.358	2.617	3.373
∞	1.282	1.645	1.960	2.326	2.576	3.291

Source: Abridged from Table III of R. A. Fisher and F. Yates, *Statistical Tables for Biological, Agricultural and Medical Research* (1948 ed.), published by Oliver & Boyd Ltd., Edinburgh, and by permission of the authors and publishers.

Appendix B

TABLE V.   Distribution of χ^2

Probability

df	.99	.98	.95	.90	.80	.70	.50	.30	.20	.10	.05	.02	.01	.001
1	.0³157	.0³628	.00393	.0158	.0642	.148	.455	1.074	1.642	2.706	3.841	5.412	6.635	10.827
2	.0201	.0404	.103	.211	.446	.713	1.386	2.408	3.219	4.605	5.991	7.824	9.210	13.815
3	.115	.185	.352	.584	1.005	1.424	2.366	3.665	4.642	6.251	7.815	9.837	11.341	16.268
4	.297	.429	.711	1.064	1.649	2.195	3.357	4.878	5.989	7.779	9.488	11.668	13.277	18.465
5	.554	.752	1.145	1.610	2.343	3.000	4.351	6.064	7.289	9.236	11.070	13.388	15.086	20.517
6	.872	1.134	1.635	2.204	3.070	3.828	5.348	7.231	8.558	10.645	12.592	15.033	16.812	22.457
7	1.239	1.564	2.167	2.833	3.822	4.671	6.346	8.383	9.803	12.017	14.067	16.622	18.475	24.322
8	1.646	2.032	2.733	3.490	4.594	5.527	7.344	9.524	11.030	13.362	15.507	18.168	20.090	26.125
9	2.088	2.532	3.325	4.168	5.380	6.393	8.343	10.656	12.242	14.684	16.919	19.679	21.666	27.877
10	2.558	3.059	3.940	4.865	6.179	7.267	9.342	11.781	13.442	15.987	18.307	21.161	23.209	29.588
11	3.053	3.609	4.575	5.578	6.989	8.148	10.341	12.899	14.631	17.275	19.675	22.618	24.725	31.264
12	3.571	4.178	5.226	6.304	7.807	9.034	11.340	14.011	15.812	18.549	21.026	24.054	26.217	32.909
13	4.107	4.765	5.892	7.042	8.634	9.926	12.340	15.119	16.985	19.812	22.362	25.472	27.688	34.528
14	4.660	5.368	6.571	7.790	9.467	10.821	13.339	16.222	18.151	21.064	23.685	26.873	29.141	36.123
15	5.229	5.985	7.261	8.547	10.307	11.721	14.339	17.322	19.311	22.307	24.996	28.259	30.578	37.697
16	5.812	6.614	7.962	9.312	11.152	12.624	15.338	18.418	20.465	23.542	26.296	29.633	32.000	39.252
17	6.408	7.255	8.672	10.085	12.002	13.531	16.338	19.511	21.615	24.769	27.587	30.995	33.409	40.790
18	7.015	7.906	9.390	10.865	12.857	14.440	17.338	20.601	22.760	25.989	28.869	32.346	34.805	42.312
19	7.633	8.567	10.117	11.651	13.716	15.352	18.338	21.689	23.900	27.204	30.144	33.687	36.191	43.820
20	8.260	9.237	10.851	12.443	14.578	16.266	19.337	22.775	25.038	28.412	31.410	35.020	37.566	45.315
21	8.897	9.915	11.591	13.240	15.445	17.182	20.337	23.858	26.171	29.615	32.671	36.343	38.932	46.797
22	9.542	10.600	12.338	14.041	16.314	18.101	21.337	24.939	27.301	30.813	33.924	37.659	40.289	48.268
23	10.196	11.293	13.091	14.848	17.187	19.021	22.337	26.018	28.429	32.007	35.172	38.968	41.638	49.728
24	10.856	11.992	13.848	15.659	18.062	19.943	23.337	27.096	29.553	33.196	36.415	40.270	42.980	51.179
25	11.524	12.697	14.611	16.473	18.940	20.867	24.337	28.172	30.675	34.382	37.652	41.566	44.314	52.620
26	12.198	13.409	15.379	17.292	19.820	21.792	25.336	29.246	31.795	35.563	38.885	42.856	45.642	54.052
27	12.879	14.125	16.151	18.114	20.703	22.719	26.336	30.319	32.912	36.741	40.113	44.140	46.963	55.476
28	13.565	14.847	16.928	18.939	21.588	23.647	27.336	31.391	34.027	37.916	41.337	45.419	48.278	56.893
29	14.256	15.574	17.708	19.768	22.475	24.577	28.336	32.461	35.139	39.087	42.557	46.693	49.588	58.302
30	14.953	16.306	18.493	20.599	23.364	25.508	29.336	33.530	36.250	40.256	43.773	47.962	50.892	59.703

For larger values of df, the expression $\sqrt{2\chi^2} - \sqrt{2df - 1}$ may be used as a normal deviate with unit variance, remembering that the probability for χ^2 corresponds with that of a single tail of the normal curve.

Source: Taken from Table IV of R. A. Fisher and F. Yates, *Statistical Tables for Biological, Agricultural and Medical Research* (1948 ed.), published by Oliver & Boyd Ltd., Edinburgh, and by permission of the authors and publishers.

TABLE VI.   Distribution of F

$$p = .05$$

n_2＼n_1	1	2	3	4	5	6	8	12	24	∞
1	161.4	199.5	215.7	224.6	230.2	234.0	238.9	243.9	249.0	254.3
2	18.51	19.00	19.16	19.25	19.30	19.33	19.37	19.41	19.45	19.50
3	10.13	9.55	9.28	9.12	9.01	8.94	8.84	8.74	8.64	8.53
4	7.71	6.94	6.59	6.39	6.26	6.16	6.04	5.91	5.77	5.63
5	6.61	5.79	5.41	5.19	5.05	4.95	4.82	4.68	4.53	4.36
6	5.99	5.14	4.76	4.53	4.39	4.28	4.15	4.00	3.84	3.67
7	5.59	4.74	4.35	4.12	3.97	3.87	3.73	3.57	3.41	3.23
8	5.32	4.46	4.07	3.84	3.69	3.58	3.44	3.28	3.12	2.93
9	5.12	4.26	3.86	3.63	3.48	3.37	3.23	3.07	2.90	2.71
10	4.96	4.10	3.71	3.48	3.33	3.22	3.07	2.91	2.74	2.54
11	4.84	3.98	3.59	3.36	3.20	3.09	2.95	2.79	2.61	2.40
12	4.75	3.88	3.49	3.26	3.11	3.00	2.85	2.69	2.50	2.30
13	4.67	3.80	3.41	3.18	3.02	2.92	2.77	2.60	2.42	2.21
14	4.60	3.74	3.34	3.11	2.96	2.85	2.70	2.53	2.35	2.13
15	4.54	3.68	3.29	3.06	2.90	2.79	2.64	2.48	2.29	2.07
16	4.49	3.63	3.24	3.01	2.85	2.74	2.59	2.42	2.24	2.01
17	4.45	3.59	3.20	2.96	2.81	2.70	2.55	2.38	2.19	1.96
18	4.41	3.55	3.16	2.93	2.77	2.66	2.51	2.34	2.15	1.92
19	4.38	3.52	3.13	2.90	2.74	2.63	2.48	2.31	2.11	1.88
20	4.35	3.49	3.10	2.87	2.71	2.60	2.45	2.28	2.08	1.84
21	4.32	3.47	3.07	2.84	2.68	2.57	2.42	2.25	2.05	1.81
22	4.30	3.44	3.05	2.82	2.66	2.55	2.40	2.23	2.03	1.78
23	4.28	3.42	3.03	2.80	2.64	2.53	2.38	2.20	2.00	1.76
24	4.26	3.40	3.01	2.78	2.62	2.51	2.36	2.18	1.98	1.73
25	4.24	3.38	2.99	2.76	2.60	2.49	2.34	2.16	1.96	1.71
26	4.22	3.37	2.98	2.74	2.59	2.47	2.32	2.15	1.95	1.69
27	4.21	3.35	2.96	2.73	2.57	2.46	2.30	2.13	1.93	1.67
28	4.20	3.34	2.95	2.71	2.56	2.44	2.29	2.12	1.91	1.65
29	4.18	3.33	2.93	2.70	2.54	2.43	2.28	2.10	1.90	1.64
30	4.17	3.32	2.92	2.69	2.53	2.42	2.27	2.09	1.89	1.62
40	4.08	3.23	2.84	2.61	2.45	2.34	2.18	2.00	1.79	1.51
60	4.00	3.15	2.76	2.52	2.37	2.25	2.10	1.92	1.70	1.39
120	3.92	3.07	2.68	2.45	2.29	2.17	2.02	1.83	1.61	1.25
∞	3.84	2.99	2.60	2.37	2.21	2.09	1.94	1.75	1.52	1.00

Values of n_1 and n_2 represent the degrees of freedom associated with the larger and smaller estimates of variance respectively.

Source: Abridged from Table V of R. A. Fisher and F. Yates, *Statistical Tables for Biological, Agricultural and Medical Research* (1948 ed.), published by Oliver & Boyd Ltd., Edinburgh, and by permission of the authors and publishers.

253

Table VI. Distribution of F *(Continued)*

$p = .01$

n_2 \\ n_1	1	2	3	4	5	6	8	12	24	∞
1	4052	4999	5403	5625	5764	5859	5981	6106	6234	6366
2	98.49	99.01	99.17	99.25	99.30	99.33	99.36	99.42	99.46	99.50
3	34.12	30.81	29.46	28.71	28.24	27.91	27.49	27.05	26.60	26.12
4	21.20	18.00	16.69	15.98	15.52	15.21	14.80	14.37	13.93	13.46
5	16.26	13.27	12.06	11.39	10.97	10.67	10.27	9.89	9.47	9.02
6	13.74	10.92	9.78	9.15	8.75	8.47	8.10	7.72	7.31	6.88
7	12.25	9.55	8.45	7.85	7.46	7.19	6.84	6.47	6.07	5.65
8	11.26	8.65	7.59	7.01	6.63	6.37	6.03	5.67	5.28	4.86
9	10.56	8.02	6.99	6.42	6.06	5.80	5.47	5.11	4.73	4.31
10	10.04	7.56	6.55	5.99	5.64	5.39	5.06	4.71	4.33	3.91
11	9.65	7.20	6.22	5.67	5.32	5.07	4.74	4.40	4.02	3.60
12	9.33	6.93	5.95	5.41	5.06	4.82	4.50	4.16	3.78	3.36
13	9.07	6.70	5.74	5.20	4.86	4.62	4.30	3.96	3.59	3.16
14	8.86	6.51	5.56	5.03	4.69	4.46	4.14	3.80	3.43	3.00
15	8.68	6.36	5.42	4.89	4.56	4.32	4.00	3.67	3.29	2.87
16	8.53	6.23	5.29	4.77	4.44	4.20	3.89	3.55	3.18	2.75
17	8.40	6.11	5.18	4.67	4.34	4.10	3.79	3.45	3.08	2.65
18	8.28	6.01	5.09	4.58	4.25	4.01	3.71	3.37	3.00	2.57
19	8.18	5.93	5.01	4.50	4.17	3.94	3.63	3.30	2.92	2.49
20	8.10	5.85	4.94	4.43	4.10	3.87	3.56	3.23	2.86	2.42
21	8.02	5.78	4.87	4.37	4.04	3.81	3.51	3.17	2.80	2.36
22	7.94	5.72	4.82	4.31	3.99	3.76	3.45	3.12	2.75	2.31
23	7.88	5.66	4.76	4.26	3.94	3.71	3.41	3.07	2.70	2.26
24	7.82	5.61	4.72	4.22	3.90	3.67	3.36	3.03	2.66	2.21
25	7.77	5.57	4.68	4.18	3.86	3.63	3.32	2.99	2.62	2.17
26	7.72	5.53	4.64	4.14	3.82	3.59	3.29	2.96	2.58	2.13
27	7.68	5.49	4.60	4.11	3.78	3.56	3.26	2.93	2.55	2.10
28	7.64	5.45	4.57	4.07	3.75	3.53	3.23	2.90	2.52	2.06
29	7.60	5.42	4.54	4.04	3.73	3.50	3.20	2.87	2.49	2.03
30	7.56	5.39	4.51	4.02	3.70	3.47	3.17	2.84	2.47	2.01
40	7.31	5.18	4.31	3.83	3.51	3.29	2.99	2.66	2.29	1.80
60	7.08	4.98	4.13	3.65	3.34	3.12	2.82	2.50	2.12	1.60
120	6.85	4.79	3.95	3.48	3.17	2.96	2.66	2.34	1.95	1.38
∞	6.64	4.60	3.78	3.32	3.02	2.80	2.51	2.18	1.79	1.00

Values of n_1 and n_2 represent the degrees of freedom associated with the larger and smaller estimates of variance respectively.

Table VI. Distribution of *F* (Continued)

$$p = .001$$

n_1 / n_2	1	2	3	4	5	6	8	12	24	∞
1	405284	500000	540379	562500	576405	585937	598144	610667	623497	636619
2	998.5	999.0	999.2	999.2	999 3	999.3	999.4	999.4	999.5	999.5
3	167.5	148.5	141.1	137.1	134.6	132.8	130.6	128.3	125.9	123.5
4	74.14	61.25	56.18	53.44	51.71	50.53	49.00	47.41	45.77	44.05
5	47.04	36.61	33.20	31.09	29.75	28.84	27.64	26.42	25.14	23.78
6	35.51	27.00	23.70	21.90	20.81	20.03	19.03	17.99	16.89	15.75
7	29.22	21.69	18.77	17.19	16.21	15.52	14.63	13.71	12.73	11.69
8	25.42	18.49	15.83	14.39	13.49	12.86	12.04	11.19	10.30	9.34
9	22.86	16.39	13.90	12.56	11.71	11.13	10.37	9.57	8.72	7.81
10	21.04	14.91	12.55	11.28	10.48	9.92	9.20	8.45	7.64	6.76
11	19.69	13.81	11.56	10.35	9.58	9.05	8.35	7.63	6.85	6.00
12	18.64	12.97	10.80	9.63	8.89	8.38	7 71	7.00	6.25	5.42
13	17.81	12.31	10.21	9.07	8.35	7.86	7.21	6.52	5.78	4.97
14	17.14	11.78	9 73	8.62	7.92	7.43	6.80	6.13	5.41	4.60
15	16.59	11.34	9.34	8.25	7.57	7.09	6.47	5.81	5.10	4.31
16	16.12	10.97	9.00	7.94	7.27	6.81	6.19	5.55	4.85	4.06
17	15.72	10.66	8.73	7.68	7.02	6.56	5.96	5.32	4.63	3.85
18	15.38	10.39	8.49	7.46	6.81	6.35	5.76	5.13	4.45	3.67
19	15.08	10.16	8.28	7.26	6.61	6.18	5.59	4.97	4.29	3.52
20	14.82	9.95	8.10	7.10	6.46	6.02	5.44	4.82	4.15	3.38
21	14.59	9.77	7.94	6.95	6.32	5.88	5.31	4.70	4.03	3.26
22	14.38	9.61	7.80	6.81	6.19	5.76	5.19	4.58	3.92	3.15
23	14.19	9.47	7.67	6.69	6.08	5.65	5.09	4.48	3.82	3.05
24	14.03	9.34	7.55	6.59	5 98	5.55	4.99	4.39	3.74	2.97
25	13.88	9.22	7.45	6.49	5.88	5.46	4.91	4.31	3.66	2.89
26	13.74	9.12	7.36	6.41	5.80	5.38	4.83	4.24	3.59	2.82
27	13.61	9.02	7.27	6.33	5.73	5.31	4.76	4.17	3.52	2.75
28	13.50	8.93	7.19	6.25	5 66	5.24	4.69	4.11	3.46	2.70
29	13.39	8.85	7.12	6.19	5.59	5.18	4.64	4.05	3.41	2.64
30	13.29	8.77	7.05	6.12	5.53	5.12	4.58	4.00	3.36	2.59
40	12.61	8.25	6.60	5.70	5.13	4.73	4.21	3.64	3.01	2.23
60	11.97	7.76	6.17	5.31	4.76	4.37	3.87	3.31	2.69	1.90
120	11.38	7.31	5.79	4.95	4.42	4.04	3.55	3.02	2.40	1.56
∞	10.83	6.91	5.42	4.62	4.10	3.74	3.27	2.74	2.13	1.00

Values of n_1 and n_2 represent the degrees of freedom associated with the larger and smaller estimates of variance respectively.

TABLE VII.   Random Numbers

Line/Col.	(1)	(2)	(3)	(4)	(5)	(6)	(7)	(8)	(9)	(10)	(11)	(12)	(13)	(14)
1	10480	15011	01536	02011	81647	91646	69179	14194	62590	36207	20969	99570	91291	90700
2	22368	46573	25595	85393	30995	89198	27982	53402	93965	34095	52666	19174	39615	99505
3	24130	48360	22527	97265	76393	64809	15179	24830	49340	32081	30680	19655	63348	58629
4	42167	93093	06243	61680	07856	16376	39440	53537	71341	57004	00849	74917	97758	16379
5	37570	39975	81837	16656	06121	91782	60468	81305	49684	60672	14110	06927	01263	54613
6	77921	06907	11008	42751	27756	53498	18602	70659	90655	15053	21916	81825	44394	42880
7	99562	72905	56420	69994	98872	31016	71194	18738	44013	48840	63213	21069	10634	12952
8	96301	91977	05463	07972	18876	20922	94595	56869	69014	60045	18425	84903	42508	32307
9	89579	14342	63661	10281	17453	18103	57740	84378	25331	12566	58678	44947	05585	56941
10	85475	36857	43342	53988	53060	59533	38867	62300	08158	17983	16439	11458	18593	64952
11	28918	69578	88231	33276	70997	79936	56865	05859	90106	31595	01547	85590	91610	78188
12	63553	40961	48235	03427	49626	69445	18663	72695	52180	20847	12234	90511	33703	90322
13	09429	93969	52636	92737	88974	33488	36320	17617	30015	08272	84115	27156	30613	74952
14	10365	61129	87529	85689	48237	52267	67689	93394	01511	26358	85104	20285	29975	89868
15	07119	97336	71048	08178	77233	13916	47564	81056	97735	85977	29372	74461	28551	90707
16	51085	12765	51821	51259	77452	16308	60756	92144	49442	53900	70960	63990	75601	40719
17	02368	21382	52404	60268	89368	19885	55322	44819	01188	65255	64835	44919	05944	55157
18	01011	54092	33362	94904	31273	04146	18594	29852	71585	85030	51132	01915	92747	64951
19	52162	53916	46369	58586	23216	14513	83149	98736	23495	64350	94738	17752	35156	35749
20	07056	97628	33787	09998	42698	06691	76988	13602	51851	46104	88916	19509	25625	58104
21	48663	91245	85828	14346	09172	30168	90229	04734	59193	22178	30421	61666	99904	32812
22	54164	58492	22421	74103	47070	25306	76468	26384	58151	06646	21524	15227	96909	44592
23	32639	32363	05597	24200	13363	38005	94342	28728	35806	06912	17012	64161	18296	22851
24	29334	27001	87637	87308	58731	00256	45834	15398	46557	41135	10367	07684	36188	18510
25	02488	33062	28834	07351	19731	92420	60952	61280	50001	67658	32586	86679	50720	94953
26	81525	72295	04839	96423	24878	82651	66566	14778	76797	14780	13300	87074	79666	95725
27	29676	20591	68086	26432	46901	20849	89768	81536	86645	12659	92259	57102	80428	25280
28	00742	57392	39064	66432	84673	40027	32832	61362	98947	96067	64760	64584	96096	98253
29	05366	04213	25669	26422	44407	44048	37937	63904	45766	66134	75470	66520	34693	90449
30	91921	26418	64117	94305	26766	25940	39972	22209	71500	64568	91402	42416	07844	69618
31	00582	04711	87917	77341	42206	35126	74087	99547	81817	42607	43808	76655	62028	76630
32	00725	69884	62797	56170	86324	88072	76222	36086	84637	93161	76038	65855	77919	88006
33	69011	65797	95876	55293	18988	27354	26575	08625	40801	59920	29841	80150	12777	48501
34	25976	57948	29888	88604	67917	48708	18912	82271	65424	69774	33611	54262	85963	03547
35	09763	83473	73577	12908	30883	18317	28290	35797	05998	41688	34952	37888	38917	88050
36	91567	42595	27958	30134	04024	86385	29880	99730	55536	84855	29080	09250	79656	73211
37	17955	56349	90999	49127	20044	59931	06115	20542	18059	02008	73708	83517	36103	42791
38	46503	18584	18845	49618	02304	51038	20655	58727	28168	15475	56942	53389	20562	87338
39	92157	89634	94824	78171	84610	82834	09922	25417	44137	48413	25555	21246	35509	20468
40	14577	62765	35605	81263	39667	47358	56873	56307	61607	49518	89656	20103	77490	18062
41	98427	07523	33362	64270	01638	92477	66969	98420	04880	45585	46565	04102	46880	45709
42	34914	63976	88720	82765	34476	17032	87589	40836	32427	70002	70663	88863	77775	69348
43	70060	28277	39475	46473	23219	53416	94970	25832	69975	94884	19661	72828	00102	66794
44	53976	54914	06990	67245	68350	82948	11398	42878	80287	88267	47363	46634	06541	97809
45	76072	29515	40980	07391	58745	25774	22987	80059	39911	96189	41151	14222	60697	59583
46	90725	52210	83974	29992	65831	38857	50490	83765	55657	14361	31720	57375	56228	41546
47	64364	67412	33339	31926	14883	24413	59744	92351	97473	89286	35931	04110	23726	51900
48	08962	00358	31662	25388	61642	34072	81249	35648	56891	69352	48373	45578	78547	81788
49	95012	68379	93526	70765	10593	04542	76463	54328	02349	17247	28865	14777	62730	92277
50	15664	10493	20492	38391	91132	21999	59516	81652	27195	48223	46751	22923	32261	85653

Source: Reprinted from Samuel M. Selby, *Standard Mathematical Tables,* 17th ed. (Cleveland: The Chemical Rubber Co., 1969), "A Table of 14,000 Random Units," pp. 626–27. © Copyright by The Chemical Rubber Co., with the kind permission of the publisher.

Table VII. Random Numbers *(Continued)*

Line/Col.	(1)	(2)	(3)	(4)	(5)	(6)	(7)	(8)	(9)	(10)	(11)	(12)	(13)	(14)
51	16408	81899	04153	53381	79401	21438	83035	92350	36693	31238	59649	91754	72772	02338
52	18629	81953	05520	91962	04739	13092	97662	24822	94730	06496	35090	04822	86772	98289
53	73115	35101	47498	87637	99016	71060	88824	71013	18735	20286	23153	72924	35165	43040
54	57491	16703	23167	49323	45021	33132	12544	41035	80780	45393	44812	12515	98931	91202
55	30405	83946	23792	14422	15059	45799	22716	19792	09983	74353	68668	30429	70735	25499
56	16631	35006	85900	98275	32388	52390	16815	69298	82732	38480	73817	32523	41961	44437
57	96773	20206	42559	78985	05300	22164	24369	54224	35083	19687	11052	91491	60383	19746
58	38935	64202	14349	82674	66523	44133	00697	35552	35970	19124	63318	29686	03387	59846
59	31624	76384	17403	53363	44167	64486	64758	75366	76554	31601	12614	33072	60332	92325
60	78919	19474	23632	27889	47914	02584	37680	20801	72152	39339	34806	08930	85001	87820
61	03931	33309	57047	74211	63445	17361	62825	39908	05607	91284	68833	25570	38818	46920
62	74426	33278	43972	10119	89917	15665	52872	73823	73144	88662	88970	74492	51805	99378
63	09066	00903	20795	95452	92648	45454	09552	88815	16553	51125	79375	97596	16296	66092
64	42238	12426	87025	14267	20979	04508	64535	31355	86064	29472	47689	05974	52468	16834
65	16153	08002	26504	41744	81959	65642	74240	56302	00033	67107	77510	70625	28725	34191
66	21457	40742	29820	96783	29400	21840	15035	34537	33310	06116	95240	15957	16572	06004
67	21581	57802	02050	89728	17937	37621	47075	42080	97403	48626	68995	43805	33386	21597
68	55612	78095	83197	33732	05810	24813	86902	60397	16489	03264	88525	42786	05269	92532
69	44657	66999	99324	51281	84463	60563	79312	93454	68876	25471	93911	25650	12682	73572
70	91340	84979	46949	81973	37949	61023	43997	15263	80644	43942	89203	71795	99533	50501
71	91227	21199	31935	27022	84067	05462	35216	14486	29891	68607	41867	14951	91696	85065
72	50001	38140	66321	19924	72163	09538	12151	06878	91903	18749	34405	56087	82790	70925
73	65390	05224	72958	28609	81406	39147	25549	48542	42627	45233	57202	94617	23772	07896
74	27504	96131	83944	41575	10573	08619	64482	73923	36152	05184	94142	25299	84387	34925
75	37169	94851	39117	89632	00959	16487	65536	49071	39782	17095	02330	74301	00275	48280
76	11508	70225	51111	38351	19444	66499	71945	05422	13442	78675	84081	66938	93654	59894
77	37449	30362	06694	54690	04052	53115	62757	95348	78662	11163	81651	50245	34971	52924
78	46515	70331	85922	38329	57015	15765	97161	17869	45349	61796	66345	81073	49106	79860
79	30986	81223	42416	58353	21532	30502	32305	86482	05174	07901	54339	58861	74818	46942
80	63798	64995	46583	09765	44160	78128	83991	42865	92520	83531	80377	35909	81250	54238
81	82486	84846	99254	67632	43218	50076	21361	64816	51202	88124	41870	52689	51275	83556
82	21885	32906	92431	09060	64297	51674	64126	62570	26123	05155	59194	52799	28225	85762
83	60336	98782	07408	53458	13564	59089	26445	29789	85205	41001	12535	12133	14645	23541
84	43937	46891	24010	25560	86355	33941	25786	54990	71899	15475	95434	98227	21824	19585
85	97656	63175	89303	16275	07100	92063	21942	18611	47348	20203	18534	03862	78095	50136
86	03299	01221	05418	38982	55758	92237	26759	86367	21216	98442	08303	56613	91511	75928
87	79626	06486	03574	17668	07785	76020	79924	25651	83325	88428	85076	72811	22717	50585
88	85636	68335	47539	03129	65651	11977	02510	26113	99447	68645	34327	15152	55230	93448
89	18039	14367	61337	06177	12143	46609	32989	74014	64708	00533	35398	58408	13261	47908
90	08362	15656	60627	36478	65648	16764	53412	09013	07832	41574	17639	82163	60859	75567
91	79556	29068	04142	16268	15387	12856	66227	38358	22478	73373	88732	09443	82558	05250
92	92608	82674	27072	32534	17075	27698	98204	63863	11951	34648	88022	56148	34925	57031
93	23982	25835	40055	67006	12293	02753	14827	22235	35071	99704	37543	11601	35503	85171
94	09915	96306	05908	97901	28395	14186	00821	80703	70426	75647	76310	88717	37890	40129
95	50937	33300	26695	62247	69927	76123	50842	43834	86654	70959	79725	93872	28117	19233
96	42488	78077	69882	61657	34136	79180	97526	43092	04098	73571	80799	76536	71255	64239
97	46764	86273	63003	93017	31204	36692	40202	35275	57306	55543	53203	18098	47625	88684
98	03237	45430	55417	63282	90816	17349	88298	90183	36600	78406	06216	95787	42579	90730
99	86591	81482	52667	61583	14972	90053	89534	76036	49199	43716	97548	04379	46370	28672
100	38534	01715	94964	87288	65680	43772	39560	12918	86537	62738	19636	51132	25739	56947

TABLE VIII. Critical Values of D in the Kolmogorov-Smirnov One-Sample Test

Sample size (N)	Level of significance for $D = $ maximum $|F_0(X) - S_N(X)|$				
	.20	.15	.10	.05	.01
1	.900	.925	.950	.975	.995
2	.684	.726	.776	.842	.929
3	.565	.597	.642	.708	.828
4	.494	.525	.564	.624	.733
5	.446	.474	.510	.565	.669
6	.410	.436	.470	.521	.618
7	.381	.405	.438	.486	.577
8	.358	.381	.411	.457	.543
9	.339	.360	.388	.432	.514
10	.322	.342	.368	.410	.490
11	.307	.326	.352	.391	.468
12	.295	.313	.338	.375	.450
13	.284	.302	.325	.361	.433
14	.274	.292	.314	.349	.418
15	.266	.283	.304	.338	.404
16	.258	.274	.295	.328	.392
17	.250	.266	.286	.318	.381
18	.244	.259	.278	.309	.371
19	.237	.252	.272	.301	.363
20	.231	.246	.264	.294	.356
25	.21	.22	.24	.27	.32
30	.19	.20	.22	.24	.29
35	.18	.19	.21	.23	.27
Over 35	$\dfrac{1.07}{\sqrt{N}}$	$\dfrac{1.14}{\sqrt{N}}$	$\dfrac{1.22}{\sqrt{N}}$	$\dfrac{1.36}{\sqrt{N}}$	$\dfrac{1.63}{\sqrt{N}}$

Source: F. J. Massey, Jr., "The Kolmogorov-Smirnov Test of Goodness of Fit," *Journal of the American Statistical Association,* vol. 46, p. 70, 1951, with the kind permission of the author and publisher.

TABLE IX. Critical Values of *r* in the Runs Test

Given in the bodies of Table A and Table B are various critical values of *r* for various values of n₁ and n₂. For the one-sample runs test, any value of *r* which is equal to or smaller than that shown in Table A or equal to or larger than that shown in Table B is significant at the .05 level. For the Wald-Wolfowitz two-sample runs test, any value of *r* which is equal to or smaller than that shown in Table A is significant at the .05 level.

Table A

n_1 \ n_2	2	3	4	5	6	7	8	9	10	11	12	13	14	15	16	17	18	19	20
2											2	2	2	2	2	2	2	2	2
3				2	2	2	2	2	2	2	2	2	3	3	3	3	3	3
4			2	2	2	3	3	3	3	3	3	3	3	4	4	4	4	4
5		2	2	3	3	3	3	3	4	4	4	4	4	4	4	5	5	5
6	2	2	3	3	3	3	4	4	4	4	5	5	5	5	5	5	6	6
7	2	2	3	3	3	4	4	5	5	5	5	5	6	6	6	6	6	6
8	2	3	3	3	4	4	5	5	5	6	6	6	6	6	7	7	7	7
9	2	3	3	4	4	5	5	5	6	6	6	7	7	7	7	8	8	8
10	2	3	3	4	5	5	5	6	6	7	7	7	7	8	8	8	8	9
11	2	3	4	4	5	5	6	6	7	7	7	8	8	8	9	9	9	10	10
12	2	2	3	4	4	5	6	6	7	7	7	8	8	8	9	9	9	10	10
13	2	2	3	4	5	5	6	6	7	7	8	8	9	9	9	10	10	10	10
14	2	2	3	4	5	5	6	7	7	8	8	9	9	9	10	10	10	11	11
15	2	3	3	4	5	6	6	7	7	8	8	9	9	10	10	11	11	11	12
16	2	3	4	4	5	6	6	7	8	8	9	9	10	10	11	11	11	12	12
17	2	3	4	4	5	6	7	7	8	9	9	10	10	11	11	11	12	12	13
18	2	3	4	5	5	6	7	8	8	9	9	10	10	11	11	12	12	13	13
19	2	3	4	5	6	6	7	8	8	9	10	10	11	11	12	12	13	13	13
20	2	3	4	5	6	6	7	8	9	9	10	10	11	12	12	13	13	13	14

Source: Taken from Frieda A. Swed and Churchill Eisenhart, "Tables for Testing Randomness of Grouping in a Sequence of Alternatives," *Annals of Mathematical Statistics,* vol. 14, pp. 83–86, 1943, with the kind permission of the authors and publisher.

Table IX.   Critical Values of *r* in the Runs Test *(Continued)*

Table B

n_1 \ n_2	2	3	4	5	6	7	8	9	10	11	12	13	14	15	16	17	18	19	20
2																			
3																			
4				9	9														
5			9	10	10	11	11												
6			9	10	11	12	12	13	13	13	13								
7				11	12	13	13	14	14	14	14	15	15	15					
8				11	12	13	14	14	15	15	16	16	16	16	17	17	17	17	17
9					13	14	14	15	16	16	16	17	17	18	18	18	18	18	18
10					13	14	15	16	16	17	17	18	18	18	19	19	19	20	20
11					13	14	15	16	17	17	18	19	19	19	20	20	20	21	21
12					13	14	16	16	17	18	19	19	20	20	21	21	21	22	22
13						15	16	17	18	19	19	20	20	21	21	22	22	23	23
14						15	16	17	18	19	20	20	21	22	22	23	23	23	24
15						15	16	18	18	19	20	21	22	22	23	23	24	24	25
16							17	18	19	20	21	21	22	23	23	24	25	25	25
17							17	18	19	20	21	22	23	23	24	25	25	26	26
18							17	18	19	20	21	22	23	24	25	25	26	26	27
19							17	18	20	21	22	23	23	24	25	26	26	27	27
20							17	18	20	21	22	23	24	25	25	26	27	27	28

TABLE X. Probabilities Associated With Values As Small As Observed Values of U in the Mann-Whitney Test

$N_2 = 3$

U \ N_1	1	2	3
0	.250	.100	.050
1	.500	.200	.100
2	.750	.400	.200
3		.600	.350
4			.500
5			.650

$N_2 = 4$

U \ N_1	1	2	3	4
0	.200	.067	.028	.014
1	.400	.133	.057	.029
2	.600	.267	.114	.057
3		.400	.200	.100
4		.600	.314	.171
5			.429	.243
6			.571	.343
7				.443
8				.557

$N_2 = 5$

U \ N_1	1	2	3	4	5
0	.167	.047	.018	.008	.004
1	.333	.095	.036	.016	.008
2	.500	.190	.071	.032	.016
3	.667	.286	.125	.056	.028
4		.429	.196	.095	.048
5		.571	.286	.143	.075
6			.393	.206	.111
7			.500	.278	.155
8			.607	.365	.210
9				.452	.274
10				.548	.345
11					.421
12					.500
13					.579

$N_2 = 6$

U \ N_1	1	2	3	4	5	6
0	.143	.036	.012	.005	.002	.001
1	.286	.071	.024	.010	.004	.002
2	.428	.143	.048	.019	.009	.004
3	.571	.214	.083	.033	.015	.008
4		.321	.131	.057	.026	.013
5		.429	.190	.086	.041	.021
6		.571	.274	.129	.063	.032
7			.357	.176	.089	.047
8			.452	.238	.123	.066
9			.548	.305	.165	.090
10				.381	.214	.120
11				.457	.268	.155
12				.545	.331	.197
13					.396	.242
14					.465	.294
15					.535	.350
16						.409
17						.469
18						.531

Source: H. B. Mann and D. R. Whitney, "On a Test of Whether One of Two Random Variables is Stochastically Larger than the Other," *Annals of Mathematical Statistics,* vol. 18, pp. 52–54, 1947, with the kind permission of the authors and publisher.

Appendix B

Table X. Probabilities Associated With Values As Small As Observed Values of *U* in the Mann-Whitney Test *(Continued)*

$N_2 = 7$

U \ N₁	1	2	3	4	5	6	7
0	.125	.028	.008	.003	.001	.001	.000
1	.250	.056	.017	.006	.003	.001	.001
2	.375	.111	.033	.012	.005	.002	.001
3	.500	.167	.058	.021	.009	.004	.002
4	.625	.250	.092	.036	.015	.007	.003
5		.333	.133	.055	.024	.011	.006
6		.444	.192	.082	.037	.017	.009
7		.556	.258	.115	.053	.026	.013
8			.333	.158	.074	.037	.019
9			.417	.206	.101	.051	.027
10			.500	.264	.134	.069	.036
11			.583	.324	.172	.090	.049
12				.394	.216	.117	.064
13				.464	.265	.147	.082
14				.538	.319	.183	.104
15					.378	.223	.130
16					.438	.267	.159
17					.500	.314	.191
18					.562	.365	.228
19						.418	.267
20						.473	.310
21						.527	.355
22							.402
23							.451
24							.500
25							.549

Table X.   Probabilities Associated With Values As Small
As Observed Values of *U* in the Mann-Whitney
Test *(Continued)*

$N_2 = 8$

U \ N₁	1	2	3	4	5	6	7	8
0	.111	.022	.006	.002	.001	.000	.000	.000
1	.222	.044	.012	.004	.002	.001	.000	.000
2	.333	.089	.024	.008	.003	.001	.001	.000
3	.444	.133	.042	.014	.005	.002	.001	.001
4	.556	.200	.067	.024	.009	.004	.002	.001
5		.267	.097	.036	.015	.006	.003	.001
6		.356	.139	.055	.023	.010	.005	.002
7		.444	.188	.077	.033	.015	.007	.003
8		.556	.248	.107	.047	.021	.010	.005
9			.315	.141	.064	.030	.014	.007
10			.387	.184	.085	.041	.020	010
11			.461	.230	.111	.054	.027	.014
12			.539	.285	.142	.071	.036	.019
13				.341	.177	.091	.047	.025
14				.404	.217	.114	.060	.032
15				.467	.262	.141	.076	.041
16				.533	.311	.172	.095	.052
17					.362	.207	.116	.065
18					.416	.245	.140	.080
19					.472	.286	.168	.097
20					.528	.331	.198	.117
21						.377	.232	.139
22						.426	.268	.164
23						.475	.306	.191
24						.525	.347	.221
25							.389	.253
26							.433	.287
27							.478	.323
28							.522	.360
29								.399
30								.439
31								.480
32								.520

TABLE XI. Probabilities Associated With Values As large As Observed Values of *S* in the Kendall Rank Correlation Coefficient

S	Values of *N*				*S*	Values of *N*		
	4	5	8	9		6	7	10
0	.625	.592	.548	.540	1	.500	.500	.500
2	.375	.408	.452	.460	3	.360	.386	.431
4	.167	.242	.360	.381	5	.235	.281	.364
6	.042	.117	.274	.306	7	.136	191	.300
8		.042	.199	.238	9	.068	.119	.242
10		.0083	.138	.179	11	.028	.068	.190
12			.089	.130	13	.0083	.035	.146
14			.054	.090	15	.0014	.015	.108
16			.031	.060	17		.0054	.078
18			.016	.038	19		.0014	.054
20			.0071	.022	21		.00020	.036
22			.0028	.012	23			.023
24			.00087	.0063	25			.014
26			.00019	.0029	27			.0083
28			.000025	.0012	29			.0046
30				.00043	31			.0023
32				.00012	33			.0011
34				.000025	35			.00047
36				.0000028	37			.00018
					39			.000058
					41			.000015
					43			.0000028
					45			.00000028

Source: Taken from M. G. Kendall, *Rank Correlation Methods* (London: Charles Griffin & Co., Ltd., 1962), Appendix Table 1, p. 173, with the kind permission of the publisher.

Appendix C

On Writing
Political Science Papers

Politics may not be a science, but its study involves quite a bit more than journalism. There are no laws that *guarantee* good results, but the following are some guidelines for writing successful political science papers.

1. Choosing a Topic

This sounds òbvious, yet many people do a bad job. A good paper will choose a clear *analytic topic*. That is, you should do more than select an area and write about it. You should even try to do more than select a question to be pondered. Sometimes descriptive or speculative papers are desired, to be sure, but most often you should pose a *hypothesis,* gather evidence, and come to conclusions about the validity of your hypothesis.

For example, a paper describing in a historical manner how Nixon was elected is usually a bad topic. A paper asking "Why was Nixon elected?" is a bit better, but is still not sharp enough. An analytic paper might pose the hypothesis that "Nixon was elected because of popular reaction against the Vietnam war under Johnson," and seek to prove or disprove this hypothesis. A good paper tries to prove something in a logical way —not just describe or speculate about something. This means you must pose a clear hypothesis at the outset.

2. Forming an Outline

This is not something "just for high school." If you can do it in your head, fine, but you really need to think out your paper in advance. For most of us, this means writing an outline. Obviously this will depend on the topic, but a typical paper will have the following general form:

A. INTRODUCTION
1. Statement of the hypothesis
2. Brief (historical) background, showing importance
3. Proposed method of analysis, integrated with proposed outline of remainder of paper
B. BODY
1. The hypothesis in operationalized form
2. Alternative hypotheses
3. Evidence on relationships, assessing significance, strength, and validity of data
4. Use of control variables as check
5. Accepting or rejecting the hypothesis
C. CONCLUSION
1. Brief summary of findings
2. Implications for political theory or larger framework

3. Setting Up the Hypothesis

It is not enough to pick an analytic topic and have a clear outline—you need to proceed logically as well. The first step, thinking clearly about your hypothesis, is the crucial one. First, make clear what, specifically, it is that you are trying to explain (what is your *dependent variable*). In a short paper it is a good idea to have just one dependent variable—for instance, Nixon's being elected—not McCarthy's failure to get the nomination as well. If you need to explain more than one thing, then you should have more than one proof, clearly distinguishing them.

After making your dependent variable clear, you should then clearly identify the *other variables* you are going to use in explaining the dependent variable. For instance, in explaining why Nixon was elected, are you going to examine variables like traditional partisan identifications, economic indicators, campaign spending, riots, foreign policy activity, personality factors, running mates, political organization, student movements, interest groups, other variables? State clearly which variables you are going to examine and explain why they are the more important. You should also explain why you are going to exclude other variables from your analysis.

Third, *operationalize your variables.* This is a very common problem with student (and professional!) papers. It is clear enough what the dependent variable in this example is: Nixon's being elected—although even here, you should decide if you are trying to explain his being elected at all, or the margin by which he was elected. But what are "economic factors," for example? Such umbrella terms must be broken into more specific variables like unemployment, cost of living, income levels. Even then, such variables must be given specific, empirical meaning. Which of the different indicators of cost of living are you going to use? You may want to use a variable like "alienation," but how, exactly, do you know it when you see it?

Fourth, *identify the causal relationships* among your variables. It is not enough to say that A and B cause X, because this could mean one of several things:

$$A\rightarrow B\rightarrow X \qquad\qquad A\rightarrow X\leftarrow B \qquad\qquad {A \atop B}{\Large >}\!\rightarrow X$$

Hypothesis 1   Hypothesis 2   Hypothesis 3

In hypothesis 1, it is asserted that A causes B, which in turn causes X. Hypothesis 2 asserts that A causes X, and B independently causes X. Hypothesis 3 asserts that the joint relation of A and B causes X. If you allow for more than three variables and if you allow for two-way (mutual) causation, identifying causal relationships becomes quite complex. Often a pictorial diagram is a real convenience. But going through this procedure becomes important when you go to gather evidence. The kind of evidence you need will depend on what exactly your hypothetical model is.

Fifth, specify the *alternative hypotheses.* You can usually assume that more than one hypothesis will fit any given set of data. Just because you show the data fit your hypothesis, your task is not complete. Other theories may well fit the data too. Ultimately, you can never prove your hypothesis is true; you can only show that alternative hypotheses are unsupported by the data and are therefore untrue. A good political science paper will therefore raise alternative hypotheses to the central one. Such alternatives may be drawn from examining the work of other writers, or from one's imagination. Creatively forming the central hypothesis *and* reasonable alternative hypotheses is half the job of writing a political science paper. The other half is gathering evidence to show your hypothesis is supported and the alternatives are not.

4. Gathering Evidence

Before you can select the types of evidence you need, you must have gone through the preceding steps. In doing so, you will have had to consider two things. First, the *level of your analysis:* are you going to explain the dependent variable on the level of biological factors (aggressive instincts, physical needs directly acted upon), ecological (demographic trends, herding), psychological (frustrations, needs), economic (relations to production, income), political (power, authority), social (group pressure), cultural (values, norms), or some combination? Second, the *method of analysis:* comparisons over time, comparisons across space; inductive, deductive; qualitative, quantitative.

Choosing the method of analysis always depends on the specific problem, but here is an example of choices that must be made. In studying power distribution, one can study particular decisions and trace relationships exhibited therein. One can ask people who they think holds power. Or one can assume that benefits indicate how power is distributed and therefore examine how benefits are distributed. And if you want to generalize, you will have to have evidence for different time periods and/or different cultures.

There is an almost infinite variety of *kinds of evidence:* archives, printed matter, surveys, interviews, participant observation, physical traces. In gathering evidence, a few rules of thumb are important:

1. The most common source of evidence in student papers is books. In using this source, focus on the author's actual evidence, not his conclusions or opinions. This sounds simple, but few observe this rule of thumb.

2. Periodicals are the next most common source, and definitely should be used in a thorough paper. But remember two points:
   a. Focus first on articles in scholarly journals, not tidbits from *Time* and *Life.*
   b. Try to consult sources representing different sides of the debate. If you're writing about another country, try to include authors from that country. If you're writing about the labor movement, include union sources, just as you would include business sources on business or communist sources on Communism (don't go to the other extreme, obviously).

3. Bring statistical evidence to bear where appropriate. Many neglect sources like the *City and County Data Book, America Votes, Handbook of World Indicators,* city, state, and country handbooks issued annually, labor and other federal department data, *Historical Statistics of the U.S. from Colonial Times to the Present,* annual presidential reports, or even the *Census.*

4. If you plan at the outset, interviewing, mail questionnaires, or even some sample surveying is possible in student papers. Remember, you don't have to rely on data collected by others— often you can collect your own.

5. Presenting Evidence on the Hypothesis

There will probably be several relationships in question in your analysis, specified when you identified the causal relationships. In presenting your evidence, deal with the different relationships in question for your analysis in some kind of logical order. One such order would be to start by presenting the evidence on relationships further from the dependent variable in your causal model, and work toward relationships directly involving the dependent variable.

Whatever logical order you choose, in presenting your evidence you should address three questions:

1. *Significance*—are you sure that the evidence you have collected isn't just the result of chance?
2. *Association*—is the evidence in support of the relationship you have posited strong enough to be consistent with your model?
3. *Validity*—would the evidence be the same at another time or place? are you really measuring what you think you are? is the surface relationship spurious because of variables omitted from the model? If your data are quantitative, there are statistical tests of significance and measures of association that may be used.

Of course, one should avoid *fallacies*. What is true for one group may not be true for another. What is true for one group may not be true overall, or vice versa. What is true between groups may not be true within groups; for example, states that are Catholic might tend to be Democratic, yet within any state there might be no relation between religion and vote—if Protestants voted Democratic in predominantly Catholic states and Catholics voted Republican in predominantly Protestant states. One may legitimately compare ideal with ideal or reality with reality, but not ideal with reality—not socialist ideal with capitalist practice, or vice versa.

6. Using Control Variables

A crucial part of determining the validity of any relationships you assert is showing they hold even when other variables are held constant (controlled). Unemployment may be associated with rioting, but does this relation hold when income is controlled for? Catholicism may correlate with voting Democratic, but does this hold when social class is taken as a control?

	Catholic	Protestant
Democratic	1a	1b
Republican	1c	1d

Low Socioeconomic Status

	Catholic	Protestant
Democratic	2a	2b
Republican	2c	2d

High Socioeconomic Status

	Catholic	Protestant
Democratic	3a	3b
Republican	3c	3d

In terms of the diagram, we may find Catholicism is associated with voting Democratic and Protestantism with voting Republican (most examples in boxes 1a or 1d, few or none in 1b or 1c). If you want to control for another variable, say socioeconomic status, divide your examples or evidence into those dealing with low socioeconomic cases and those dealing with high cases. If the examples are still concentrated in the *a* and *d* boxes (in tables 2 and 3), then the relationship holds even when socioeconomic status is controlled for. This may be done in a qualitative way with descriptive examples, or in a quantitative way with aggregate data. In statistics, control variables may be handled by multivariate analysis or partial correlation, among others.

7. Accepting Or Rejecting Your Hypothesis

The preceding steps should lead logically to your conclusion—acceptance or rejection of your hypothesis. The soundness of the evidence gathered will, of course, determine the assurance with which you may come to a conclusion. You will want to show that the evidence leads to rejection of the alternative hypotheses formed earlier, but is consistent with your own views. This whole process is not, of course, as mechanical as these notes might suggest, nor need it be quantitatively oriented or even follow the suggested outline. But the elements of logical proof must be present in a sound social science paper.

8. Drawing Implications

Aside from avoiding various fallacies and keeping one's generalizations within those warranted by the kind of evidence one has gathered, a good political science paper should attempt to relate its findings to existing political science literature, to contemporary issues, or to some larger framework. Relations to disciplines other than political science should not be neglected. At the same time, the limits of the study should be made explicit; don't overstate a good case.

RESEARCH AIDS

Benson, Oliver, *Political Science Laboratory* (Charles E. Merrill, 1969).
An introductory paperback manual covering the basic elements of a
quantitative political science paper, which requires no mathematical
background beyond use of tables and graphs, yet is still advanced
enough to be well worthwhile.

Irish, Marian, ed., *Political Science: Advance of the Discipline* (Prentice-
Hall, 1968).
A paperback reviewing the general state of each of the several traditional areas of political science, such as public administration, international relations, public law and judicial behavior, etc. A good
source to start to find out how your concerns fit into the field of
political science.

Other paperbacks of a similar nature are:

Dahl, Robert, *Modern Political Analysis* (Prentice-Hall, 1963).

Young, Oran, *Systems of Political Science* (Prentice-Hall, 1964).

Mackenzie, William J., *Politics and Social Science* (Pelican, 1967).

Two hardbound books that review the field are:

American Political Science Association, Ithiel de Sola Pool, ed., *Contemporary Political Science: Toward Empirical Theory* (McGraw-Hill,
1967).

Golembiewski, Welsh, and Crotty, *A Methodological Primer for Political
Scientists* (Rand McNally, 1969).

Berelson, Bernard, and Gary Steiner, *Human Behavior: An Inventory of
Scientific Findings* (Harcourt, Brace & World, hardbound or abridged
paperback, 1964).
An inventory of social science studies, this is a good starting point
to find how your study relates to other social science studies.

For a general treatment see:

Lipset, Seymour M., ed., *Politics and the Social Sciences* (Oxford University Press paperback, 1969).

Becker, Leonard, and Clair Gustafson, *Encounter With Sociology: The
Term Paper* (Glendessary paperback, 1968).
A sound handbook, equally useful for political scientists.

Merritt, Richard, and Gloria Pyszka, *The Student Political Scientist's
Handbook* (Schenkman paperback, 1969).
A guide to sources.

Index